STUDIES ON THE CHINESE ECONOMY

General Editors: Peter Nolan, Lecturer in Economics and Politics, University of Cambridge, and Fellow and Director of Studies in Economics, Jesus College, Cambridge, England; and Dong Fureng, Professor, Chinese Academy of Social Sciences, Beijing, China

This series analyses issues in China's current economic development, and sheds light upon that process by examining China's economic history. It contains a wide range of books on the Chinese economy past and present, and includes not only studies written by leading Western authorities, but also translations of the most important works on the Chinese economy produced within China. It intends to make a major contribution towards understanding this immensely important part of the world economy.

Published titles include:

Shangquan Gao
CHINA'S ECONOMIC REFORM

Xiaoping Xu
CHINA'S FINANCIAL SYSTEM UNDER TRANSITION

Malcolm Warner
THE MANAGEMENT OF HUMAN RESOURCES IN CHINESE
INDUSTRY

Tim Wright (*editor*)
THE CHINESE ECONOMY IN THE EARLY TWENTIETH CENTURY

Yanrui Wu
PRODUCTIVE PERFORMANCE OF CHINESE ENTERPRISES

Haiqun Yang
BANKING AND FINANCIAL CONTROL IN REFORMING PLANNED
ECONOMIES

Shujie Yao
AGRICULTURAL REFORMS AND GRAIN PRODUCTION IN CHINA

Xun-Hai Zhang
ENTERPRISE REFORMS IN A CENTRALLY PLANNED ECONOMY

Ng Sek Hong and Malcolm Warner
CHINA'S TRADE UNIONS AND MANAGEMENT

China's Price and Enterprise Reform

Wang Xiao-qiang
Senior Research Fellow
Research Institute of Economic System and Management
State Council's Commission for Restructuring Economic Systems
People's Republic of China

Foreword by Peter Nolan

First published in Great Britain 1998 by
MACMILLAN PRESS LTD
Houndmills, Basingstoke, Hampshire RG21 6XS and London
Companies and representatives throughout the world

A catalogue record for this book is available from the British Library.

ISBN 0–333–69635–2

First published in the United States of America 1998 by
ST. MARTIN'S PRESS, INC.,
Scholarly and Reference Division,
175 Fifth Avenue, New York, N.Y. 10010

ISBN 0–312–17698–8

Library of Congress Cataloging-in-Publication Data
Wang, Hsiao-ch'iang.
China's price and enterprise reform / Wang Xiao-qiang.
p.   cm. — (Studies on the Chinese economy)
Includes bibliographical references and index.
ISBN 0–312–17698–8
1. Prices—Government policy—China.   2. Price regulation—China.
3. Government business enterprises—China.   4. Industrial policy-
-China.   5. China—Economic policy—1976–   I. Title.   II. Series.
HB236.C55W355 1997
338.5'26'0951—dc21   97–2567
                                                                   CIP

This book is printed on paper suitable for recycling and made from fully managed and sustained forest sources.

10   9   8   7   6   5   4   3   2   1
07   06   05   04   03   02   01   00   99   98

Printed and bound in Great Britain by
Antony Rowe Ltd, Chippenham, Wiltshire

Contents

List of Tables

List of Figures

List of Abbreviations

CESRRI-a   Chinese Economic System Reform Research Institute
CESRRI-b   Development Research Office of Chinese Economic System
            Reform Research Institute
CESRRI-c   Microeconomics Research Office of Chinese Economic
            System Reform Research Institute
CESRRI-d   The delegation of field study in Japan, the Chinese Economic
            System Reform Research Institute
SSB   State Statistical Bureau

Foreword

I am delighted to be asked to write a Foreword for this book. The subject of the book is of the highest importance. It examines one of the most important phenomena in China's modern history, namely the debates over economic policy in China in the 1980s. At the heart of these were arguments over ownership and price reform. Wang Xiao-qiang's book analyses these in a fresh and vigorous fashion.

Few people are as well qualified as Wang Xiao-qiang to write a book such as this. He was closely involved in the policy-making process surrounding the great reforms in the Chinese countryside in the early 1980s. He then worked at the Rural Development Research Centre, under the Directorship of Du Rensheng, who played a key role in this process.[1] Wang Xiao-qiang's pioneering book on poverty in sparsely populated areas, *The Poverty of Plenty*[2] (co-authored with Bai Nanfeng) was one of the best-selling Chinese books of the 1980s. For several years he was Deputy Director of the Chinese Economic System Reform Research Institute (CESRRI), the leading reformist policy 'think tank' of the 1980s. In this capacity he was intimately involved in the cut-and-thrust of policy debate at the very highest levels. While in this position, he was responsible for promoting and organising a great deal of research on different aspects of China's economic reforms. The results of the largest of these projects was the book *Reform in China: Challenges and Choices* (1987). The book's editor, Bruce Reynolds, believes that this research project was 'arguably the most extraordinary empirical investigation undertaken in twentieth century China' (Reynolds, 1987, p. xv).

China's economy has grown at high speed since the late 1970s. Because it has been so successful it is hard to imagine that it could have been anything other than successful, just as it is hard for most people to imagine that with different policy choices, the Soviet reforms could also have 'grown rapidly out of the plan'. However, as Wang Xiao-qiang shows, it was far from a foregone conclusion that in China successful reform policies would be chosen. The reform path was never clearly charted: the reformers were indeed 'groping for stones to cross the river'. Wang Xiao-qiang's book re-evaluates the arguments that raged over the choice of reform path. Many of these were ill-constructed at the time. The debates were often conducted at high speed, with the ideas based frequently on intuition, rather than being the result of long-maturing economic research programmes. Policy could not wait. Decisions had to be made. With the benefit of hindsight, Wang Xiao-qiang is able to develop the key arguments in a rigorously worked-out form.

From the beginning there were those who argued for 'one cut of the knife', for dramatic changes in the ownership and price structure. They used as their intellectual support the principles of Western neo-classical economics and the arguments of Western scholars and policy advisers.[3] These ideas were presented in their most powerful form by Janos Kornai and Jeffrey Sachs. It was far from a foregone conclusion that those who argued against these ideas, who argued instead for experimentalism and caution, for a 'muddy' approach to policy, would succeed in having their policies implemented. Indeed, as this book shows, in the mid-1980s the leadership came very close to adopting the radical path.

Wang Xiao-qiang's book is not the account of a neutral observer. Rather, it is written by someone who participated vigorously in those debates. Wang Xiao-qiang does not personalise the criticism of his opponents within China. He could easily have done so, since the debates were hard. Instead, he confines himself to analysing the arguments. The positions which Wang Xiao-qiang defends in this book constitute a deep criticism of the arguments of those who supported the radical 'one cut of the knife' approach. The book carefully reconstructs and amplifies the case for experimental reform and for cautious changes of price and property relations which build on existing institutions rather than destroy them. It is of the utmost interest to anyone trying to understand the logic of China's reform path as perceived from the inside of the policy-making process.

Had the Chinese leadership adopted the big bang of price and ownership reform, it is highly unlikely that the China's economy would have experienced the success it has. Indeed, it is likely that there would have been great disorder in the economic system, leading to political turbulence much greater than that which culminated in the Tiananmen Square protests. The resulting chaos would have propelled China along a completely different path of political economy. It is one thing for a sophisticated, industrialised economy (such as Russia's) to experience politico-economic collapse; it is another thing for a huge poor economy such as China's to experience this. The result would, in all probability, have been immense suffering for a large part of the Chinese population.

Wang Xiao-qiang himself draws a comparison with the Soviet debates of the 1920s. The triumph in Russia of the Stalinist, command economy approach had profound consequences for that country, as well as, of course, for many other countries. Similarly, had the Chinese policy discussions in the 1980s taken a different turn, then the course of China's history in the two or three decades after Mao's death might well have been very different. The impact would not just have been felt within China. Its successful growth under its reform policies has had a huge impact upon the world economy, greatly altering the trends in international trade and capital movements as well as the whole global balance of economic and political power. If China's huge process of 'transition' had been executed badly, then China might have had to wait a long time for another chance to 'catch up'. Moreover, the growth prospects and even the share price of many leading capitalist firms would not have risen as fast as they have done, since this growth has been based to a significant degree upon the enticing prospects offered by the explosive growth in East Asia in general and China in particular. In other words, the stakes involved in the debates analysed by Wang Xiao-qiang were extremely high, especially for the Chinese people, but also for the whole global economy. The analogy with the Soviet debates of the 1920s is far from overdrawn.

Wang Xiao-qiang's book does not suggest that by the early 1990s all was clear for Chinese policy-making. Despite having grown faster than any other country in the world for the past two decades, China still faces huge policy dilemmas. There is deep debate about how best to shape policy in respect to the challenges that face China's political system, in respect to the explosion of migration from the countryside, in respect to the continuing pressure of population upon food supply, in respect to the ecological consequences of China's explosive industrialisation, in respect to the sharply widening differentials of income and wealth between classes and regions, in respect to the way ahead for loss-making state enterprises, in respect to the relationship between emerging big Chinese businesses and the global corporations of the advanced capitalist world, in respect to the huge cultural transformation that modernisation is producing, and in respect to dealings with the USA, whose hegemonic position of the past half century is threatened by China's rise. However, many of these problems are the consequences of accelerated growth and marketisation. Had China made the wrong policy choices in the 1980s, it would have had a very different, and much more severe, set of difficulties to face.

In a vast country such as China in the midst of a colossal process of modernisation and system change, the only useful way to approach policy is to think from first principles, applying logic and common sense. As Wang Xiao-qiang's book shows, there are no easy solutions to be found in textbooks for the complex policy choices that confront China's leaders.

His book will be essential reading for those attempting to make sense of the vast process known as the 'transition'.

PETER NOLAN

Notes

1.   His book of essays, *Reform and Development in Rural China* (Macmillan, 1995) is also published in this series.
2.   Translated into English by Angela Knox, and published in this series by Macmillan (1991).
3.   Of course, there was no unanimity among Western scholars. Leading commentators such as Dwight Perkins, Tom Rawski and Barry Naughton all broadly supported the experimental approach towards system reform.

Preface

This book arose from my own involvement in China's reform process from 1978 to the present. The arguments in it reflect the intense debates that took place among policy-makers in China. After almost 20 years of successful 'reform' and growth it is easy to forget that China's policies could have taken a very different path. I believe that history will come to realise that these debates are of as great a significance for China's history as those in the Soviet Union in the 1920s were for Russia. I hope that my book may help to shed light on these debates. With the benefit of hindsight, some of the arguments that were not explained so clearly then by those involved in the tense discussions may now be explained more satisfactorily.

I was Deputy Director of CESRRI, at the State Council's Commission for Restructuring Economic Systems in China, from 1984 to 1989. Since 1994, I have been Senior Fellow of the Institute of Economic Systems and Management, at the State Council's Commission for Restructuring Economic Systems in China. I have been fortunate enough to participate in a series of practical studies on China's economic reform since 1979. Some ideas represented in this book have benefited from my working experiences with different scholars and officials, especially my colleagues at CESRRI.

The original version of this book was my PhD thesis in the Faculty of Economics and Politics, Cambridge University, entitled 'Industrial price reform and enterprise reform in transitional economies: theory, and evidence from China'. In writing the book, I owe my biggest thanks to my supervisor, Peter Nolan, who helped me to have the opportunity to write a work of this nature. He granted me the use of his office at any time with all the books and materials he has collected. He was always willing to listen to my half-baked ideas and discuss them until I could clarify them. Our two year (1994–6) collaborative field study on 'The emergence of the modern corporation in China', funded by the British Economic and Social Research Council, has been of great help in enabling me to understand the arguments presented in this work more fully. Finally Peter Nolan has corrected my English expressions word by word. I particularly wish to thank Thomas Chan, head of the China Business Centre at Hong Kong Polytechnic University. The Centre has financially supported me in organising research groups on several different topics in China since 1994. He also read the final draft word by word, and commented not only on theoretical issues but also on English expressions. The help of both these people gave me great moral encouragement to deal with the broad and complicated issues involved.

John Thoburn, Geoffrey Meeks, Dwight Perkins, Adrian Wood and Lo Dic all read carefully, and gave critical comments on the earlier drafts.

I am grateful to David Newbery. Through him the early drafts of each of the two parts of this work have been printed separately (in 1993 and 1996) in *Discussion Papers on Economic Transition*, No. 9305 and No. 9603, Department of Applied Economics, University of Cambridge.

Finally I would like to thank my wife, Guo Peihui, a former ballerina with the Central Ballet of China. She has fully supported me during all the uncertainties of life abroad since 1989. She has undertaken all the housework, including taking care of our son, when I had only a very limited student scholarship. I definitely could not have finished this book without her support.

None of these people can be held responsible for any errors or omissions in what follows.

WANG XIAO-QIANG

Introduction

Since 1989, transition from the command to the market economy has spread to all pre-socialist countries. Price liberalisation and enterprise reform are the two core elements of transition. The former provides the new rule of market mechanism, while the latter creates new players for the game of competition. Sachs and Kornai delivered two oversimplified but influential principles: the big-bang programme to establish the market; and privatisation to reform state-owned enterprises.

SHOCK THERAPY

Kornai argues: 'The reform process has a forty-year history in Yugoslavia, twenty in Hungary, and almost a whole decade in China. All three countries represent specific mixtures of amazing results and disastrous failures' (1990b, p. 210). Transferring the economic system from a command to a market system, it is argued, needs radical and comprehensive 'shock therapy'.

What is 'shock therapy' in this context? The proposal calls for implementing a series of *laissez-faire* policies in one shock. According to Sachs and Lipton, Poland's classic 'big-bang' programme in 1989 consisted of stabilisation, price liberalisation, trade liberalisation, promotion of the private sector and privatisation of state-owned enterprises (1990, p. 55). These five components are fundamental and powerful enough to set up a textbook perfect market mechanism. Price liberalisation eliminates distortions and subsidies, while providing the correct signals for reallocating resources efficiently. The development of the private sector and the privatisation of state-owned enterprises invigorate classical profit-seekers to compete with each other, favouring market demand. Trade liberalisation further clarifies prices and stimulates competition, not only domestically but also internationally. Stabilisation, through enforcing constrictive monetary and fiscal policies to counter inflation, ensures that the entire transition process is under control. With its simple, lucid and convincing logic, the big bang has become the most influential proposal.

Kornai argues that all measures of big bang, 'one stroke' or 'surgery' reflect 'a major operation on a patient involving a whole package of measures' (in Lipton and Sachs 1990, p. 139). The 'major operation' is not only for a specific patient. Regarding his 'feasible' and 'educational' book, *The Road to a Free Economy*, Kornai declares: 'I am confident that the core of ideas presented here is applicable not only in Hungary, but in all other countries in transition from a socialist regime to a free economy' (1990a, pp. 13–24).[1] With more confidence, Sachs delivered the 'package of measures' to many different patients around the world, including (so far) Poland, Russia, Yugoslavia, Mongolia, Bolivia, Venezuela and Slovenia, according to Hutton (1992). Moreover, long before transition in Eastern Europe, Sachs believed that the same 'shock' programme had successfully cured a number of patients, such as Argentina, Bolivia, Brazil, Israel and Peru most recently, Germany, Austria, Hungary and Poland after the First World War, and Japan, South Korea and Taiwan after the Second World War (Sachs 1987, p. 317). The shock therapy is not only universal but perpetual.

China is not exceptional. The 'price-reform school' or the 'integrated-reform school' was established as early as 1984, when urban reform officially began (Hsu 1991, pp. 156–61).

> They seek (a) independent enterprises responsible for their own profit and loss, (b) a free-price market that encourages competition, and (c) an indirect control mechanism. To pave the way, according to their scenario, it is necessary to reform the price system by first adjusting, and then freeing, all the prices within a short period of time, while at the same time setting up a new government budgetary system and a new monetary system. (Wu and Zhao 1988, pp. 26–7)

Actually, China almost executed the big-bang programme twice (once in 1986 and again in 1988).

THEORETICAL UPGRADING

Sachs and Lipton promised that there were profound possibilities for 'rapid improvements in living standards', if the East European countries could make the transition from central planning to the market economy (1990, pp. 46–7). Having performed their surgery, instead of these 'rapid improvements in living standards' some transitional economies were locked into inflation, substantial budget deficits, stagnant or declining production, high unemployment, heavy foreign debts, and difficulties in increasing exports. *The Economist* summed up the Soviet transition thus: 'Plenty of shock, no therapy' (1991c, p. 71). Confronted with these results, there was a theoretical upgrading. Sachs told his patients that there was always a 'valley of tears' to accompany the big bang (Sachs 1991, 1992a, 1992b). From the tears, Sachs (1994) obtained his theoretical innovation. In contrast to the ordinary 'good' equilibrium, he created a new concept of 'bad equilibrium' in which the state is unable to finance itself, or to provide basic public goods. Kornai names the 'valley of tears' as a unique 'transformational recession' (1993, p. 2):

> To improve their trade and current account balances, several countries need to devalue their currencies more than they have done so far; doing so, however, will certainly speed up inflation. To halt the production decline and stimulate recovery, countries need to use fiscal means ranging from tax concessions for private investment projects to publicly financed investment; but these measures could further increase the budget deficit. To improve the fiscal balance and encourage financial discipline, countries need to observe a hard budget constraint, with no bailouts for persistent loss-makers. Such an uncompromising stance, however, could result directly and by slipover in higher unemployment, lower aggregate demand, lower output or, in the short-run, slower growth. (Kornai 1994, p. 5)

> What present themselves are painful trade-offs and choices between bad and worse. (Kornai 1992a, p. 18)

What is wrong with this contradiction between the theory and the consequences of implementing the theory? No matter in how bad a condition they are in the surgery, usually patients do not have enough knowledge of medicine to argue with doctors, and besides, the theory is being upgraded. Unfortunately or fortunately, one big patient has not yet been honoured with the same surgery. China started reforms in 1978. Without both the big-bang programme and massive privatisation, in the last 16 years China's real gross national product (GNP) grew by an average of almost 9 per cent a year. In 1994, the economy was four times that of 1978. While Russia has suffered from hyper-inflation and a 20 per cent per annum fall in industrial output from an even poorer economic base China became the eleventh largest exporter in the world in 1992 (*Economic Reference* [Chinese], 10 December 1992).

The exception has made the doctors embarrassed. Sachs and Woo (1994) wrote a paper to explain why China had not yet been the subject of shock therapy. They list a series of Chinese 'advantages of backwardness'. The reason that China escaped from the surgery was just because China was too poor. They predict that the future will be problematic unless

China goes back to their hospital. In this book, based on Chinese experience, I argue that what is wrong is the oversimplified theory of Sachs and Kornai. First, transition is not only a process of transferring the economic system from a command to a market one, but also an economic development process of re-industrialisation that includes adjustment of the existing industrial structure and establishment of new industries, in order to create a new industrial structure more responsive to the market demand both domestically and internationally. Growth itself can facilitate and promote system changes. Second, the nature of transition is not a process of copying some simple principles from the textbook, but the process of innovation, in terms of firm organisation, and the relationship between the state and business. These are not yet available in the textbook.

STRUCTURE OF THE BOOK

The book consists of two independent papers: price reform and enterprise reform.

Part I focuses on price reform. Chapter 1 examines the non-feasibility of the big-bang programme. In practice, without enterprise reform, the big-bang programme could not achieve equilibrium because of the problem of a return to the original price relativities, in which unreformed enterprises raised their output prices to cover increased costs, thereby reproducing price distortions with inflation in addition. Moreover, since inflation was the consequence of enterprise behaviour rather than a purely macroeconomic matter, stabilisation could not work well. There is a discussion of the linkage between price liberalisation and re-industrialisation. This was disregarded by the big-bang theorists.

Chapter 2 explains the 'gradual approach' of price reform in China since 1978. Along with the adjustment of the industrial structure, the government decontrolled prices one by one under buyer's market conditions. China also introduced the dual-track price system, in which part of production was still distributed by official rationing at fixed prices, while enterprises were free to sell what they produced or to buy what they needed above the mandatory quota at free prices in the market. Under the dual-track system, economic growth is influenced by market signals. Economic growth, together with the growing impact of the market, accelerated competition, re-industrialisation and technological advance. In particular, expansion of large state-owned enterprises in upstream industries was an essential part of China's remarkable growth.

Part II analyses enterprise reform. Chapter 3 reviews the modern history of the large firm. Individuals only own a small percentage of shares in modern corporations. The owners trade shares in the stock market, but do not actually operate the firm. Large Japanese corporations hold shares in each other's firms. Competition, however, is even fiercer in the Japanese 'manager-controlled firm' than it was in the traditional 'owner-controlled firm'. Therefore, this chapter argues that enterprise reform in the transition should focus on enhancing managerial autonomy.

Chapter 4 analyses enterprise reform in China. The state sector has been withdrawing from downstream industries and concentrating on upstream industries. There have been four types of enterprise reform in China: the 'contract responsibility system', the enterprise group, the joint-venture and the joint-stock company. They are leading to an enhancement of managerial autonomy rather than privatisation. The 'ownership maze' in China leaves a huge space for the state to intervene. Therefore, reform of the government is another core of the transition.

The conclusion makes two main points: first, because of the lack of a blueprint, transition in China has followed a purely pragmatic philosophy. It has focused more on economic development than on reform in itself. Second, China has combined the 'gradual approach' of transition with the gradual process of economic development. The combination of transition and development gave China a chance to try something new in price reform and enterprise reform.

Note

1. Hungary has not yet adopted the big-bang programme (Hare and Revesz 1992).

Part I

Growth and Re-Industrialisation: China's Price Reform versus the Big Bang

Price liberalisation is often the first topic of reform in transitional economies. However, those economists who argued that it should come first could not provide a clear explanation of how it could be implemented first. The 'big bang' proposal calls for freeing prices in one go, such as in Poland and Russia. China, on the other hand, has practised a 'gradual approach' which has combined economic reform with economic development since 1978. Around 700 kinds of producer goods were allocated by the plan in 1978, but by 1991 the number was below 20 (*The Economist* 1992). In 1993, the Chinese government declared that most price controls had been abolished. Based on Chinese experience, this part will argue that price reform cannot succeed without fruitful enterprise reform and adjustments of the industrial structure. In China, the 'gradual approach' – the combination of the so-called buyer's market price reform and dual-track price system – was a profound innovation.

Introduction:
The Inconsistencies
of the Big Bang: Is it a
Comprehensive Package?

What is the big-bang programme? According to Sachs and Lipton, Poland's classic big-bang programme in 1989 consisted of stabilisation, price liberalisation, trade liberalisation, promotion of the private sector and privatisation of state-owned enterprises (1990, p. 55). The five components are fundamental to the setting-up of a textbook perfect market mechanism. Nevertheless, if one examines the big bang carefully, it is easy to see that the programme is not a comprehensive one. In practice, it consists only of price liberalisation in the product market.

COMPREHENSIVE AND SIMULTANEOUS?

Piecemeal reform is said to fail in coping with the interactions of the economic system. As the foremost distinction between piecemeal reform and the 'big bang', 'comprehensiveness' and 'simultaneity' have always been emphasised by 'big-bang' theorists:

> The problem lies in the fact that implementation of these changes is inconsistent and sluggish. The ambiguity that prevails in one set of measures reduces the efficiency of another set. The sum total of ten different kinds of half results is not five full successes but five full fiascos. All of the above-named measures are conditional upon one another. Stopping inflation requires a balanced budget. Balancing the budget, in turn, can be achieved only if the tax system is placed on a radically new basis. The budget cannot be balanced in the midst of inflation, since revenues are always delayed by comparison with expenses, so that inflation makes itself felt more strongly in the income side than on the expenditure side. Stopping the subsidisation of loss-making firms is conditional upon the introduction of a new tax system and also upon the possibility of finding out which firms are genuine profit or loss makers through the use

of market-clearing equilibrium prices. Genuine market prices cannot emerge, however, amid accelerated inflation. While the partial price adjustments do not converge to a rational system of relative prices, they themselves speed up the inflationary spiral. The list of these concentric and interdependent problems could well be extended by a dozen more examples. Taken together, they provide an economic explanation for the need to execute the operation at one stroke. (Kornai 1990a, p. 159)

The indispensability of the 'big bang' lies in the fact that it is a comprehensive package including all necessary changes simultaneously (Lipton and Sachs 1990; Prybyla 1991).

THE LAG OF ENTERPRISE REFORM

Lipton and Sachs declared 'the transition process is a seamless web' (1990, p. 99). However, the lag in enterprise reform is a big 'seam' in the comprehensive 'big-bang' programme:

Britain's prime minister, Margaret Thatcher, who may be regarded as the most fervent privatizer of the 1980s, had presided over some two dozen privatisations in the past decade, most of which were carried out by public offerings of shares of state companies. In Poland, however, there are over 7000 state enterprises that are candidates for privatisation. Poland must therefore find new privatisation means that are administratively feasible, economically efficient and politically viable (Sachs and Lipton 1990, p. 61)

Not surprisingly, Poland executed the 'big-bang' programme before the 'new privatisation means' had been found. Again, Russia was strongly persuaded to go for the 'big bang' without the 'new privatisation means', although Sachs knew that privatisation is much more complex in Russia than in Poland (1992c, pp. 46–7). Experiences in Poland and Russia seem to demonstrate that it is impossible to accomplish many necessary changes simultaneously, if the changes must occur as one shock. State-owned enterprises often produced 70–90 per cent of total industrial output in transitional economies. Meanwhile, the state sector predominated in most other economic areas, such as the commercial network, producer goods distribution, trade business, financial system, transportation, communication, power supply, infrastructure, and so on. The lag of enterprise reform means that the whole picture of the economy cannot be changed too much, even by a 'big bang' programme. Actually, the real 'big bang' was mainly price liberalisation.

Lipton and Sachs acknowledge that privatisation 'is likely to take many years' (1990, p. 101). But the lagging behind of enterprise reform is inconsistent with the supposedly comprehensive 'big bang'. As a result, two years after Poland's 'big bang', Sachs provided the following bizarre description: 'Indeed, Poland already can be considered to have a market economy, but one that still has an overwhelming state ownership of large industrial firms. Poland has so far achieved a form of "market socialism"' (1992b, p. 14). Kornai also admits: 'It is impossible to privatise in a "big bang"' (in Lipton and Sachs 1990, p. 142). He even referred to the co-existence of the state and private sectors as a *'dual* economy' and considered that the symbiosis would endure for the next two decades (1990a, p. 101). Neither Sachs nor Kornai, however, has said what kind of mechanism can handle an economy consisting of market-determined prices and enterprises which have not been privatised for 'many years' or for the next two decades.

WHO IS THE 'DRIVER'?

The definition of price liberalisation, according to Sachs and Lipton, was that 'Prices had to be decontrolled and subsidies eliminated, in order to establish a demand-and-supply-driven system of price determination' (1990, p. 55). Undoubtedly, having eliminated government control, prices must be determined by demand and supply in the market. The crux is: who, instead of the government, would physically be the 'demander' and 'supplier' to drive prices?

Eventually the 'demand-and-supply-driven system', in large measure, must be driven by the unreformed enterprises instead of the government. These enterprises are the sellers of their products and the buyers of raw materials, intermediate and investment goods. Through paying wages to employees, they also indirectly influence individuals' consumption demands.[1] Samonis has observed:

state enterprises, integrated horizontally and vertically to cover the country and the branch, produce well over 80 per cent of industrial output. More than half of industrial output comes from the sole producer [who] either pass on price increases (as a cost-pushed inflation) to the buyers of their output or, failing that, limit output to increase the monopoly rent. That's how they maximise their profit in an easy

way. And that's what largely accounts for a drop in output in Poland.
(1991, pp. 9–13)

ADMINISTRATIVE STABILISATION

Price liberalisation must be accompanied by macroeconomic stabilisation.
Restrictive fiscal and monetary policies are always emphasised by the
big-bang proponents. The suppression of inflation by tight policies is
universal truth. In a transitional economy, the question is: what causes
inflation? What, therefore, should macroeconomic policies seek to control:
the money supply, government expenditure, or the behaviour of unreformed enterprises?

A decade ago Kornai found that in a socialist economy the authorities
withstand the tendencies towards price-drift generated within the enterprises, not determined by fiscal and monetary policies (1980, p. 274). In
China, inflation was a consequence of enterprise behaviour rather than a
product of macroeconomic policies. China introduced stabilisation measures in 1986 and 1989–91. The best way to describe the nature of stabilisation was how it worked to reduce money supply. In China in the 1980s
there was no financial market. All banks were branches of the government
administration, the same as other ministries (World Bank 1988b), so that
there was no place for open market operations. Enterprise managers were
appointed by the government and their positions were incorporated into the
bureaucratic hierarchy of the government. How could investment be
reduced? 'Investment hunger' was insensitive to interest rates. Enterprise
managers' bureaucratic position was determined by the size of their enterprises and therefore the size of investment, regardless of the firm's
profitability. How could wages be reduced? Wages were inflexible in a
downward direction, because the manager's appointment partly rested on
his evaluation by employees. So the stabilisation programme had no choice
but to resort once again to administrative means. Government officials set
credit ceilings and distributed loan quotas, set investment ceilings and distributed investment quotas, and imposed a surtax on bonuses as a form of
wage ceiling. The would-be macroeconomic stabilisation was exactly what
government officials had done under the pre-reform command economy.
The economic authorities had the option of either controlling prices administratively or controlling investment and wages administratively. Of course,
price distortions lead to misallocation. But how could price distortions be
eliminated under administrative stabilisation, which meant that all credit
and investment ceilings, loan and investment quotas (capital allocation),

and rates of bonus tax (labour allocation) were set administratively and distributed administratively by the same bureaucrats?

Using these traditional means of reducing the money supply, the consequence was, in Perkins's words: 'At the user end, quotas were set that cut off credit to efficient and profligate borrowers alike. The result was a sharp drop in the growth of industry and increasing lay-offs' (1992, p. 25).

RE-INDUSTRIALISATION

Since the goal of price liberalisation is to establish a demand-and-supply-driven system of price determination, it is necessary to inquire what the 'demand' demands and what the 'supply' can supply, as well as how to bridge the gap between the two.

Under the pre-reform command economy, planned prices functioned as a tool of revenue distribution – the 'revenue-generating mechanism' – rather than as the signals of resource allocation. In order to carry out the 'forced draft' industrialisation strategy, the state monopolised industry. The government set the prices of basic goods low and the prices of processing industries high. From these price differentials, the state extracted revenue directly from the turnover of state-owned enterprises to speed up industrialisation (Naughton 1992). In other words, *the 'distorted' prices were associated with a 'distorted' industrial structure*. Consequently, price liberalisation was not only a means to change the price determination mechanism from the planning system to the market, but also implied an adjustment of the industrial structure. This is what Amsden, Kochanowicz and Taylor (1994) call 're-industrialisation'.

Re-industrialisation is wholly outside the vision of the 'big-bang' proponents. It may be handled by the invisible hand. For example, Kornai says nothing about industrial structure in his two influential books, *The Road to a Free Economy* and *The Socialist System*. Sachs sees reform and re-industrialisation as being two perspectives: 'The reforms themselves can and should be introduced quickly, in three to five years. The restructuring, on the other hand, will necessarily last for a much longer period, presumably a decade or more' (1992b, p. 6).

FREEING THE PRODUCT MARKET ALONE?

Although proponents of 'big-bang' theory have principally focused on allocative efficiency, somewhat surprisingly in practice, the real 'big-bang' was only executed in the product market. Reforms at the deeper level aiming to establish a series of factor markets, such as capital, labour and housing markets, are always left out of the practicable scheme of the 'big bang'. In a command economy, the 'distortions' in factor markets misallocated resources much more seriously than price distortions did in the product market (Byrd and Tidrick 1987; World Bank 1988b). Indeed, the reforms in factor markets are crucial conditions for enterprise reform.

Structural adjustments need accurate allocation signals. Therefore, price liberalisation is a prerequisite, so that the factors of production can follow market signals. Aside from indecision over whether product prices could be cleared in the absence of factor markets, the debate about the 'big-bang' programme in China also concentrated on whether the signal for resource movement or resource movement itself was more decisive. It is not right to say that price liberalisation is unimportant. If there were no reform of factor markets within the 'big-bang' programme, without factors of production following market signals to move, allocative efficiency would be more hypothetical than real (Perkins 1988, 1991a; Portes 1992). In both theory and practice, reforms in factor markets are obviously more fundamental than price liberalisation in the product market alone. In fact, Kornai himself pointed out the non-feasibility of the 'big bang' which he strongly and repeatedly recommended: 'It is impossible to reach a satis-factory price system in some areas of the economy – those outside the sphere directly controlled by the state – while the basic characteristics of the old price system survive at the heart of the economy, in the state-controlled sphere' (1992b, p. 525).

SUMMARY

As enterprise reform, structural adjustment and the establishment of factor markets could not be accomplished simultaneously with price liberalisa-tion, the would-be comprehensive 'big-bang' programme turned out to be solely price liberalisation in the product market. Much has been written about *why* price liberalisation *should* come first; in contrast, there is no clear explanation of *how* prices *can* be freed first.

1 Why did China Avoid the Big Bang?

The big-bang proponents call for instituting all necessary changes simultaneously (Steinherr 1991, p.4). In practice, enterprise reform and adjustments of the industrial structure cannot happen all at once. Thus the comprehensive big bang turns out to be price reform first. What mechanism can handle an economy consisting of market-determined prices and unreformed state-owned enterprises: that is, *market prices and non-market enterprises*? The big-bang theorists have not answered this question.

In this chapter, based on Chinese experience, we outline what would happen in an economy consisting of 'market prices and non-market enterprises'. The first section delineates the mechanism of the so-called return to the original price relativities, in which unreformed enterprises simply raise their output prices to cover the increase in their costs, thus reproducing price 'distortions' but with inflation in addition. The following section further argues that stabilisation could often induce a fall in production rather than a fall in inflation. Moreover, inter-firm trade credits can become a powerful weapon with which unreformed enterprises can frustrate a monetary squeeze. In the final section, we argue that there is a corresponding connection between the shock of price liberalisation and the task of re-industrialisation. All these considerations led China to avoid the infeasible big bang.

A RETURN TO THE ORIGINAL PRICE RELATIVITIES: IS THERE EQUILIBRIUM?

'There are interactions between the socialist enterprises and prices. In one direction of cause and effect the firm is not a passive price-taker but, to a considerable extent, a price-maker' (Kornai 1980, p. 323). How do socialist enterprises make prices? Kornai has given an excellent description in his book, *Economics of Shortage* (1980, chs 4, 5, and 14). He concludes: '*The socialist firm, both as seller and as buyer, had an incentive to increase prices. Both the cost-push tendencies (shifting increases in costs onto the buyer in the form of higher prices) and the demand-pull*

9

tendencies (the unsatisfied buyer offers a higher price) can be discerned in the behaviour of the firm' (p. 363, italics in original).

Table 1.1 bears out Kornai's assertion. In China, a survey of 77 large-and-medium state enterprises in machinery industry in Hunan Province in 1985 showed that more than 57 per cent of state enterprises simply passed on more than 100 per cent of the increase in their costs (caused by input price increase) through their output prices. Some 70 per cent of enterprises gained more than 30 per cent of their increased profit directly by raising their output prices.

Table 1.1   Price reaction of Chinese state-owned enterprises, 1985 (%)

Profit increase from output price increase/ cost increase from input price increase	*Enterprises as % of total sample*	*Profit increase from output price increase/ selling profit*	*Enterprises as % of total sample*
< 30	10.67	< 30	29.33
30–60	20.00	30–60	38.67
60–100	12.00	60–100	14.67
> 100	57.33	> 100	17.33

Source: CESRRI-c (1988), Table 1.3.

'Return to the Original Price Relativities'

As important evidence of the failure of gradual reform and the indispensability of the big bang, Kornai has frequently cited and criticised the phenomenon of what in China is called the return to the original price relativities:

The prices of products belonging to group 'A' are raised, on the premise that they are too low in comparison with those of groups 'B,' 'C,' etc., but the price increase for 'A' pushed up the costs of 'B,' 'C,' etc., or if consumer articles are involved, the cost of living. Sooner or later, the costs of the groups of products 'B,' 'C,' etc., will outpace their prices, which will then have to be raised, just as the rise in the cost of living will provoke a rise in nominal wages, which in turn will push up the cost level. The series of partial price adjustments inevitably engenders a cost-price-wage spiral thus diminishing the change in relative prices initially pursued through partial increases. At the date of the increase, the price of the group of products 'A' rose, say, by 30 per cent relative to groups 'B' and 'C,' whereas in three to five users' time the prices of the products 'B' and 'C' will also have been raised to the same level by the inflationary process ... During the process, the relations between costs, demand and supply will also be constantly shifting, and distortions will be reproduced ... The problem can be solved only through a *general and comprehensive* price reform which places the entire price system on a market basis in a relatively short time. I am convinced that from the economic point of view, the solution must be applied in such a way that it resembles a single big shock. (1990b, pp. 50–1, italics in original)

Naughton (1992) used the profit rates of different industries to explain the function of price distortions in China. Figure 1.1 reveals an apparent

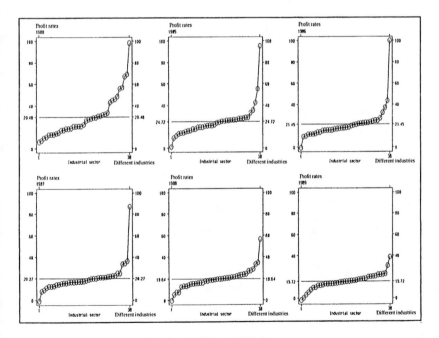

Figure 1.1   Sectoral profit rates in China, 1980–9
Source: SSB (1990b), pp. 153–9.

tendency of sector variations of profit rates to fall from time to time, thus converging towards the horizontal average profitability line.

If we assume that all differences in profitability come from price distortions, the line of profit rates in Figure 1.1 can be seen as the relative price lines.[1] The average profitability line, therefore, can symbolise the line of theoretical price equilibrium. In a perfect market economy with full employment, an industry with a profit rate below the equilibrium should be in shortage, and above the equilibrium, oversupplied. Then we shift the diagram of profit rates from Figure 1.1 into Figure 1.2 as diagram (B). The oblique line RP-1 represents the relative price line. The horizontal line represents the theoretical equilibrium line. By using the method of mechanical drawing, diagram (A), as with the vertical sections of diagram (B), represents the industry A with its price P below equilibrium point E_1 and P^*, displayed by the supply curve S_1 and the demand curve D_1 while the shortage remains Q_1 to Q_2. And diagram (C) represents industry C with its price P above equilibrium point E_1 and price P^*, displayed by the supply curve S_1' and the demand curve D_1', while the surplus remains Q_1' to Q_2'. Now, Figure 1.2 can schematically delineate the proposition of return to the original price relativities.

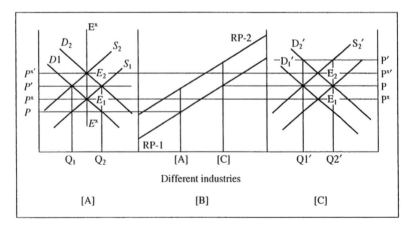

Figure 1.2   'Return to the original price relativities'

Diagram (A) represents an industry in scarcity. After its input price increases as a result of 'supply-push', the supply curve shifts from S_1 to S_2 and its price rises from P to P'.[2] Matching the shift of the supply curve, the reasons given by Kornai (quoted earlier) shift the demand curve from D_1 to D_2.[3] As a consequence, the equilibrium point moves from E_1 to E_2. The new price P' is lower than new equilibrium price $P^{*\prime}$, and the shortage remains within $Q1 - Q2$. Through the chain effect of one industry on another, the demand for a slack industry (C) can be raised from $D1'$ to $D2'$ thus raising its price from P to P'. This thereby enables its supply curve also to shift $S1'$ to $S2'$ in compensation for its input price increases, while the new price P' becomes higher again than new equilibrium price $P^{*\prime}$, and the quantity of surplus (inventory) is maintained in $Q1' - Q2'$ at a higher price level. In general, the industries with low prices can increase their output prices. Their increased revenue can build up an increasing demand for other industries whose prices might already be higher than that in the previous equilibrium. The supply and demand curves take turns to shift, finally resulting in the shift of the relative price line from RP-1 to RP-2 as shown in (B), and the shift of the equilibrium line from P^* to $P^{*\prime}$.

Figure 1.2 suggests two interesting implications. First, Kornai is right. If a piecemeal price reform was stopped at any stage, the price distortions must be still there, so price reform can never succeed because of the reproduction of price distortions. Second, Kornai is wrong. If one decontrolled all prices in one go, the same mechanism of a return to the original price relativities must reproduce price distortions repeatedly. As long as there are industries whose prices are relatively low, they can increase their output prices as the cost-push force of the next cycle of price rises. Along with the supply and demand curves taking turns to shift, the equilibrium point E in (A) will move dynamically along the vertical line $E^* - E^*$. Therefore equilibrium can never be reached, but inflation results.

In reality, the equilibrium point E cannot be fixed at one position. The chain effect of 'cost-push' and 'demand-pull' exists even in a typical market economy. *A more meaningful concept is the degree of the return to the original price relativities.* If the slope of line RP-2 was approximately zero, the shock caused by price liberalisation should be once-and-for-all; otherwise it will appear repeatedly. In other words, if the 'big-bang' programme is executed in a market economy, as, for example, in Erhardt's reform in West Germany in 1948, the distortions of relative prices would be replaced by equilibrium in one shock, at a higher price level. After price liberalisation, there was no serious effect of the return to the original price relativities.[4] Contrarily, in a transitional economy, the slope of relative price line is unlikely to reach zero very soon. As shown in Figure 1.1, in China, the lines of profit rates were converging to the horizontal average line only gradually.

The slope of the relative price line, in the dimension we are discussing, is determined by how enterprises respond to price changes. According to Kornai, enterprise responsiveness to price is the function of the degree of the hardness of the budget constraint.[5] The slope of the relative price line, or the degree of success of price liberalisation, depends on the extent of enterprise reform. The deeper the enterprise reform, the more sensitive the enterprise responsiveness to price changes, the smaller impact of the return to the original price relativities and, *ceteris paribus*, the smaller the inflationary impact of the 'big-bang' programme.

In China in 1987, the prices of raw materials, fuel and power increased more than 9 per cent. Over 80 per cent of all producers' prices of industrial products increased by around 8 per cent. Capital goods prices increased 7.8 per cent. Consumption goods prices increased by 8.4 per cent (SSB 1988, p. 4). From 1986 to 1988, the producers' prices in mining industries increased by 25.5 per cent, with an average rate of 7.9 per cent a year. The producers' prices in processing industries increased by 27.4 per cent, with an average rate of 8.4 per cent a year. The producers' price of raw materials increased by 30.4 per cent, with an average rate of 9.3 per cent a year. The ratio of the increase rates of three was 0.995:1:1.1. It can be seen that the relative price distortions were not ameliorated, but regressed equi-proportionally at a higher price level (SSB 1991, p. 8).

Irreducible Demand-and-Supply

Given the extent of 'cost-push', the slope of the relative price line is determined by the movement of the demand curve. In a market economy, when price increases, demand decreases *ipso facto*. In Figure 1.2, demand should move back horizontally from $Q2$ (and $Q2'$) towards $Q1$ (and $Q1'$), and not just shift from $D1$ (and $D1'$) to $D2$ (and $D2'$). The farther the demand moves back horizontally, the smaller will be the demand curve shifts from $D1$ (and $D1'$) to $D2$ (and $D2'$), and the bigger will be the reduction of the slopes between *RP-1* and *RP-2*. Nevertheless, reducing demand is costly, especially when prices of inelastic goods, such as energy and materials, sharply increase. Sometimes the reduction in demand introduces bankruptcy for many firms as it did in the 'oil shock' of the 1970s in many market economies.

In China, there was no institutional device for state enterprises to go bankrupt. Throughout the last decade, only three small state-owned enterprises have gone bankrupt as an experiment (Singh 1992, p. 94). Without the bankruptcy option, all existing enterprises had to keep running; more precisely, they had to buy their input and sell their output. For a given industry, no matter how much its input price increased, the demand for these inputs could not be cut significantly. By the same token, no matter how much its output was oversupplied, this output could not be seriously reduced. A certain quantity of the demand and supply was irreducible because of the 'non-bankruptcy' system.

Behind irreducible demand-and-supply was the 'non-dismissal' system. In China's cities, there was no institutional device to accommodate unemployment. Employees were not hired by enterprises, but distributed by the government's labour department. In 1983, 'fixed workers' comprised 96.8 per cent of the state work force; these workers enjoyed the right to remain in their initial enterprise for life (White 1989, p. 153). They received housing, medical benefits, and a pension from the enterprises. In 1986, only 0.007 per cent of the state work force was fired because of 'violation of discipline' (White 1989, p. 164). In 1988, only 0.8 per cent of workers in the state sector left their jobs for reasons other than death or retirement (Lardy 1992, p. 122).[6] Unable to be fired, all employees had to receive their wages. Until 1990, fixed wages still constituted more than 60 per cent of total wages in both the state and collective urban sectors (SSB 1991, p. 120). According to the national unified wage system, the fixed wage, called the 'basic wage', could not be altered by changes in either enterprise profits or government revenues. Even when many enterprises made huge losses or the government budget turned out a serious deficit, the 'basic wage' as the minimum wage was the legitimate entitlement of every worker and had to be paid by either enterprises or the government.

The system of 'non-bankruptcy' and 'non-dismissal' built up a bottom line for the horizontal movement of demand, no matter how big the 'big bang' would be.

Wage Emulation

As wages in one sector rise sharply, workers in other enterprises or industries press for 'matching' wage hikes from their 'home base'. This is called 'wage emulation' in China. After reform began in cities, the wage emulation, in addition to the traditional 'investment hunger', became a stubborn problem for macroeconomic management.

Workers demanded 'more pay for more work'. During the process of enterprise reform, linking wages to profits was perhaps the only way to motivate workers. This reform altered state-owned enterprises from being plan-oriented to being profit-oriented (Perkins 1988). It also triggered wage emulation.

An enterprise's performance is affected not only by the enthusiasm of its workers but also by a mix of other factors, including changes in price, and the enterprise's level of investment and technology. Figure 1.3, arranged by growth rate of labour productivity, shows the changes in profit rate and labour productivity in the 101 largest enterprises in 14 heavy industries from 1984 to 1985, revealing that there was no clear relationship between the two (adjusted R square = 0.0059, T test = 1.263, and F test = 1.59).

With no labour market in which wages could be determined by demand and supply, 'more pay for more work' in reality could only be practised as 'more profit, more pay'. Workers in an enterprise with increased profits assume that they are working harder and deserve better pay. Workers who

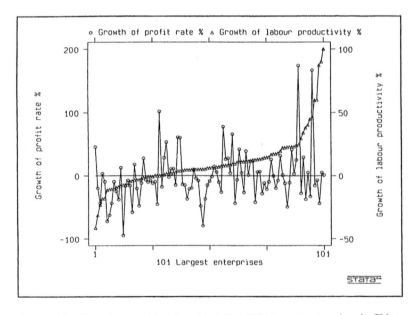

Figure 1.3   Growth of profit and productivity of 101 largest enterprises in China, 1984 and 1985
Sources: SSB (1986), pp. 341–54; (1987), pp. 331–44.

work harder also assume that they deserve a wage rise whether or not their enterprise increases its profits. This mixture of 'more pay for more work' and 'more profits, more pay' replaced the old wage system with an incalculable, and hence unmanageable, principle. Wages surged.

Table 1.2   Productivity and average wage in China, 1978–90

Year	Growth rate of industrial productivity (1)	Growth rate of industrial average real wage (2)	(2)/(1)
1978	11.5 (2.1)	9.6 (6.7)	83.5 (319.0)
1979	3.0 (4.9)	8.2 (7.5)	273.3
1980	5.3 (5.6)	7.5 (5.5)	141.5 (98.2)
1981	3.6 (−3.3)	5.5 (−1.8)	−
1982	2.0 (2.3)	2.1 (−0.3)	105.0
1983	6.5 (6.6)	2.1 (0.1)	32.3
1984	11.2 (9.5)	19.9 (17.6)	177.7 (185.3)
1985	13.8 (12.6)	7.5 (4.6)	54.3 (36.5)
1986	2.5 (3.0)	20.7 (7.8)	828.0 (260.0)
1987	6.4 (6.9)	8.9 (1.7)	139.1 (24.6)
1988	9.9 (13.2)	8.6 (−0.2)	86.9
1989	1.7 (4.8)	−3.5 (−3.0)	−
1990	(5.3)	(8.7)	(164.2)

Note: Data within parentheses are from SSB (1991). There is no explanation about the change.
Sources: SSB (1990), p. 64; (1991), p. 63.

Table 1.2 shows how the index of average real wages in industry generally overshot the index of labour productivity from 1978. According to the text book, 'the rate of price inflation equals the rate of wage inflation minus the rate of labour productivity growth' (Ehrenberg and Smith 1991, p. 639).

Hidden Wage Emulation

The government took energetic steps towards deflating the wage surge through administrative measures. However, as cash wages were restricted, the non-pecuniary benefits expanded, especially housing. Figure 1.4 shows the amazing expansion of 'non-productive' and housing investments after 1978.[7] With an increase in the urban population of 129 million, the average living area per citizen increased from 3.6 square metres in 1978 to 6.7 square metres in 1990 (SSB 1991, pp. 79, 306).

Summary

In China, 'higher input prices will lower the demand for those inputs, but only to a limited degree. Put in more technical language, the price elasticity of demand for industrial inputs is not zero, but it is much lower than it would be in a true market system' (Perkins 1991a, p. 162). The irreducible supply-and-demand corresponds to a certain quantity of production which can ensure that all enterprises make enough profits to meet their wage bills. The 'basic wage' is the bottom line, and the remaining wages are determined by the extent of 'wage emulation'. Only variations in the government subsidy paid as wages can make some inroads on the irreducible demand-and-supply.

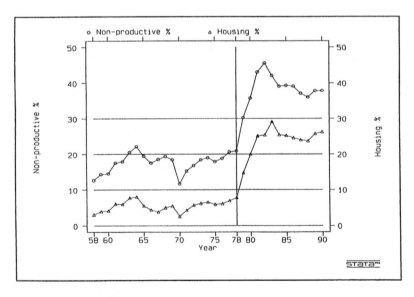

Figure 1.4   Proportion of 'non-productive' and housing investment in China, 1958–90
Sources: SSB (1983), p. 339, (1989), p. 477; (1991), p. 143.

TRIANGULAR DEBT: IS IT A MACROECONOMIC MATTER?

Stabilisation is the key device of the big bang for coping with inflation during price liberalisation. Although it became 'administrative stabilisation' in practice, it did not work well in China. This section examines the reasons for this.

Rigid Wages versus Elastic Output

In 1986 the first administrative stabilisation programme was put in effect to rein in double-digit inflation. Credit and investment funds were tightened by using every variety of administrative measure. This 'cold turkey' method was unable significantly to slow down wage emulation, but led to a radical reduction of enterprises' deposits, and a corresponding fall in output.

In a typical market economy, 'cold turkey' methods force firms to shrink their investments first and bonuses second. Working capital is relatively rigid, because it affects enterprises' daily life.

> By contrast, in China credit restrictions have virtually no impact on final demand. Consumer purchases are virtually unaffected, and investment is reduced only when specific bank-financed investment projects are suspended. Instead, the immediate impact comes on enterprises, which experience much greater difficulty in getting the credit they need to purchase inputs and carry on normal production. (Naughton 1991, p. 155)

Therefore, 'the retrenchment would, on the whole, suppress supply even more than demand' (Song and Zhang 1990, p. 38).

The annual growth rate of industrial output dropped from 21.4 per cent in 1985 to 0.9 per cent by February 1986 (year-on-year), but nominal wages rose by 19.4 per cent in February (year-on-year rate). This paradox confused policy-makers: the former outcome was an 'excessively cold' depression, and the latter an 'excessively hot' prosperity. The unexpected reduction in output obliged the government to refresh illiquid enterprises with huge loans of working funds.[8] Under the first stabilisation programme, industrial labour productivity rose 2.5 per cent, while average real wages increased by 20.7 per cent in 1986.[9]

Song and Zhang argued that this does not mean that tight money cannot bring about a balance between supply and demand and a reduction of prices, because there is no absolute rigidity. However, if a 5 per cent reduction of output is needed to produce a 1 per cent cut in prices, is there any sense in exercising that kind of control (1990, p. 45)? From 1985 to 1986, the annual growth rate of the retail price index fell from 8 to 6 per cent, and the annual growth rate of industrial output declined from 21.4 to 11.7 per cent (SSB 1989, pp. 53, 687). The rigid wages induced rigid prices, and made enterprises' working funds elastic, which in turn caused output to be elastic with respect to the money supply.

Rigid 'Non-Productive' Investment

The growth of housing and 'non-productive' investment seem to be particularly insensitive to changes in overall investment. Apart from rigid wages and elastic output in the short term, the rigid 'non-productive' investment was a source of concern for long-term growth.

Table 1.3 presents the elasticities for different types of investment with respect to total investment. The elasticity of housing investment was, without exception, less than one after its proportion reached 25 per cent in 1981. The elasticity of 'productive' investment was, except in 1980 and 1982, always more than one. In 1981 and 1989, the growth rate of overall investment was negative, while the elasticity of housing investment dropped to its lowest levels of 0.01 and 0.02; and the elasticity of 'productive' investment reached its highest level since 1981. This suggests that the stricter was the stabilisation programme, the slower was the decline in housing investment, and the greater the cutback in 'productive' investment.

The rigid wages and housing investment created a formidable difficulty for the authorities in their efforts to deal with inflation. There was a trade-off between inflation and a fall in output in the short term and inadequate 'productive' investment for long-term growth.

Triangular Debt

Beginning in 1989, under the slogan of 'adjustment and rectification', the second administrative stabilisation lasted for more than two years. In 1989, the price index declined by 0.7 percentage points while industrial output fell by 12.3 percentage points. Then, a miracle occurred. In 1990, the price index dropped 15.6 percentage points, and output remained virtually unchanged (SSB 1991, pp. 229 and 49). In 1991, there was a slight price increase (around 3.5 per cent), and industrial output grew 12.9 per cent (*China Daily* [Chinese], 14 January 1992).

The second 'cold turkey' was so 'cold' that many township-village enterprises died from frost-bite. From 1988 to 1990, the number of town-

Table 1.3   Different investment elasticities with respect to total investment in China, 1978–90

Year	Ph (%)	It (%)	Ip (%)	In (%)	Ih (%)	Ep (3)/(2)	En (4)/(2)	Eh (5)/(2)
	(1)	*(2)*	*(3)*	*(4)*	*(5)*			
1978	7.83	31.02	30.57	32.76	24.54	0.98	1.06	0.79
1979	14.76	4.49	−7.85	51.16	48.55	−1.75	11.40	10.81
1980	19.98	6.76	−1.60	26.06	22.24	−0.24	3.85	3.29
1981	25.10	−20.75	−29.74	−4.57	−0.21	1.43	0.22	0.01
1982	25.39	25.43	19.99	32.63	13.43	0.79	1.28	0.53
1983	29.10	157.42	173.72	137.89	97.50	1.10	0.88	0.62
1984	25.40	28.18	33.12	21.33	5.95	1.18	0.76	0.21
1985	25.23	38.75	39.90	37.02	18.90	1.03	0.96	0.49
1986	24.15	18.73	19.12	18.14	6.84	1.02	0.97	0.36
1987	23.95	20.57	24.60	14.30	9.78	1.20	0.70	0.48
1988	24.00	22.13	23.43	19.93	11.18	1.06	0.90	0.51
1989	25.71	−6.95	−9.08	−3.22	−0.15	1.31	0.46	0.02
1990	26.17	7.53	7.63	7.30	4.73	1.01	0.97	0.63

Ph = Proportion of housing investment = [(Housing investment)/(Total investment)] × 100.

It = Index of total investment = [(Increment of total investment)/(Total investment of last year)] × 100

Ip = Index of 'productive' investment = [(Increment of 'productive' investment)/('Productive' investment of last year)] × 100.

In = Index of 'non-productive' investment = [(Increment of 'non-productive' investment)/('Non-productive' investment of last year)] × 100.

Ih = Index of housing investment = [(Increment of housing investment)/(Housing investment of last year)] × 100

Ep = Elasticity of 'productive' investment with respect to total investment.

En = Elasticity of 'non-productive' investment with respect to total investment.

Eh = Elasticity of housing investment with respect to total investment

Note: The calculations are at current prices. In fact, inflation had different impacts on different types of investment (Chen, Jefferson, Rawski, Wang and Zheng 1988). This table only indicates the attitude of different types of investment.

Sources: Calculated from SSB (1983), p. 339; (1989), p. 447; (1991), p. 143.

ship-village enterprises fell by 378 600, while the number of employees fell by 2.8 million from 1988 to 1990 (SSB 1991, p. 377). Meanwhile, total profits (after tax) of the state industrial sector were reduced by 56.5 per cent. Total losses in the state sector multiplied 3.3 times. The proportion of loss-makers in the state sector grew from 10.9 to 27.6 per cent of enterprises (*People's Daily* [Chinese], 25 November 1991). Unlike rural township-village enterprises, the 'non-bankruptcy' system in cities meant that enterprises had no way to exit from production. They all had to keep going. Under the 'non-dismissal' system, workers could not be forced to 'exit' from their enterprises, and everyone had the legal right to receive at least the 'basic wage'.

With the 'no bankruptcy' option, all enterprises had to keep going and pay their wage bills, no matter how 'cold' the 'cold turkey' was. Conversely, the 'non-bankruptcy' system presupposed that enterprises had unlimited responsibility for their liabilities. Put differently, socialist enterprises were the safest borrowers, because any debt had to be paid either by enterprises themselves or ultimately by the government. Therefore, the 'non-bankruptcy' system gave enterprises '*no way out*', but it did give them *a way to borrow*. Enterprises were confident that the supply of liquidity would be refreshed by the government sooner or later. This 'rational expectation' was indeed correct and guaranteed by the 'non-bankruptcy' system. Consequently when the money supply was severely squeezed, 'triangular debt' proliferated spontaneously.

In China, the abnormally overdue trade credit is known as 'triangular debt' because of its circular inter-enterprise characteristic: enterprise A owes money to enterprise B, enterprise B owes money to enterprise C, and enterprise C owes money to enterprise A. Even in market economies, simply extending the period of trade credit is a useful weapon for firms to frustrate a monetary squeeze (Brechling and Lipsey 1963). Triangular debt is not difficult to generate in a transitional economy when an enterprise knows that its buyers can never go bankrupt and payment is eventually bound to come either from its buyers or from the government, and when the enterprise knows that its suppliers have to sell their output, and its suppliers also know their buyers can never go bankrupt and will eventually pay.

Inter-firm credit plays an important role in the reformed planned economies of Hungary (since the 1970s), Yugoslavia, Poland, and China. In Yugoslavia the stock of inter-firm credit was estimated at 43 per cent of gross social product in 1987; in Poland at around 48 per cent of GDP at the end of 1989. In China the phenomenon is particularly relevant, and in the package of policy measures implemented by the Chinese government in 1989, the solution to this problem was deemed as one of the main targets. It is estimated that, in 1990, arrears in payments of inter-firm credit amounted to about 20 per cent of the working capital of all state enterprises, and arrears in payments of working capital credits from the banking system were of analogous size. (Calvo and Coricelli 1992, p. 79)

In China, from August 1988 to August 1991, triangular debt rose from RMB78.9 to 226.5 billions[10] with a growth rate of 42 per cent a year.[11] The huge triangular debt as a substitute for money was good enough for enterprises to keep running. Although 378 600 township-village enterprises closed down and 2.8 million employees left rural industry, in the urban areas no enterprise went bankrupt and no worker lost his or her 'basic wages' because of the existence of irreducible demand-and-supply. Inflation cooled down. Depression was avoided. The macroeconomic indices looked superficially satisfactory, except for the triangular debt and excess-inventory ones.

Excess Inventories

Triangular debt did not grow in response to aggregate demand, but to the demand for state enterprises to survive. Consequently, the products whose output was sustained by triangular debt were difficult to sell, and turned into excess inventory. When triangular debt grew, excess inventory also grew. Moreover, the soaring inventories further squeezed enterprises' working capital. As a result of extension of overdue payments, even well-managed enterprises became illiquid. The vicious circle was: stabilisation → shortage of working funds → triangular debt → excess inventory → shortage of working funds. In this circle, the 'multiplier' was 3: that is, one unit of shortage of working capital resulted in approximately three units of triangular debt.[12]

In 1990, about 31 per cent of the total working funds in the machine-building industry were tied up in inventories, and interest payments on the inventory exceeded the total profits made by this industry (*Economic Information* [Chinese], 8 January 1992). State industrial enterprises hoarded an amount of inventories and triangular debt equivalent to 29.3 per cent of the total output of state industry (*Financial Times* [Chinese], 27 November 1991; SSB 1991, p. 391).

The vicious circle of triangular debt and excess inventories permeated the entire economy, forcing the State Council to establish a clearing-house to eliminate triangular debt. The enterprises' 'rational expectation' was realised again. From 1988 to 1990, the government issued loans for working capital at the fastest rate ever, increasing by 20.6 per cent each year (*Financial Times* [Chinese], 6 October 1991). In a market economy, whether and to what extent trade credit can frustrate macro policies has been the subject of long-standing debate (Crawford 1992). In China, however, it is difficult to see how the authorities could have controlled the money supply. The panacea of stabilisation was limited within a trade-off between inflation and depression, as well as the combination of triangular debt and excess inventories. In addition, triangular debt further complicated the techniques of macroeconomic management. In former Yugoslavia 'inter-firm credit' functioned as a kind of 'self-managed money' (Schonfelder 1990). In China also, triangular debt was 'self-managed' by the enterprises. It was not clear to what extent stabilisation of a given severity would force enterprises to issue how many triangular debts, and neither was it clear what the policy target should be in seeking to control triangular debt: its size, or the length of its overdue period?

It is probably true that when stabilisation affects the irreducible demand-and-supply, triangular debt will be generated. The size of the irreducible demand-and-supply can be reduced by enterprise reform, but not by either price liberalisation or stabilisation.

Summary

Lipton and Sachs have asserted:

> Prices should be deregulated quickly, in parallel with the macroeconomic austerity program, because the proper relative prices are crucial for all the necessary resource reallocations. Price deregulation might lead to a one-time jump in prices, but not to an ongoing inflation, as long as macroeconomic policies remain tightly constrained. (1990, p. 100)

In China, the 'proper relative prices' were unlike to emerge from a once-and-for-all jump, because the return to the original price relativities reproduced price distortions. Therefore the big-bang programme would result in either ongoing inflation or stagflation (Calvo and Coricelli 1992). Stabilisation could not remedy depression, and neither could the combination of triangular debt and excess inventory. Neither price liberalisation nor stabilisation could work well without fruitful enterprise reform.

THE TWO GAPS VERSUS RE-INDUSTRIALISATION: HOW BIG IS THE BIG BANG?

Sachs and others demonstrate the gains from the big bang by applying the utility model to deal with abstract goods (Lipton and Sachs 1990: Berry and Sachs 1992). The nature of the goods is not important. In theory, for any given good, utility will be increased by eliminating price distortions. In practice, however, the nature of the goods could be decisive if one was waiting for expected responses from supply and demand after implementing the big bang. Butter and cannons have different supply and demand elasticities which determine the size of the big bang. If price distortions were primarily concentrated in consumer goods, such as bikinis and mini skirts, the big bang would be a little bang, and vice versa: the big bang would be really big if price distortions were concentrated in energy and material goods, such as oil and steel.

As mentioned earlier, the structure of price distortions is associated with a 'distorted' industrial structure. Full price liberalisation implies the adjustment of the industrial structure built by central planning in a closed economy, to a new structure led by market demand in an open environment. This is a process of re-industrialisation. In this process, there are two gaps which need to be filled. One is the structural gap between the command and market economies, and the other is the structural gap between the closed and open economies.

The 'First Gap': domestic structural gap

The 'first gap' is domestic, namely that between the existing industry built up by central planning and a new industrial structure steered by market demand. The price gap between the planned and market prices reflects this first gap to some degree.

The price gaps, as indicated in Table 1.4, have an apparently structural pattern. Compared with market prices, the planned prices of energy and raw materials were low, while those of finished products were relatively high.[13]

Table 1.5 provides additional information about the size of the big bang. The figures in the final column indicate how big the price jump would be if price controls on energy and some key materials were lifted.

According to Bruno and Sachs, the 'oil shock' in the West was the jump in oil price of 69 per cent in nominal terms, and in real terms of 44.4 per cent, from 1973 to 1975 (1985, p. 164). In the USA, the real fuel price increased 38.8 per cent from 1973 to 1975. To manage this oil shock, one of the most popular textbooks wanted the US government to adopt 'accommodating polices' (Dornbusch and Fischer 1991, pp. 489–90). In a staggering contrast, the big-bang theorists advocated the 'banging' together of the ten or twenty oil shocks, shown in Tables 1.4 and 1.5, with a ruthless austerity. Calvo and Coricelli observed that in Poland's big bang, under strict stabilisation, the enterprises' liquidity crunch was also caused by the

Table 1.4   Planned, market and world prices in China, 1988

Product	Planned price (RMB/ton) (1)	Market price (RMB/ton) (2)	Border price (US$/ton) (3)	(2)/(1)	(3)/(2)
A. Raw materials					
Crude oil	100	500	127	5.00	1.40
Coal	60	200	65	3.33	1.79
Phosphate ore	80	–	59	–	–
Pyrites	130	200	55	1.54	1.51
Sulphuric acid	280	400	130	1.43	1.79
Calcium carbide	600	1200	500	2.00	2.29
Caustic soda-solid	1500	2000	600	1.33	1.65
B. Intermediates					
PVC	3600	7000	1300	1.94	1.02
Polyethylene	4000	9000	1300	2.25	0.79
Caprolactam	10 150	14 000	2000	1.38	0.78
Nylon chips	14 000	17 000	2200	1.21	0.86
Viscose filaments	18 000	30 000	1300	1.67	0.24
C. Finished products					
SSP fertiliser	180	200	–	1.11	–
Synthetic fatty alcohol	7000	7000	1800	1.00	1.41
Vitamin C	42 000	50 000	–	1.19	–
Penicillin	200 000	300 000	–	1.50	–
Mesacycline	380 000	450 000	–	1.18	–

Note: The final column is calculated at the exchange rate of RMB5.5 = US$1.
Source: Statistical Annex, Jiangsu Chemical Sector Report, cited in Singh (1992), Table 3.6

unaffordable increases in the prices of energy and materials.[14] Moreover, in transitional economies, the 'material intensity' of production, namely the use of input and energy per unit of output, was often very high (1992, p. 72).[15]

Price liberalisation in transitional countries is different from the oil shock in the West. Initially, in these 'shortage economies', the excess demand could not always be met by supply at low planned prices. As Lipton and Sachs (1990) have described in their 'model of repressed inflation', the annoyance of having to 'queue' decreased utility. This is why some people were happy to pay more for the same goods instead of waiting in queues. For non-inferior consumer goods with high demand

Table 1.5   Material price gaps in China, 1985–6 and 1988 (RMB/ton)

Product	Planned prices (1)	Market prices (2)	(2)/(1)
1985–86			
Coal	38.6	91	2.36
Crude oil	100	545	5.45
Diesel fuel	330	700	2.12
Fuel oil	65	460	7.08
Cement	62	210	3.39
Plate glass (RMB/square metre)	2	6	3.00
1988			
Wire rod	610	1680	2.8
Thin plate steel	870	4602	5.3
Medium thick plate	570	1804	3.2
Pig iron	293	752	2.6
Aluminium	4000	16 077	4.0
Cement (No. 425)	90	193	2.1
Soda ash	390	1192	3.1
Caustic soda	640	2986	4.7
Timber (RMB/cubic metre)	119	636	5.3

Note: For 1988, the market prices are posted prices, not market clearing prices.
Sources: 1985–86 section taken from Ma and Sun, cited in Lardy (1992), Table 4.3; 1988 section from *China Price*, cited in Singh (1992), Table 3.2.

elasticity and diversified preferences, some people preferred dealing with the clearing market prices to having to receive the goods from the government by administrative distribution. The excess demand caused by low planned prices had to be cut down. The time spent queuing could be used for leisure or to do something else.

This model, however, has only limited usefulness even with in its own terms.[16] It is illogical to apply this model to the staple food ration of a pensioner, and say: 'You don't need to wait in line for rations any more. If you don't get food to eat, you can have more time to relax or to do something else.'

The problem of producer goods in a socialist economy is more analogous to the pensioner's story. First, energy and materials are the 'staple food' of industry. Their supply and demand elasticities are very low anyway. Second, as discussed earlier, unreformed state-owned enterprises are not as rational as households who are often willing to use their queuing time to do something else. Third, even if enterprises do want to do something other than 'wait in line', there is often nothing else for them to do because of the absence of factor markets. For example, during price liberalisation, if enterprises were all well-developed factor markets, as in the USA, they could do a number of different things, including go bankrupt. If there was only a labour market, as in Eastern Europe, enterprises had the option of laying off employees. If there was no labour market, as is the case in Chinese cities, enterprises could do nothing except increase output prices, generate triangular debt and excess inventories, or bargain with the government for subsidies.

If this supposition is correct, the 'model of repressed inflation' must be misplaced.

The 'Second Gap': International Structural Gap

The 'second gap' is that between the existing industrial structure within a closed environment and the new industry established with greater integration into the world economy.

The final column of Table 1.4 shows the gap between domestic and international prices. In the raw materials category alone it can be seen that after prices had cleared domestically, there would have been several other oil shocks lying in wait if the economy had opened up instantly. It is worth calculating the size of the big bang before deciding to jump from planned to market prices, and then to international market prices. Kenen believes: 'A two-step reform, moreover, involving a move to domestic market prices, then to world prices, would be far more expensive than an immediate move to world prices; it would require two steps of shifts in resource allocation' (1991, p. 247). Blanchard and others are hesitant: 'The unfettered market process could lead to too many bankruptcies and too much labour shedding, and that protracted high unemployment is just as undesirable for social reasons as it is for resource allocations' (1991, p. 93).

Regarding the two gaps, Soviet reformers appeared 'sometimes to believe that a set of market-clearing prices can be made to rise from the ruins of the planned economy, like the Phoenix from the ashes' (Kenen 1991, p. 248). It is easy to see how the single jump can lead to 'ashes'; it is less easy to see how the Phoenix can rise.

Price liberalisation could lead to a substantial adjustment of the industrial structure. Crossing the first gap, from planned to market prices, would lead to an adjustment of the industrial structure: principally, a shift from heavy to light industry. Crossing the second gap, opening up the economy to the world, would require an upgrading of the technological capacity of existing industry. The former needs to *shift* production *horizontally* at the existing technological level. The latter requires the economy to *climb vertically* from a low to a high technological level.

Table 1.6   Energy structure between the two Germanies, 1989 (%)

Energy	East Germany	West Germany
Total (t.c.e.)	127 million tons	383 million tons
Brown coal	69	8
Mineral oil	14	40
Natural gas	9	17
Hard coal	4	15
Nuclear energy	3	17
Other sources	1	3

Source: *The Economist* (1991b), p. 65.

Table 1.6 illustrates the different energy structures between the two Germanies. It suggests that filling up the second gap is a *dynamic process of upgrading technological capacity rather than a static process of reallocating available resources*. Prices can jump to world prices in one go, but one cannot change the energy structure without essential technological advance.

The 'Old Four' and 'New Five' Durables

China tried to bridge the two gaps for over a decade. This was reflected in the rise of two groups of consumer durables – the 'old four' (watches, radios, sewing machines and bicycles) and the 'new five' (television sets, electric fans, tape recorders, refrigerators and washing machines). Table 1.7 shows two broad stages, corresponding to the two gaps, in the process of re-industrialisation.

The first stage was *changing* the product-mix. China had produced the old four since the early 1950s. Due to the planning regime focusing on heavy industry while ignoring the market demand, the supply of the old four was constrained at a low quantity for more than two decades. The old four were so extraordinarily scarce that the State Statistical Bureau used ownership of the old four as an official indicator of people's living standards (SSB 1981,

Table 1.7   Output volume of the 'old four' and 'new five' consumer durables in China, 1978–90

Product	Output volume (10 000)			Peak earlier than 1990	(4)/(1)	Annual growth (%)	
	1978 (1)	1984 (2)	1990 (3)	(10 000) (4)	(5)	1978–84 (6)	1984–90 (7)
Old four							
Sewing machine	486.5	934.9	761.0	1286.0 (1982)	2.6	11.5	–3.4
Bicycle	854.0	2861.4	3141.6	4140.1 (1988)	4.8	22.3	1.6
Watch	1351.1	1798.2	8352.6	–	6.2	18.8	14.0
Radio	1167.7	2220.3	2103.0	4057.2 (1981)	3.5	11.3	–0.9
New five							
Refrigerator	2.80	54.74	463.06	757.63 (1988)	270.6	64.1	42.7
Television set	51.73	1003.81	2684.7	2766.54 (1989)	53.5	63.9	17.8
Recorder	4.7	776.4	3023.5	–	643.3	134.2	25.4
Washing machine	0.04	578.10	662.68	1046.80 (1988)	26170.0	394.5	2.3
Electric fan	137.8	1770.7	5799.3	–	42.1	53.0	21.9

Source: SSB (1991), pp. 422–4.

p. 450). When production shifted from planning instructions to responding to market demand, output of the four rocketed. As Table 1.7 shows, they quickly reached saturation levels.

The second stage was to produce *new* products, as the market began to demand superior products. With the satisfaction of traditional demands, new demands at an upgraded technological level sprang up as the economy opened up to the world, income levels rose and tastes changed. Table 1.7 indicates the explosive expansion of the new five. Besides the old four, ownership of the new five was added to the official statistics after 1986 as an indicator of people's living standards (SSB 1986, p. 688). Except for a few black-and-white televisions, these new consumer durables did not exist in the existing production structure. There was no output recorded for washing machines or electric fans before 1978 (SSB 1991, p. 424). All five, with other new products as well, were linked to foreign technology.

There is a clear distinction between the old four and new five: the former could be produced by existing industry, whereas the latter are new products which existing industry was technologically incapable of producing.

The Rigidity of the Industrial Structure

How is it possible to speed up the process of re-industrialisation? It depends on not only the correct price signals, but also resource mobility. China had virtually no factor markets in the 1980s (Byrd and Tidrick 1987; Perkins 1988). The 'non-bankruptcy' system resulted in irreducible supply and demand which was identical to actual output produced by the existing industrial structure. When the volume of irreducible supply and demand was constant (because of the 'non-bankruptcy' system), the existing industrial structure was correspondingly rigid to some degree.

Before 1978, all profits made by state enterprises were turned over to the state. The government collected all financial resources, then invested them in its planned projects. Although state-owned enterprises could not go bankrupt, some of them obtained funds for investment from the government. *Some did not.* During the transition, the government expanded enterprise autonomy. Utilising retained profits and bank loans, enterprises were able to invest. However, given the absence of factor markets, especially the financial market, enterprises were only able to reinvest in themselves. This enabled the existing structure to be reinforced by vigorous new investment (Deng and Luo 1987). Based on data from state-owned enterprises, Singh concludes that there was only a slight change in the investment structure (1992, pp. 2–3).

Under the 'non-bankruptcy' system, these enterprises' self-reinvestment strengthened the existing industrial structure, reinforcing the effect of the return to the original price relativities during price reform. Figure 1.2 shows that the smaller the slope of the relative price line, the faster price liberalisation will achieve equilibrium. In the short term, the slope of the relative price line is determined by the elasticity of supply and demand. In the long term, it is determined by the flexibility of the industrial structure.

Summary

Price distortions and the distorted industrial structure determine the size of the big bang. In the spring of 1986, the Chinese State Council set up a special office to design the reforms. Under this office, all economic ministries were mobilised in serious preparation for a comprehensive one-shot price reform. After six months, Prime Minister Zhao Ziyang abandoned the big-bang programme, partly because careful calculations revealed the prohibitive cost.

More fundamentally, it was realised that existence of the two structural gaps necessitated re-industrialisation, which is a comprehensive development issue far beyond a narrow question of price reform. The big bang proposal made no provision for structural adjustment, which was critical for China as the biggest developing country in the world.

2 'Groping for Stones to Cross the River': Price Reform in China

Having avoided the big bang, Chinese reform missed the orthodox path, and was able only to 'grope for stones to cross the river'. This famous slogan was officially promulgated by the central government. It referred to the fact that no one knew how to handle the transition. Policy-makers can only experiment, identify the problem, and then decide where, when and how to take the next step. This strategy of 'no strategy at all' made the Chinese reform path obscure and controversial.

This chapter pays special attention to how China's unseasonable experiments challenged the holistic 'big bang'. Along with the adjustment of the industrial structure, China decontrolled prices one by one under buyer's market conditions, which resulted in decreasing prices. China also introduced the dual-track price system, in which a part of production, subject to mandatory plan requirements, was still distributed by official rationing at fixed planned prices, while enterprises were free to sell what they produced, or to buy what they needed, above the mandatory quota at free prices in the market.

'GOLDEN PERIOD OF REFORM' VERSUS BUYER'S MARKET PRICE REFORM

Socialist economies are 'shortage economies' because of the 'insatiable demand' coming from numerous sources of 'investment hunger' and 'consumption hunger' (Kornai 1980). In these 'shortage economies', tourists can witness ubiquitous scenes of people queuing up in long lines to buy simple commodities that are always oversupplied in the West. It may thus seem strange that some 'shortage economies' encountered a drastic fall in output after they implemented the big bang.

The fall in output suggests there must be surplus supplies. These surpluses, dubbed 'wasteful and unwanted production', were designed to meet the requirements of the state plan, not market demand. Hence, 'output could fall sharply as nonviable production was cut and unemployment would rise' (IMF, World Bank, OECD and EBRD 1990, p. 18). If the fall in output represents waste, the welfare of the society should not decrease, and may even increase.

Whether welfare was changed by the fall in 'wasteful and unwanted production' in Poland or Russia is not the concern of this study.[1] My question is: do the unwanted products indicate redundant production capacity?

'Golden Period of Reform'

Surveying the reform experiences in Yugoslavia, Hungary and China, one could find the so-called 'golden period of reform' in the early stages. From 1956 to 1964 in Yugoslavia, from 1967 to 1973 in Hungary, and from 1978 to 1984 in China, there was fast economic growth coupled with a rapid improvement of living standards of the population, in the absence of a serious inflation (Balassa 1985; Gao, Chen and Wang 1988).

The 'golden period of reform' can be attributed to three preconditions of supply, demand and the price structure.

First, on the supply side, most transitional economies were semi-industrialised with a sizeable modern industry. In certain areas, their technological capabilities were even comparable to advanced countries. 'On a sectoral level, the industrial structure in every country is strongly skewed toward heavy industry and capital goods and away from light industry, services, and consumer goods' (Lipton and Sachs 1990, p. 82). While there were extreme shortages of consumer goods, some products of heavy industry were overproduced. Thereafter, to shift production from the plan to market demand suggests a shift of production from heavy to light industry, *not the reverse*. This is the first favourable precondition for transitional economies. Most simple consumer goods, including the durables of the 'old four', were easy to produce, unlike the products of heavy industry which require an intensive scale of capital, labour and technology, and require a long gestation period. The reform made the massive products of heavy industry 'wasteful and unwanted', but did not make these production capacities redundant. In any case, the existing industry was capable of producing what the market needed in the early stages of transition.

Second, on the demand side, there was a chronic shortage of many simple consumer goods. In the late 1970s, the Chinese government issued a variety of rationing coupons to deal with the severe shortage of consumer goods, including the old four. The old four were so scarce that the Ministry of Material Distribution used them as the standard units for material exchanges among different agencies. The severe shortage of consumer goods indicates that, even without any improvement in their quality, the existing products had a large domestic demand. This is a second favourable precondition for the transition.

Third, in the existing price structure, production of most consumer goods, except for a few household necessities, was profitable. The old four were extremely scarce, but also extremely profitable at planned prices: for example, the profit rate of watch production was around 360 per cent before the reform (calculated from Byrd and Tidrick 1984). In the early 1980s, most industrial consumer goods were in short supply and profitable under the pre-reform price structure. This is a third favourable precondition for the transition.

The supply capacity was adequate, the market demand was hungry, and the price structure was appropriate. These favourable preconditions, inherited from the old command regime, pointed towards structural adjustment: a production shift from heavy to light industry. Then the government introduced the scheme of 'profit retention', under which the government

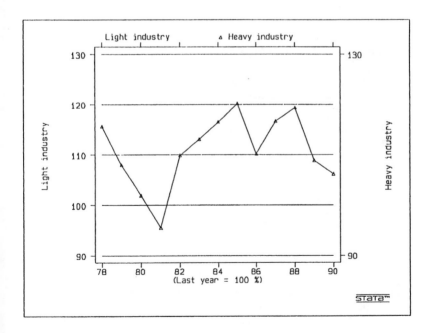

Figure 2.1   Growth rates of light and heavy industry in China, 1978–90
Source: SSB (1991), p. 56

allowed enterprises to keep part of the profits they had generated. Enterprises could use a part of retained profits as bonuses, and they also were given autonomy over what to produce. Without significant investment or sophisticated reform, the three favourable preconditions alone gave rise to the 'golden period of reform'.

Figure 2.1 illustrates a drastic output shift from heavy to light industry after 1978, with a relative fall in 'unwanted production' (heavy industry), and a rise in 'wanted production' (light industry). As 'wanted production' increased, parts of the 'unwanted production', the 'overgrown' heavy industry, became 'wanted' too.[2] From 1978 to 1984, gross industrial output increased by 72.92 per cent, with heavy industry increasing by 52.19 per cent and light industry increasing by 100.70 per cent. As shown in Table 1.7, the old four durables experienced an abrupt upsurge with an annual growth rate of more than 10 per cent. Meanwhile the ownership of the old four during the same period increased by 270 per cent for bicycles, 290 per cent for sewing machines, 300 per cent for watches and 1 270 per cent for radios (SSB 1988, p. 804; 1991, p. 274, 287; 1986, p. 688). During this period neither price reform nor enterprise reform made much progress. Nevertheless, the easily achieved 'golden period of reform' made everyone happy.

Buyer's Market Price Reform[3]

The 'golden period of reform' built up advantageous conditions for carrying forward price reform. Due to the shift from heavy to light industry, a number of consumer goods previously in chronic shortage soon became oversupplied. For example, output of sewing machines and radios reached their peak as early as 1981 and 1982 (see Table 1.7).

In 1981, the 'profit-retention' reform was introduced in the commercial agencies. Thereafter, they were made aware of the negative effect on profits that came from holding an excessive inventory of consumer goods. Although the government administratively lowered prices several times, oversupplied goods continued to be produced. Consequently, commercial agencies became harsher to suppliers. Many of them eventually stopped procuring surplus products, forcing producers to sell the oversupplied goods elsewhere. This forced producers to sell these products in a real market with free prices! Byrd and Tidrick did an excellent case study on a watch producer. From 1980 to early 1983, the government reduced watch prices three times. The total reduction was more than 20 per cent of the original price. Nevertheless, the producer still produced far more watches than the production limitation issued by the planning authorities. Commercial agencies preferred to accept only those watches which were easier to sell at planned prices. Finally, the producer had no chance but to mobilise its workers to sell the rest on the streets at, of course, market (1984) prices.

According to Byrd, 17 per cent of all industrial consumer goods were directly retailed by producers themselves in 1983, compared with less than 11 per cent in 1979. As early as 1980, 'direct sales outside the state plan accounted for 46 per cent of total sales by enterprises under the First Ministry of Machine Building (compared with 13 per cent in 1979) and 33 per cent of sales by all machinery producers' (1987, p. 237).

Byrd (1987) shows that the proportion of products self-marketed by enterprises was directly related to the buyer's market condition. Furthermore, negotiation between commercial agencies and producers increasingly focused on products for which there was a seller's market. As a kind of compensation for self-marketing of oversupplied products, commercial agencies allowed producers to sell part of their products for which there was excess demand at above-planned prices. There was no 'bang' at all. *The process proceeded so spontaneously and smoothly that no one can even tell exactly when price liberalisation started.* The old four durables had been extremely scarce and had been heavily controlled for decades in respect both to price and distribution. During the 'golden period of reform', when most industrial consumer goods became oversupplied one by one, prices of the old four were also liberalised. Naturally the freeing of prices in a buyer's market placed downward pressure on these prices. It is easy to imagine how pleased ordinary people were when the prices of more and more consumer goods fell while their income increased at an unprecedentedly fast pace.

The data in Table 2.1 illustrate the 'buyer's market' price reform. From 1978 to 1984, as the overall price index went up, the prices of industrial consumer goods, in columns (4), (6) and (7), including clothing and consumer durables, successively fell.

Of course, the easy 'golden period of reform' also embraced inefficiency because of the incompleteness of reform. Nevertheless, the aim of utilising existing production capacity more efficiently (by shifting production from surplus to shortage sectors) was a superior solution to simply cutting surpluses.

Which Should Be Done First?

The Chinese 'golden period of reform' provides a counter-example to the big-bang sequencing schedule. In 1990, Sachs and Lipton set up an agenda for Poland's transition: 'the actual restructuring of economic activity, involving the rise of small and medium-size firms in the private sector and

Table 2.1   Retail price indexes in China, 1978–90 (1977 = 100%)

Year	Overall (1)	Of which: consumer goods (2)	Of which: food (3)	Clothing (4)	Goods for daily use (5)	Recreational goods (6)	Of which: electrics (7)
1978	100.7	101.5	101.5	100.2	100.1	100.6	–
1979	102.7	103.6	107.1	99.7	100.6	102.4	100.0
1980	108.9	111.0	118.3	99.7	102.2	97.8	93.6
1981	111.5	113.9	122.7	99.3	103.5	95.8	91.0
1982	113.6	116.0	126.1	97.2	104.1	93.2	87.4
1983	115.3	117.4	129.2	96.0	103.4	91.4	83.1
1984	118.5	119.4	132.5	96.0	103.6	91.2	82.9
1985	129.0	130.7	151.6	96.9	106.4	92.6	83.6
1986	136.7	139.1	162.8	100.0	112.9	93.5	83.2
1987	146.7	149.4	179.3	103.5	119.8	95.8	83.4
1988	173.8	177.8	220.5	116.7	134.4	109.4	96.2
1989	204.7	209.0	256.2	137.8	155.0	125.0	109.6
1990	209.1	212.3	257.0	147.6	157.9	121.9	102.0

Note: (7) includes television sets, radios, cassette recorders, electric organs, and so on.
Source: Calculated from SSB (1991), pp. 231–3.

a shift of production from heavy industry to light industry, services and housing construction, will occur only in the course of the coming decade' (1990, p. 48).[4] The underlying logic is self-evident. Unless private enterprises are allowed to function in a free market, economic development cannot be on the right track.[5]

Compared with China, Russia had a deeper industrial foundation, more hungry domestic demand and a similar price structure. Soros believes that one of the reasons why Russia did not have a 'golden period of reform' was that 'the bureaucracy was totally unprepared for functioning in the new environment' (1990, p. 106).

Lipton and Sachs do not believe that the old bureaucracy is capable of doing anything useful in the transition (1990, p. 88). Nevertheless, in a typical command economy, all transactions went through the administrative distribution system run by these bureaucrats. Industrial enterprises obtained inputs from this system. They delivered their outputs to the system. Industrial enterprises often did not know much about their suppliers and buyers. In China in 1990, the state materials distribution and commercial systems employed nine million people, equivalent to one-quarter of the industrial work force in the state sector.[6] The materials distribution and commercial systems, which owned 558 000 agencies, together distributed inputs and outputs for all industrial enterprises (SSB 1991, pp. 393, 483, 571). Before the transition started, the entire system of distribution was governed by the administrative mechanism. Unsurprisingly, it worked. Goods could be distributed administratively, but only if prices were also set administratively. To liberalise all prices in a single day would have broken up the entire system. Every producer would have had to find his or her own suppliers and buyers under suddenly fluctuating market prices. The shock would have been comparable to, if not much bigger than, breaking all existing contracts in one single day in a market economy. The more all-embracing the distribution system, the more destructive would the shock be.

When Sachs and others constructed their utility models to demonstrate the gains from the big bang, they assumed there was a 'parallel market': the black market (Lipton and Sachs 1990, p. 90; Berry and Sachs 1992, pp. 120–1). This assumption implied that there was a market system ready to substitute for the existing distribution system. If such a well-developed 'parallel market' for producer goods did not exist, then the big bang was an erroneous strategy.

Summary

Sachs and others emphasised that the big-bang programme brought a 'rapid shift from a shortage to a surplus economy' in Poland (Lipton and Sachs 1990, p. 119; Sachs 1991, 1992a, 1992b). Poland arrived at the status of a surplus economy through a 'pure' market approach. The Chinese 'golden period of reform' just muddled through with both planning and the market mechanisms. The difference between the two is that in Poland, the surplus was achieved by driving down demand.[7] In China, because demand was rigid, the surplus was realised by increasing supply.

DUAL-TRACK ECONOMY: DIVISION AND UNIFICATION

The 'golden period of reform' was easy, but further reform was tough. Unlike consumer goods, which were scarce with lucrative prices, material inputs were in short supply but with unprofitable prices. In the area of material inputs, on the one hand, it was clear how the reform should proceed in the absence of price liberalisation to provide allocative signals. On the other hand, if prices were freed comprehensively, price increases in those 'staple foods' of industry would result in a return to the original price relativities, thus reproducing price distortions but with inflation in addition. The dilemma raises the question again: what kind of mechanism could operate the new hybrid economy consisting of market-determined prices and state-owned enterprises which had not yet been completely reformed?

The Chinese answer was the notorious dual-track system. Under this system, through the 'plan-track', as required by the mandatory plans, part of industry's output was distributed by central redistribution with fixed, planned prices. Meanwhile, enterprises were free to sell what they produced or to buy what they needed above the mandatory quota, both at market prices (the 'market-track'). Interestingly, the emergence of the dual-track system dated back to 1958, soon after the command economy was established in China. There have always been a variety of transactions between regions and enterprises outside the planning system, a minor market economy, normally at prices higher than planned prices. These economic relations have been euphemistically called in China 'co-operation relations,' and the goods purchased in this fashion, 'co-operation materials' (Wu and Zhao 1988, p. 20). The introduction of the dual-track system was nothing new, but simply legitimised the reality of the crevices of the command economy. There was also no 'bang' at all.

Clear Signals

With the dual-track system, most products had some part of their sales in the free market, with the price determined by demand and supply. As early as 1985, around 99 per cent of a sample of 429 enterprises relied to some degree on the market for both sourcing their inputs and selling their output (Reynolds, or CESRRI-a, 1987, p. 5). From the basic principle of economics, price is determined by marginal cost and revenue. For individuals, producers and consumers alike, the possibility of selling an additional, marginal, unit of output or the need to buy an additional, marginal, unit of input at free market prices means that for each additional unit of output or input produced or saved, a given enterprises would experience increased sales, or reduced costs, in relation to market prices. This would be irrespective of the amount of inputs obtained or output turned over to the planning authorities at planned prices (whether these be higher or lower). As long as the market does exist, market prices provide clear signals of resource allocation with no distortion. Moreover, the government introduced the policies of 'new product, new price' and 'new plant, new prices'. Thus more and more new products were produced and new plants

operated in response to pure market prices. If the objective of price liberalisation is to get accurate allocative signals, then the dual-track system
achieved this. Byrd concludes:

> In any case, where the two-tier system remains, planning plays a
> primarily redistributional rather than an allocative role ... At a
> fundamental level, the issues of market allocation and to a lesser extent
> price reform are becoming passé, and they no longer need to be the
> prime concern for reformers. The focus of attention thus can shift to the
> next 'level' of resource allocation – China's factor allocation system,
> which is full of rigidities and problems. (1988, pp. 16–17)

'Big-bang' theorists do not focus attention on factor markets, yet it is
here that the real problems lie. Kornai found: 'in many respects the resulting dualism combines the drawbacks of bureaucracy and the market'
(1992b, p. 515). Wu and Zhao appeal for a comprehensive price reform in
order 'to put an end to the impasse of duality', because of its four well-
known problems:

> *First, hypocritical behaviour by enterprises.* On the one hand, they try
> to hide their production capacity so that they will get lower production
> quotas from the state, while on the other hand they strive to claim as
> large an allocation of material as they can from the state...
> *Second, loss of objective standards for performance assessment by
> the state.* State production quotas are based on past enterprise perform-
> ance. Now, a well-managed enterprise that receives a larger production
> quota from the state is less able to produce extra for its own profit
> through the free market, while a less efficient factory is in a better posi-
> tion to profit in this way...
> *Third, induced smuggling in distribution.* Knowing that profit can be
> made by reselling allocated materials, smugglers avail themselves of
> numerous wide-open loopholes...
> *Fourth, irrational utilisation of resources.* The high prices and profits
> in the free market attract investment. The investment is flowing to the
> 'right' industry, but the flow hatches a number of small and inefficient
> enterprises. This gives rise to irrational utilisation of resources due to
> the loss of economies of scale. (Wu and Zhao 1988, pp. 24–6, italics in
> original)

The four problems, however, cannot be attributed to the wrong prices.
For example, in the case of the first problem, although Hungary never had

a dual-track price system, Kornai described the fact that enterprises negotiated 'hypocritically' with the government in many other areas, such as tax, capital, labour and investment. In the case of the second problem, in a typical command economy, all the factors of production that form an enterprise were administratively allocated by the state. Even if there are market prices in the product market, it is still impossible to find the 'objective standards for performance'. Enterprises can make 'easy profits' from such sources as cheap labour, easy credit, free investment and free land.

Clearly, these four problems are not problems of price reform, but the problems of enterprise reform and reforms of factor markets. These problems cannot be resolved by price reform, whether of the dual-track system of the big-bang variety.

Gradualist Dynamics

In tandem with the buyer's market price reform, the dual-track system could achieve price liberalisation in a way that the big-bang programme could not. Using the same approach as diagram (B) of Figure 1.2, Figure 2.2 shows the gradual dynamics of price reform in China: that is, a combination of the buyer's market price reform starting from the

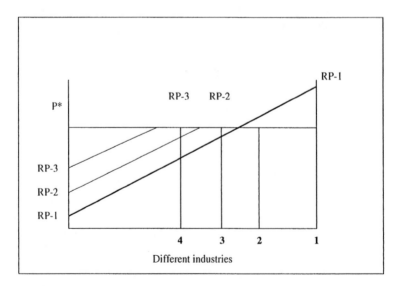

Figure 2.2   Gradual dynamics of buyer's market price reform and the dual-track price system in China

consumer goods market and the dual-track price system in the producer goods market, especially raw materials.

1. *RP-1* represents the original relative price line, in which the prices of some industries, say industries 1 and 2, were higher than equilibrium price *P**, and the prices of other industries, say industry 3 and 4, were lower. Along with those profitable products successively becoming overproduced, their prices were decontrolled by the government one by one from right to left. This buyer's market price reform started from consumer goods and brought downward pressure to bear on prices, from industry 1 to 2. The same process spread into producer goods industries, especially the overproduced machinery industry (Byrd 1987). Meanwhile, *with the market for producer goods developed*, more and more products' prices were decontrolled, regardless of whether they were oversupplied or not. The distribution of some 256 materials was a state monopoly in 1979. Their number had been reduced to 27 in 1988 (World Bank 1990a, p. 60). According to one estimate, in 1990, some 70 per cent of goods were distributed through the market (Li 1992).

2. Under the dual-track system, market prices provided accurate allocation signals shown by the horizontal line *P**.

3. *RP-2* and *RP-3* represent planned relative price lines below the market price *P**. With the material distribution system as a kind of subsidy, those cheaper goods were conveyed through the plan-track to meet the irreducible supply and demand, thus lessening the effect of a return to the original price relativities.

4. When enterprise reform went deeper and with supply increasing, the share of materials distributed by the plan-track could be reduced from time to time. Altogether, 'between 1980 and 1988, the central allocation of steel declined from 74 to 59 per cent; of coal, from 54 to 42.3 per cent; of timber, from 81 to 24 per cent; and of cement, from 36 to ten per cent' (Singh 1992, p. 30).

5. Represented by the movement from *RP-2* to *RP-3*, the gap between the planned and market prices also could be reduced from time to time by raising planned prices while market prices were falling.[8] For example, on 1 April 1991, the dual prices of cement were abolished in favour of a unified market determined price, since the distance between the planned price and the market price became very small (Li, quoted in Perkins 1992, p. 18).

6. Like any administrative measure, the plan-track could control prices by following a static price list. It could not control the prices of new products outside the list. Thus the policy of 'new product, new price' became an important part of price reform. It stimulated enterprises to introduce new products outside the control price list. This policy not only promoted

new products 'growing out of plan', but also encouraged enterprises to compete with each other by bringing out new products, thus prompting both re-industrialisation and technological advance. A survey of the 3356 so-called 'key industrial enterprises' showed that, as early as 1985, the output of new products accounted for 12.45 per cent of their gross output value (SSB 1989, p. 47).

7. Also importantly, the plan-track was useful for the state to ensure the construction of its priority projects. The final section in this chapter will discuss this issue.

'Growing Out of Plan' (Byrd 1988, p. 12)

Hitherto, the discussion has not considered the question of growth. Based on the non-bankruptcy system, there was downward rigidity in the irreducible supply and demand, the rigid wages, and the rigid non-production types of investment. If a big-bang programme attempts to *cool down* the economy in order to squeeze out a pure market system, these rigidities would be resistant to reforms, including administrative stabilisation which itself re-deployed all the traditional measures to enforce restrictive policies. The tighter the squeeze on the economy was, the stronger anti-reform resistance would be. In contrast, if policies encouraged growth, the *warmed up* economy would be more flexible. For example, Table 1.3 suggests that 'non-productive' and housing investments were inelastic both downwards and upwards. In the downward direction, the larger the decline in overall investment was, the smaller the decrease of 'non-productive' investment and the larger the decrease of productive investment would be; whereas, in the upward direction, the greater the increase in overall investment, the smaller the increase in 'non-productive' investment and the greater the increase in productive investment.

Under administrative stabilisation, interest rates could not function well as a mechanism to help the selection of efficient projects and to resist inefficient investments. Administrative measures, such as setting investment and credit ceilings, distributing investment and credit quotas, always faced difficult negotiations with different ministries, local governments and enterprises. Thus the effect of an austerity programme would inevitably be a cut in investment equiproportionally among different sectors, regions and enterprises, regardless of efficiency and structural priority. Therefore, the more severe the austerity was, the more rigid the existing industrial structure would become. Conversely, when overall investment increased, investors could have more chances to choose profitable projects from among others in the market. Hence a structural adjustment might be more desirable than austerity. Under the dual-track

Table 2.2   Key materials allocated by the central authorities in China, 1979–88

Product	Proportion of central allocation in total output (%)		Output volume		Growth of output (%)	Centrally allocated volume		Growth of central allocation
	1979	1988	1979	1988	[(4)–(3)] /(3)	1979 (1)×(3)	1988 (2)×(4)	[(7)–(6)] /(6)
	(1)	(2)	(3)	(4)	(5)	(6)	(7)	(8)
Steel	77.0	46.8	2 479	4 689	89.1	1908.8	2194.4	+ 14.9
Coal	58.9	43.5	6.4	9.8	53.1	3.8	4.3	+ 13.2
Cement	35.7	13.6	7 390	21 014	184.4	2638.2	2857.9	+ 8.3
Timber	85.0	25.9	5 439	6 218	14.3	4623.2	1610.5	− 65.0

Note: Units are 10 000 tons for steel and cement, 100 million tons for coal, and 10 000 cubic metres for timber.
Sources: Calculated from World Bank (1990a), Table 4.1; SSB (1992), pp. 424–5.

system, high market prices might be paid by those who are rich enough to pay. In an ideal situation, those who produce and sell more output above the plan quotas would be able to pay higher prices for their inputs. When the fixed irreducible supply and demand was accommodated by the plan-track, any increase in output beyond that would be guided by market demand. *Without growth, the dual-track system would be meaningless*: that is, the entire economy would shrink back to a single plan-track. In contrast, the faster the economy grew, the faster the market portion of the economy would expand. The dual-track system was useful, *if and only if* the economy was growing.

Table 2.2 shows the result of the implementation of the dual-track system under growth. The proportions of centrally allocated steel, coal and cement declined, because of the expansion in overall supply of these products. While the proportions of centrally allocated steel and coal came down rapidly, the absolute volumes of steel and coal allocated by the central government increased considerably. For instance, while the proportion of centrally allocated steel contracted from 77.0 per cent of the total output in 1979 to 46.8 per cent in 1988, the absolute volume under central allocation increased by 14.9 per cent, because total steel output increased by a large margin (89.25 per cent) during the period.

The dual-track system enabled the economy to grow out of the plan. The buyer's market price reform was brought forth by economic growth.

The success of the dual-track system was also dependent on economic growth. In sum, therefore, China's price liberalisation depended on economic growth for its success.

Division and Reunification

The dual-track system divided the original materials distribution system into two parts, the plan-track and the market-track. Together with other reforms, typically those promoting enterprise autonomy and economic decentralisation, it worked to break up the traditional command economy into two parts: one planning, the other market. This division opened the door for the part of the economy that had previously been excluded from the process of industrialisation.

In China before the reform, the economy had been divided into two parts, namely, the planning economy and the extra-planning economy. The former consisted of industries that were concentrated in a limited number of cities, and the latter was almost identical to agriculture, located in the vast countryside. Industry in China, then, was a state monopolised system that covered material production and distribution. Outsiders had no way of engaging in industrial production simply because they could not have access to materials. The successful reforms in the rural areas released a surplus labour force of hundreds of millions away from their tiny plots who wanted to join the process of re-industrialisation.

The dual-track system was able to open the door for these newcomers. The number of industrial enterprises in China increased from 348 000 in 1978 to 9 563 200 in 1993. Of new enterprises, 83.35 per cent (or around eight million) were private firms. Together with township-village enterprises, they made up 99 per cent of the new industrial enterprises emerging after 1978 (SSB 1983, p. 207; 1994, p. 373). Not surprisingly, because of their non-state-owned status, most of them could not get materials from the plan-track and they had to be fed by the market (Byrd and Zhu 1990).

Being castigated as the fourth defect of the dual-track system by Wu and Zhao, there were many stories about those newcomers scrambling for materials from the state sector. Since state-owned enterprises usually shouldered more tax, higher product quotas, better employment welfare and so on, they were less able to afford the high market prices of materials. The competition for materials in scarcity often resulted in irrational utilisation of resources. While the production capacity of some well-equipped state enterprises stood idle, small and inefficient township-village enterprises produced low quality products at much higher costs, because they could pay the market prices for materials (Wu and Zhao 1988, pp. 25–6). This was especially true at the beginning of the reform.

From a static point of view, competition generated by the dual-track system would lead to a conflict between the two tracks. The more the non-state sector got materials from the market-track the less available they would be to the well-equipped state sector from the plan-track. Nevertheless, as Table 2.2 indicated, the absolute volume of steel and coal distributed by the plan-track did not decrease, but increased considerably. Evidently, the proposition of irrational utilisation of resources needs to be examined further: to what extent were the huge numbers of new industrial firms fed by the huge increase in materials supply?

Newcomers to the industrial sector also contributed in part to the expansion of materials supply. For example, the number of small coal mines jumped from 16 000 in 1982 to 50 000 in 1985 (*Economic Daily* [Chinese], 10 May, 1985). By the end of the 1980s, collective and individual mines produced some 35 per cent of national output of coal (Albouy 1991, p. 4). They sold their output not only to the non-state sector but also to the state sector. In the 1980–8 period, over 30 per cent of the growth of China's total materials production was attributed to township-village enterprises (Chen, Jefferson and Singh 1992, p. 205). They not only ate but also produced (Perkins 1992, p. 24).

Without the dual-track system, it could have been difficult for the non-state industrial sector to compete with the state sector. Consequently, for more than two decades, huge resources in the vast countryside, which contained 80 per cent of China's total population, had been idle, outside the industrialisation process. Today, competition between the two sectors in many different industries suggests that the previously separated two parts have been integrated into the process of re-industrialisation. By 1992, township-village enterprises employed more than 100 million workers and accounted for 30 per cent of total national social product (BBC, 13 January 1993, p. 1). From the point of view of resource mobilisation, the development of rural industry has ended the history of the state's industrial monopoly, or the planned economy. The dual-track system mobilised enormous resources from the countryside and put them into the process of re-industrialisation. Put differently, the ability of the planning system to mobilise resources was so weak and limited that it had been incapable of utilising the vast resources of labour and capital at the local level for more than two decades. Industrialisation in China had been restricted to a few cities. Now, re-industrialisation has accelerated all over the country.

Summary

Although many economists do not like the dual-track system, they often acknowledge that this system could allay the pains of price liberalisation by changing one big earthquake into several small tremors (Wu and Zhao 1988). The function of the dual-track system, however, is far beyond that of being a 'pain-killer'. Riding economic growth, it has broken up the monopolistic planning economy into two parts, thereby mobilising innumerable idle resources into the process of re-industrialisation. Viewed in this light, the dual-track system was the key to integrating transition and re-industrialisation.

ECONOMIC GROWTH: A VEHICLE FOR REFORM AND RE-INDUSTRIALISATION

In general, growth can improve people's living standards and reduce social friction, thus fostering public support for further reform. This section explores the proposition that growth itself is a necessary condition for both successful transition and re-industrialisation.

Growth of the Non-State Sector

Under the dual-track system, growth was steered by market demand. The non-state sector simply reacted to market demand, and its growth was faster than the state sector. From 1978 to 1990, the gross industrial output value (at constant prices) of the country increased by 195 per cent, whilst that of the state sector rose by 142 per cent and the collective sector (mainly township-village enterprises) by 617 per cent. The large differential in growth rates greatly reduced the state sector's share of total output, falling from 77.63 per cent of total industrial output in 1978 to 43.13 per cent in 1993 (SSB 1994, p. 375).

The expansion of the non-state sector was not achieved by cutting down the state sector, but by 'making the pie bigger'. In contrast, under stabilisation, the non-state sector would normally suffer more because it did not have the same protection from the non-bankruptcy system as the state sector had. In 1989–90, the number of firms and employees of township-village enterprises in industry fell respectively by 515 200 and 1.32 million employees, whereas the state sector increased by 5300 enterprises and 1.35 million employees (SSB 1991, pp. 105, 377, 391). The slow down in economic growth hurt the non-state sector first.

Intensifying Competition

Usually economic prosperity makes it easier for everyone to make money. Pressure from competition should be less than under austerity, when many firms close down. This is why the big-bang theorists proposed an austerity programme: to intensify competition. But the conventional wisdom is questionable, at least for China. First, as mentioned in the first section in Chapter 1, there was irreducible supply and demand. As restrictive policies encountered a certain minimum quantity of production, the economy would become inflexible. Second, as discussed in the next section in Chapter 1, administrative stabilisation would itself directly obstruct market competition by the use of administrative measures. Third, as just stated, a slow down in economic growth would disproportionately reduce the share of market-track activity, where market competition occurred. In view of these specific conditions in China, growth did not undermine, but instead intensified, market competition.

From 1978 to 1990, the number of industrial enterprises in China increased by eight million. In the newly created market environment, most new firms, *including new state-owned enterprises*, were seeking profits. By entering into profitable industries, they brought competitive pressure to those industries. For example, from 1978 to 1982, the number of enterprises engaged in the bicycle industry increased from 38 to 140. The excessive supply of bicycles in the market led to a stockpiling of 1.34 million in 1980 and 3.47 million in 1983. All the excessive stocks were produced by the new entrants, and it resulted in a price cut in 1984 (Guo 1992, pp. 97–109). The story was replicated in all other profitable light industries.[9]

Naughton has used the convergence of profit rates across sectors in state industry and the erosion of profitability in rural industry as evidence of the intensification of competition (1992). Table 2.3 shows clearly both the trend of profit equalisation in the state sector and the erosion of profitability

Table 2.3 Deviation of industrial profit rates in China, 1980–9

Year	1980	1985	1986	1987	1988	1989
Standard deviation	19.70	14.94	15.18	13.06	9.36	7.43
Mean	29.48	24.72	21.45	20.27	19.64	15.72
Coefficient of variation	0.67	0.60	0.71	0.64	0.47	0.47
Average profit rate of township-village enterprises	32.5	23.7	19.7	17.0	17.9	15.2

Note: Deviation of profit rates in 38 industries, except tobacco, which is officially monopolised by the state.
Sources: Calculated from SSB (1990), pp. 153–9; (1991), p. 379.

in the non-state industry. It suggests that competition pressure did increase in both the state and non-state sectors (Mcmillan and Naughton 1991).

The New Industries

The non-bankruptcy system made the industrial structure rigid. To adjust the structure, it was less easy to squeeze existing industry. Re-industrialisation in China has relied very much on creating new firms to establish new industries in the fast-growing economy.

Increased marketisation was intimately connected with the process of re-industrialisation. The shift of production from heavy to light industry attracted numerous new enterprises. Many of them were previously outsiders to the planned economy. It constituted a positive feedback or symbiotic process in Chinese reform. The growth of market activities contributed to re-industrialisation; structural adjustment attracted and accommodated the growth of market activities. *Without the growth of market activities, structural adjustment could not advance fast and smoothly. Coincidentally, without re-industrialisation, the numerous new enterprises and the non-state sectors would have had no room in which to achieve the fast growth they enjoyed in the last decade.*

The final section of Chapter 1 discussed the concepts of the two gaps. Re-industrialisation is not a simple matter of cutting unwanted production. Parallel to reform, it changes the product-mix and initiates *new industries.* One estimate shows that of the total incremental industrial output produced during 1980–5, 30.8 per cent was contributed by new consumer goods industries (CESRRI-b 1988, p. 15).

To fill up the first gap in the old four consumer durables sector, new entrants played a key role as competitors pushing through the shift of production from heavy to light industry. To fill up the second gap in the new five consumer durables sector, new entrants played an even more crucial role as founders of, or pioneers in, new forms of production introducing new technology to China. For example, from 1978 to 1988, the annual output of electric fans increased 33 times, that of television sets 48 times, refrigerators 271 times, tape recorders 540 times and washing machines 26 170 times (see Table 1.7). After 1987, China became the world's biggest producer of television sets (SSB 1990, p. 63). China has become the biggest producer of electric fans in the world and in the early 1990s, its output exceeded 50 per cent of the world's total output (Qu 1992). These new products were outside the originally planned economy. All their production capacities were established after 1978; for example, the number of washing machine producers jumped from two in 1978 to 300 sub-sequently, and remained at 147 in 1985.

The second gap is a gap between different technological levels. It cannot be filled simply by supplying domestic technology to existing industry. It can be filled only by building up new industries using imported technology. *It is a process of industry-building, which cannot take place without economic growth.* The big-bang theorists focus on static efficiency of resource allocation, ignoring the dynamic nature of re-industrialisation. *No matter how much unwanted production can be cut out, it is impossible to squeeze out new industries from the existing economy.*

Growth-Productivity Dynamic

The driving force of economic growth is usually thought of as technological invention and innovation to enhance productivity, and productivity improvement drives economic growth. In such a growth relationship there is no reverse causality. Growth cannot generate technological advance, and thus productivity improvement. Beside the famous Verdoorn's law, which implies that growth improves productivity through economies of scale or through competitive incentives (Chenery, Robinson and Syrquin 1986), Amsden presents the growth-productivity dynamic:

> Ignoring for the moment the institutional setting, it can easily be appreciated that if foreign technology is embodied in plant and equipment, then to raise productivity by importing technology will depend on the rate of investment in new plant and equipment. The faster output is rising, the faster one may expect investment to rise, and hence technology imports to rise. If growth and investment are low, the import of foreign technology will also be low. Similarly, it will be easier to realise scale economies embodied in imported foreign technology when output is growing. When output is growing, income is also growing, and hence the size of the market is expanding, making it easier to reach minimum efficient scale. Finally, how efficiently foreign technology is used will depend on the experience of the user. The faster output is rising, the faster experience accumulates. In other words, learning-by-doing, which is one critical aspect of learning in general, depends on cumulative output.
>
> If growth depends on productivity, then as just stated, productivity also depends on growth. The growth-productivity momentum is a closed loop. Once growth starts and invades newer industries, it gathers momentum by triggering increases in productivity (Amsden 1989, p. 111).

Table 2.4   Investment and foreign trade in China, 1978–90 (%)

Year	Investment / GNP	Growth of trade / growth of GNP
1978	36.5	100
1979	34.6	110
1980	31.5	111
1981	28.3	111
1982	28.8	112
1983	29.7	120
1984	31.5	122
1985	35.0	141
1986	34.7	137
1987	34.1	140
1988	34.5	128
1989	33.8	234
1990	32.8	66
1991	32.8	227
1992	34.3	154

Sources: SSB (1993), pp. 33, 43, 633; Lardy (1992), Table B.2.

Table 2.4 reveals an extremely high investment rate in China throughout the last decade. Up to 1990, the state sector investment was 65.6 per cent of total investment. In productive investment, the state sector covered as much as 77.6 per cent of the total (SSB 1991, p. 146). This investment surge was the malign result of traditional investment hunger. Nonetheless, the same investment hunger could have a different outcome due to three changes.

First, the state emphasised technological advance. Within the state sector, investment for technical upgrading increased sharply relative to capital construction investment. 'Technical transformation investment' represented 25 per cent of total investment in the late 1970s, 37.6 per cent in 1983, and 33 per cent in 1987 (Singh 1992, p. 18). Second, the investment surge was pushed by the same investment hunger, but this time it was guided by market demand, and subject to more and more vigorous competition. Third, much more profoundly, this investment surge happened in a more open environment. As shown in Table 2.4, the rate of increase in foreign trade consistently exceeded the growth of GNP.[10] According to Lardy, the average annual growth rate of national income was 5.7 per cent in 1952–77, and 8.7 per cent in 1978–89; but that of foreign trade was 8.5 per cent and 13.3 per cent respectively (1992, p. 14).

Imports of machinery and transport equipment, essential to upgrading China's technological base, rose from US$5.1 billion in 1981 to US$18.2

billion in 1989 (SSB 1991, p. 617). As early as 1985, 19.7 per cent of total equipment in the state sector was imported (compared to 8.2 per cent in the collective sector). For large enterprises, 30.1 per cent of their total equipment was imported (SSB 1989b, p. 32). Moreover, the World Bank remarks: 'Recent Chinese policy has stressed the need to import "software" (know-how) in addition to, or instead of, "hardware" (equipment)' (1988a, pp. 45–7).

In the 1980s and 1990s China's very high growth rate was combined with an extremely high investment rate. *The combination resulted in a complete capital reformation. The sum of investment made during 1978–90 was twice that in 1952–77.*[11] Like economic growth, the investment surge also embraced inefficiency because of the incomplete reform. Nevertheless, due to the three changes, the investment reformation must have been greatly different from the traditional pattern mobilised by the planning authorities from their offices. Economists increasingly believe that there was a significant productivity growth in China in the last decade. Chen and others calculate that the total factor productivity in the state industry grew at a rate of 4–5 per cent per annum during 1978–85 (1988). Nolan estimates the growth rate of output/capital was –0.8 per cent in 1957–78, but 3.7 per cent in 1978–85 (1992b, p. 106). Perkins reckons that 43 per cent of the total 8.78 per cent annual growth in 1976–85 was thanks to productivity increases (1988, p. 628). Jefferson, Rawski and Zheng estimate the productivity gain amounted to 2.4 per cent per annum for state industry and 4.6 per cent for the collective sector in 1978–88.[12] Significantly, 'if productivity growth is divided into two components representing technical change and scale economies, the contribution of the former component is far larger than the latter' (1991, p. 257).

Summary

Economic growth in China included both allocative inefficiency and X inefficiency on a grand scale, due to the absence of factor markets and the maintenance of the non-bankruptcy system in the state sector. Nevertheless, during the transition, economic growth had three important implications. First, growth was mainly led by market demand, and partly driven by the non-state sector in which the mechanism of closure and unemployment operated forcefully. Therefore, growth could facilitate the development of market activities, thereby intensifying competition. Second, growth accommodated numerous new entrants into industry, thereby accelerating re-industrialisation. Third, growth stimulated the surge of investment often using imported equipment with advanced technology, thus raising productivity. These three special implications could improve both static and dynamic efficiency enough to compensate for the inefficiency generated by the non-bankruptcy system.

In an empirical study of 16 countries from 1870 to 1979, Abramovitz has established his 'catch-up' proposition: 'The combination of technological gap and social capability defines a country's *potentiality* for productivity advance by way of catch-up' (1989, p. 224, italics in original). If an economy is technologically backward but socially advanced, it will tend to catch up faster. The bigger the technological gap, and the higher the social capability, the faster the economy will catch up with advanced ones. According to this theory, social capability includes such factors as education, experience with organisation and management of large-scale enterprises, and capability of mobilising resources. Many socialist countries as semi-industrialised economies were capable of catching up. The command economy generated both a technological gap and social capability. One could expect a respectable growth in such an economy. If inappropriate 'surgery' injures the country's 'social capability', *the real loss is not just a fall in output, but the missing of a historical development opportunity*; for example, re-industrialisation in China, in terms of adjustment to the industrial structure, establishments of new industries and capital reformation.

THE BACKBONE OF GROWTH: THE 'PLAN-TRACK' AND THE STATE SECTOR

The remarkable growth in China during the 1980s was not only led by the market but also supported by the plan-track. The main advantage of the dual-track system was to keep both the old central planning and new market mechanism working together. This main advantage was criticised by the big-bang theorists as its principal disadvantage. By and large, the co-existence of the planned and market mechanisms must result in chaotic signals and rules, as well as giving rise to corruption. The following discussion acknowledges this disadvantage. Unfortunately, it is difficult to enjoy the advantage without suffering from the disadvantage, since the advantage and the disadvantage are but two sides of the same coin.

An Essential Part of Growth[13]

In the Chinese experience, there were two categories of material production. One was material production that was elastic to price changes: for example, small coal mines have produced 54 per cent of total coal output in 1988 since the higher market prices made production profitable (Zinser

1991). The second category was material production that was inelastic to price changes: for example, the market price of steel was so high that thousands of 'bucket-size blast furnaces' were established to make money in 1985. Those mini-furnaces did not produce a significant amount of steel. Unlike the small coal mines, the steel industry needs to mobilise considerable resources.

By 1992, the average output per enterprise in the state sector was more than RMB16 million or US$2.16 million; in the collective sector it was around RMB0.8 million or US$0.1 million, while in private enterprises it was some US$4 500 (SSB 1993, pp. 409, 413). Most non-state enterprises are so small that they concentrate on light industries and are unable to engage in large projects (Chen, Wang and Colleagues 1988). The absence of factor markets is a crucial obstacle to augmenting the scale of non-state enterprises (Byrd and Zhu 1990, p. 109). It was not until as late as the 1990s that China started to develop the markets for land and labour. Financial resources were predominantly distributed by the administratively managed banking system. Although different factor markets were growing up, often informally (from as early as 1978), they were still embryonic. They were removed from the point at which the market alone could run the whole economy. Willing or unwilling, only the state sector was capable of mobilising resources on a large scale:

> Until now, the government has relied heavily on its 'state key projects' program to achieve the necessary shift of resources into priority sectors. This program consists of large projects in priority sectors which have been assigned 'key project' status by the State Council. These projects are financed through a combination of budgetary resources, mandatory bank loans, and voluntary 'cost sharing' arrangements with the province in which the project is located. The importance of this program derives from two factors. First, the supply of materials to these projects is planned with a degree of sophistication and precision to be expected only from a centrally planned economy. Second, *most of the materials are made available at state plan prices*, so the nominal size of this program understates its real importance. (Singh 1992, pp. 36–7, my emphasis)

As mentioned in the first section of this chapter, goods could be distributed administratively if the prices were administratively set. Until the market was sufficiently mature enough to mobilise resources on a large scale, it was indispensable for the state sector to do so administratively. As long as administrative distribution was indispensable, planned pricing was indispensable. Unintentionally, under the plan-track, planned prices were super-stable in the face of inflation during the transition. More importantly, *administrative distribution was super-assured in the face of numerous uncertainties during the transition.* These two characteristics made the plan-track conducive to the constructions of giant projects which involved not only a long-term pay-off period but also a long gestation period. In 1985–90, for instance, the average construction cycle of the 'large and medium' projects was six years and 11 months (calculated from SSB 1992, p. 151).

Only Loss-Makers?

In 1990, state industry suffered losses of RMB34.88 billion, equal to 23 per cent of the total of profits and taxes made by the state industry (SSB 1991, p. 408). The government subsidy to loss-makers reached RMB57.89 billion, or 17 per cent of total government expenditure (SSB 1991, pp. 209, 212, 408). Loss-making has always been evidence of inefficiency in the state sector.

As can be seen in the second column of Table 2.5, by 1990 the losses made by the state sector were concentrated in the four industries of coal mines, oil and gas, machinery, and textiles. They accounted for 53.15 per cent of total losses. The two downstream industries, machinery and textiles (loss ranks third and fourth), were almost fully liberalised in the pricing of their products. The low state share in the second column reflects the fact that there were many non-state enterprises competing against the state sector. The losses in these two industries, accounting for 18.83 per cent of total losses, can be attributed, to a certain degree, to competition. The losses in the 'coal mines' and 'oil and gas' (first and second loss ranks) categories, with their low profitability and high state shares, account for 34.32 per cent of total losses, these were apparently not caused by competition from the non-state sector, but were predominantly caused by the low planned prices. According to Albouy, the centrally controlled mines, for example, sold 85 per cent of their output at planned prices and 15 per cent at 'guidance prices' which were 200 per cent of the average planned price, but only 69 per cent of the average market price (Albouy 1991, p. 11).

These loss-makers are not always inimical to economic development (Chang and Singh 1993). Being upstream industries, some of them provided staple but cheap inputs for the profit-makers at downstream industries where non-state firms were concentrated. Although most non-state

Table 2.5   State sector's shares, losses and profit rates in China, 1990

Industry rate	State share*	Profit rate (state sector)†	Loss share‡	Loss Rank	Rank of profit rate
Total	67.26		100.00		
01. **Oil and gas**	**99.91**	**0.16**	**13.59**	**2**	**27**
02. Timber	97.59	7.57	1.00	17	21
03. Tobacco	96.49	134.55	2.51	12	1
04. Oil refining	96.44	30.87	0.39	26	2
05. Power	96.11	13.42	4.85	6	8
06. Water	91.09	3.61	0.83	19	25
07. Ferrous metals	86.58	16.87	3.08	9	7
08. Chemical fibre	84.53	21.42	0.22	28	4
09. Food	79.54	9.41	6.55	5	16
10. **Coal mines**	**78.82**	**–6.45**	**20.73**	**1**	**30**
11. Chemicals	77.90	17.30	4.02	7	6
12. Coking and town gas	77.70	–0.39	1.21	14	29
13. Non-ferrous mines	76.05	10.55	0.67	20	13
14. Beverages	74.60	17.50	2.65	10	5
15. Fodder	73.34	8.24	0.42	25	18
16. Transport machines	71.30	6.90	2.52	11	23
17. Rubber	68.05	26.44	0.44	24	3
18. **Machinery**	**67.50**	**5.83**	**10.83**	**3**	**24**
19. Electronics	66.02	8.75	1.78	13	17
20. Ferrous mines	65.96	7.90	0.12	30	19
21. Instruments	61.20	7.36	0.52	22	22
22. **Textiles**	**56.52**	**11.16**	**8.00**	**4**	**12**
23. Building materials	51.16	9.41	3.90	8	15
24. Electric machinery	48.72	13.27	1.16	15	9
25. Wood products	42.49	–0.14	0.88	18	28
26. Non-metal mines	41.47	9.63	0.34	27	14
27. Metal working	26.00	11.63	0.57	21	11
28. Plastics	21.81	7.61	0.44	23	20
29. Non-ferrous metals	17.83	12.18	1.02	16	10
30. Furniture	12.35	2.00	0.13	29	26

* State share = output of state sector/total output, calculated from SSB (1991), pp. 399–340, 471.
† Profit rate = (tax + profit)/total capital.
‡ Loss share = loss in this industry/total loss, calculated from SSB (1991), p. 408.
Notes: These figures relate to aggregate values of all 'independent accounting' industrial enterprises, excluding those industrial enterprises which are subordinates of non-industrial enterprise. Their gross output value is equal to 78.12 per cent of the nation's industrial gross output. By this definition, some small enterprises are not included. It makes the output share of the state sector higher (SSB 1991, pp. 394–7).

firms could not directly obtain planned materials, these cheap inputs satisfied inter-industry demand. For example, steel used a lot of cheap coal and electricity as inputs. Cheap rail transportation, bearing 40.53 per cent of the total turnover volume of cargo transport in 1990, relied heavily on coal for fuel. In 1989, coal was 76 per cent of total energy consumption in China (SSB 1991, pp. 453, 499). The coal processing industry, other upstream industries and the transport sector received a RMB3.3 billion transfer due to the low price of coal (Albouy 1991, pp. 10–12), equivalent to 66 per cent of total losses in state coal mines in the same year (SSB 1990, p. 442).

'Wrong Prices, Right Direction'?

According to Amsden (1989), South Korea distorted its relative prices but did so in the 'right' direction, towards exports.[14] In China, with an administrative jungle encompassing currency inconvertibility, licensing, differential tariffs, subsidies, tax rebates, retention of export-earned foreign currency, export contracts, and mandatory plans, it is difficult to estimate whether the domestic price distortions were biased towards or against exports (Lardy 1992, p. 100).

The upsurge of imports relied on the expansion of exports (Lardy 1992). In 1990, China registered a US$8.7 billion trade surplus, and 74.4 per cent of its exports were manufactured products (SSB 1991, pp. 615–18), compared with 64 per cent for 'upper-middle-income countries' and 49 per cent for 'lower-middle-income countries' in 1989 (World Bank 1991, p. 234). In 1990, China became the third largest developing country exporter of manufactured goods (Yeasts 1991, p. v). 'China shot up to become the sixteenth largest exporting country in the world by 1987 and the thirteenth largest by 1989' (Lardy 1992, p. 13), and the eleventh in 1992 (*Economic Reference* [Chinese], 10 December 1992).

China's manufactured exports were largely from light industry, favoured by China's domestic price structure. In 1990, textiles and garments accounted for 30 per cent of China's total manufactured exports (SSB 1991, p. 618). In 1992, China became the world's biggest textile exporter (*United Daily* [Chinese], 10 October 1992). Labour-intensive light manufacturing was where China's comparative advantage lay (World Bank 1988a). Both domestic planned and market price structures favoured processing industries. As shown in Tables 1.4 and 1.5, domestic prices of inputs, such as of materials and energy, were much lower than world prices. On the demand side, the price structure encouraged irrational exports of materials for energy generation (Lardy 1992, pp. 95–6).[15] On the supply side, the cheap inputs enhanced the competitiveness of manu-facturing exports.[16] In the past decade, providing materials at low planned prices through the plan-track has been a powerful means for the Chinese government to promote manufactured exports.

The prices of non-tradable goods, such as power and transportation, were also low, compared with that in the destination countries of Chinese manu-facturing exports, say the USA and the UK. In addition, the lack of markets helped make the factors of production, including labour, land and capital, much cheaper than they are in a typical market economy. As for land, by the 1990s, there was no open market. Most enterprises paid no rent or other charges for the land they occupied (World Bank 1988b). As for labour in the urban areas, besides free education, medical care, social security, housing, and so on, city dwellers also benefited from abundant 'price subsi-dies' from the government budget. In 1990, the item 'price subsidy' (apart from a small proportion paid to agricultural machinery and fertilisers, it mainly benefited the urban population) reached RMB38.08 billion, equiva-lent to 11.5 per cent of total government expenditure or 98.11 per cent of total industrial profit of the state sector (SSB 1991, pp. 209, 223, 408). As for capital, after 1978, bank loans increasingly financed investments at interest rates well below the market clearing level (Perkins 1992, p. 25).

Summary

The plan-track which distorted relative prices had several positive and indis-pensable functions. First, as discussed above, it was the prerequisite for the goods distribution system, thus saving the economy from collapse. Second, as already discussed, being a source of subsidy, it reduced the impact of a return to the original price relativities while the price of products produced above plan quotas was able to be decontrolled in the market. Third, as a super-stable mechanism, it enabled the state to invest in giant projects, thus recharging a key force for economic growth. Fourth, underpricing of some basic goods was advantageous to light manufactured exports. Finally, in these price-inelastic industries, the state sector and the plan-track provided cheap industrial inputs, thereby becoming the driving force propelling the economy forwards rather than merely the target of privatisation.

Conclusion to Part I: The Reversible Big Bang

Sachs and others employ oversimplified utility models to explain why the big bang must work. In order to let the models work, they assume there is a 'parallel market' capable of substituting for the existing goods distribution system. Then they use consumer goods and household behaviour to demonstrate the benefits of price liberalisation in general. In their model, they use household behaviour with consumer goods to illustrate enterprise behaviour with producer goods (see Lipton and Sachs 1990, p. 90; Berry and Sachs 1992, pp. 120–1). The simple facts in China were: first, enterprises' 'responsiveness' to price changes was not as rational as households'. Second, there did not exist a 'parallel market' available for producer goods distribution. Third, consumer goods and producer goods have different situations in the original price structure, and have different responses to price liberalisation and reindustrialisation.

The big-bang theorists emphasised correctly that transition must be comprehensive and that 'many of the changes have to be introduced simultaneously' (Prybyla 1991, p. 16). The transition process is, indeed, a seamless web (Lipton and Sachs 1990, p. 99). Price reform alone is only capable of changing the economic system at the superficial level of the product market. As long as enterprise reform, reforms in factor markets and re-industrialisation have not been effectively pushed forward, price reform would be easily held back if it had gone too far. In 1968, implementing the 'New Economic Mechanism', the Hungarian government intended to abolish all administrative controls simultaneously, including administrative pricing. However, the resulting pressure of price increases forced the government to renegotiate with large state-owned companies more and more frequently, until 300 different types of 'indirect co-ordination' measures had been introduced (Kornai 1990b, p. 31; see also Balassa 1987; Gao, Chen and Wang 1988). In 1986, the Chinese government declared the elimination of compulsory purchase of grain, but there was no corresponding reform of state-owned grain procurement agencies. These agencies were affiliated to the government at different levels and districts. They were incapable of buying and selling grain across administrative boundaries. Consequently, in the same year, the government had to set up the so-called 'contracted purchases', which was exactly the same as the compulsory purchases before the reform.

As long as several key reforms have not proceeded far enough, the authorities have to renegotiate with (or administratively control) enterprises in order to control individual prices, whether directly or indirectly, under whatever guise. The more monopolistic the economy was, the easier it would be for the authorities to control prices. Sooner or later, the big-bang programme would have to be reversed. Administrative stabilisation was eventually a step backwards in price liberalisation when the authorities distributed investment quotas administratively. To what extent price liberalisation which has gone too far can be reversed depends on how deep and how fast enterprise reform and reform in factor markets has gone.

Surgery may be painful. A high level of pain is not proof that surgery has been successful. If the reforms try to split up the 'seamless web' and carry out inappropriate surgery, the transition will be more painful than is necessary. Perhaps this is the reason why *The Economist* discusses Soviet economic reforms under the title 'Plenty of shock, no therapy' (1991c, p. 71).

In 1994 China downgraded two important departments, the State Bureau of Price Management and the Ministry of Material Supply. The government incorporated the former into the State Planning Commission, and the latter into the Ministry of Domestic Trade. By then most prices were free in the market, and price reform in China was no longer the main topic. Nevertheless, there were still direct price controls over rail and air transport, power supply, oil, gas, grain and cotton, and indirect price controls through the 'state guidance prices' over steel, coal and other materials. Facing the problems of inflation and recession, as well as triangular debt and excess inventory, administrative stabilisation is sometimes necessary. Further academic work still needs to be done to reveal the complexity of the process.

Part II

Transcending the Logic of Private Ownership: China's Enterprise Reform versus Privatisation

Enterprise reform is at the heart of transition in pre-socialist economies. The IMF, World Bank, OECD and EBRD define enterprise reform as ownership reform:

> Enterprises must be able to make decisions with the guidance of price signals. This will require financial autonomy, with owners and managers taking responsibility for the full range of business decisions and for the financial benefits and costs of those decisions. Experience shows that this is most likely to happen when assets are privately owned. Private ownership also creates opportunities for individuals and reduces political interference in managerial decisions. (1990, pp. 16–17)

The logic of privatisation dominates enterprise reform in all transitional economies, including China. All transitions have exercised some forms of privatisation in small businesses. What remains problematic is the privatisation of large state-owned enterprises. Large and medium state-owned enterprises often produced about 50 per cent of industrial output in transitional economies. Moreover, they dominated most other economic areas, including the commercial network, the distribution system of producer goods, trade, the financial system, transportation, communication, power supply and infrastructure. Without reform in these large state-owned enterprises, the prosperity of small businesses alone cannot change the nature of the economy.

In fact, enterprise reform is a broad issue of political economy rather than a narrow question of ownership reform *per se* (Rowthorn and Chang 1993). Compared with privatisation in the West, Ferguson (1992) lists ten necessary preconditions that Eastern Europe does not possess, while

Hare (1990) produces an even longer list. Meanwhile, the various non-commercial functions, and the actual efficiency of public enterprises in developing countries, are still highly debated issues (Chang and Singh 1993). Furthermore, the explosive growth of township-village enterprises in China challenges the necessity of privatisation even in the small business sector (Nolan 1993, p. 311). Based on these arguments, Part II argues that privatisation is infeasible for many large state-owned enterprises in transition. Enterprise reform should focus on managerial autonomy rather than privatisation.

Introduction: The Self-Contradictory Privatisation

How are state-owned enterprises to be reformed? Privatisation seems to be the obvious solution (Lipton and Sachs 1991, p. 232). In theory, 'only private property can supply enough incentive to permanently guarantee effective use of the resources' (Kornai 1990a, p. 91). However, in practice, privatisation of large state-owned enterprises is so problematic that a series of seemingly technical problems backfire on the principle of privatisation itself. Since there is no feasible way to privatise, the question how to privatise becomes the question why to privatise.[1]

PRIVATISATION BY 'TURNING BACK THE REEL TO THE BEGINNING'?

Kornai, Lipton and Sachs argue for wholesale privatisation. They reject any option other than transferring property rights from the state to 'truly private hands' (Kornai 1990a, 1992b; Lipton and Sachs 1991). According to Kornai: 'public property belongs to all and none. The hazy nature of property is the ultimate reason why the interest of the manager of a firm is hazy, ambiguous, and replete with contradiction' (1992b, pp. 504–5). Hence, state ownership must be thoroughly privatised:

> It is my firm conviction that history is not like a film reel that can be stopped at any moment, or run on fast forward or backward at will. Socialist state ownership means the complete, 100 per cent impersonalisation of property. We cannot simply reverse this process in an attempt to reduce the percentage gradually to 95, 90, 85 per cent and so on. The reel must be fully rewound and played from the beginning (1990a, p. 73)

I call Kornai's hypothesis the theory of 'turning back the reel to the beginning'. It has three distinctive underlying principles.

First, there is no 'third way'. All attempts at 'market socialism' failed, including self-management, co-operatives, local state-ownership, and simulating joint-stock companies, capital market and stock exchange.[2]

> The market mechanism is the natural co-ordinator of private sector activities ... It is futile to expect that the state unit will behave as if it were privately owned and will spontaneously act as if it were a market-oriented agent. It is time to let go of this vain hope once and for all. Never, no more ... This kind of bureaucratic co-ordination is as much the *spontaneous* effect and natural mode of state property's existence as market co-ordination is of private property. Twenty years of Hungarian experience together with the experience of all other reform-minded socialist state demonstrate that this is no longer a debating point, but simply a *fact* that must be accepted. (Kornai 1990a, pp. 58–9, italics in original)

Second, the impersonalised institutions in the West are 'the germs of socialism'. They are the wrong example for transitional economies to learn from:

> Ironically, the germs of socialism are already present in today's capitalism. There are many who believe that ownership has become inordinately impersonal in the insurance industry, health services, and banking. In the United States we see today a classic example for the softening of the budget constraint, namely in the sphere of savings and loan associations specialising in financing housing projects ... Now it is the state's turn to reach deep into its pocket and rescue these associations. If the state failed to do this, depositors would trigger a run on these units, and this in turn might result in a grave financial crisis similar to the recession of 1929. But is this really an example for us to follow? Certainly not! (1990a, pp. 76–7)

Certainly not! No one wants to follow the USA back into the recession of 1929. For this reason, transition must go back beyond 1929. Kornai raises the question: should Hungary 'adopt the market economy in its 19th or 20th century form'? Do we need 'identifiable "flesh and blood" entrepreneurs or impersonal joint-stock companies instead'? He answers: 'The reel must be fully rewound and played from the beginning ... Hungary today does not have to imitate the contemporary United States or Japan' (1990a, pp. 50–76). Kornai does not say that we should beware lest Western impersonalised investors disturb our transition, yet all the transitional countries are trying hard to attract foreign investments from the West.

Third, based on the above two propositions, Kornai, Lipton and Sachs object to giving managerial autonomy to state-owned enterprises before privatising them: '*The private sector must be wholly and truly liberalised*', while 'it is necessary to *restrict* the independence of the state firm in terms of credit, subsidy, wage, hard currency, investment and the sale of enterprise assets' (Kornai 1990a, pp. 38–50, 64–7, italics in original).

Kornai blames not only nationalisation but also impersonalisation in general, thereby advocating the *personalisation* of property. Since impersonalisation in the West is 'the germ of socialism', neither Sachs nor Kornai likes the stock market and voucher privatisation. Kornai refuses to replace the 'quite impersonal state ownership' by 'an equally impersonal private ownership' (1990a, p. 91). He suggests granting credits to the private sector to buy state property. But this credit 'should be granted to real flesh-and-blood persons instead of distributing it through an intangible stock market' (1990a, p. 85).

Kornai actually wants the 'traditional capitalist firm'. Chandler has termed it the 'personal enterprise' (1977, p. 9), in which an entrepreneur, or owner-manager, single-mindedly operates the firm to maximise profits (Fama 1980, p. 288). Though the enterprise grows, 'real flesh-and-blood persons' should retain control over management, and 'the manager is only a paid employee' (Kornai 1990a, p. 67).

The logic of privatisation is unambiguous. Privatisation brings back visible and tangible private owners in control. But the logic leads to an impasse: if it was impossible to introduce control over management in large state-owned enterprises by 'real flesh-and-blood persons', why should we attempt to privatise them?

SPONTANEOUS PRIVATISATION

'Spontaneous privatisation', as Lipton and Sachs observe in Poland, is the process whereby managers of state-owned enterprises appropriate state property by making sweetheart deals with an outside partner (1991, p. 236).

The logic of privatisation is easy to understand, but difficult to implement. At the beginning of capitalist history, most firms were directly operated by 'real flesh-and-blood persons', and there were few large industrial enterprises. However, in China in 1990, the largest 500 state-owned industrial enterprises accounted for 22 per cent of total industrial output, 23 per cent of total sales and 50 per cent of total profit before tax (*Management*

World 1991, p. 30).[3] The second largest industrial enterprise, Anshan Steel Company, employs 400 000 people, and possessed RMB8.6 billion (US$1 billion) of net fixed assets, with an annual production capacity of 22 million tonnes of iron, steel and steel products (Anshan Steel Company 1991, p. 1; *Management World* 1991, p. 2). It is not easy to deliver such a big firm into the hands of a few 'real flesh-and-blood persons'.

No matter what method is adopted, privatisation is time-consuming (Lipton and Sachs 1990). Kornai reckons the process will last for two decades (1990a, p. 101). Unfortunately, the next two decades are rather dynamic. Before they have been fully privatised, state-owned enterprises, as the main economic force, will still need to produce output. The existing managers and workers wish to improve their living standard. Apart from just waiting to be privatised, neither Kornai nor Sachs indicate what they are to do for the next two decades. Portes terms this 'un-conscientious neglect' – one of the 'transition traps' – 'state desertion', in which the pro-ponents of privatisation put the large numbers of state-owned enterprises into an irresolvable quandary. In theory, all state-owned property has to be privatised. In practice, there is no way to privatise the huge assets of state-owned enterprises in a short period. In the two decades before the 'real flesh-and-blood persons' take over, the existing managers have to make decisions daily on all economic activities.[4]

A king pronounced that all residents of his kingdom should be sen-tenced to death. However, he did not have an efficient guillotine to kill the masses overnight. All these prisoners facing the death sentence were freed to roam the streets instead. No one told them what they should do except wait to be killed later on. It is easy to imagine what those 'free prisoners' might do before their inescapable death:

> They would grant the foreign partner a highly favourable stake in the enterprise, and in return the foreign partner would grant the manager an attractive position in the new venture. The manager effectively traded the state property for personal gain ... Even more egregious cases ensued in which the state enterprises entered into contracts with newly established private firms in which the manager had a personal stake. The manager might then lease to the private firm the plant and machin-ery of the state enterprise at highly favourable terms. The profits of the state enterprise would thereby be transferred to the private firm. (Lipton and Sachs 1991, p. 236)

Lipton and Sachs imply that the awful picture is a result of 'Communist-appointed managers' (1991, p. 236). Nevertheless, they have not said what the right behaviour for these managers should be. In fact, *'spontaneous privatisation' is just the spontaneous consequence of privatisation theory.* In Kornai's words: 'state-owned enterprises expecting privatisation are practically paralysed; and state managers are not prepared to commit themselves to any enterprise development before property questions are settled' (1994, p. 5). All managers are in the position of 'who knows who will be dismissed when' (Kornai 1992a, p. 3), while they have to continue to carry out the enterprise's day-to-day business. Facing this contradiction, it would be surprising if there was anything other than 'spontaneous privatisation'; even the managers are appointed, or replaced, by Lipton and Sachs themselves.

SIMULATING PRIVATE OWNERSHIP?

Privatisation generates spontaneous privatisation. Spontaneous privatisation becomes the new reason to try to speed up privatisation (Lipton and Sachs 1991).

Attempting to speed up privatisation makes it even more difficult to deliver property rights. Some odd agencies are recommended to assume the role of private owners (at least temporarily). In China, people became tired of searching for these agencies (Hsu 1991). Despite variations in the details of the different proposals, the common element is that all these agencies or boards are not 'real flesh-and-blood persons'. They are often 'quasi-private' (Nellis 1991), impersonalised, or even government-appointed (Lipton and Sachs 1991, p. 240). Lipton and Sachs, for example, have no choice but to divide their wholesale privatisation into two steps:

> The first, and urgent, task is to introduce a provisional system of corporate governance that can monitor the management and prevent the managers and workers from squandering the capital income and capital assets of the firms before full privatisation takes place. The second, and long-term, task is to foster a structure of ownership in which the new private owners will be in a strong position to manage their newly acquired assets. (1991, p. 248)

The criticisms Kornai and Sachs have directed at all enterprise reform other than 'true privatisation' turn a full circle. The reasons for which they argue that 'true privatisation' is necessary fatally weaken the internal consistency of their privatisation scheme:

It would involve nothing other than the transfer of state property from one state hand to the other state hand, regardless of whether the other hand is characterised a 'firm,' a 'bank,' or an 'insurance company.' In fact, every new owner would be a firm with a soft budget constraint, this is, a more or less bureaucratic formation. There cannot be a real market in capital without capitalist private owners. (Kornai 1992b, pp. 503–4)

The past decades were replete with pseudo-reforms; what we are experiencing today is the latest wave of these fake, illusory changes. We have seen that an organisation is out there with the authority to spend the money of the state, and which does so irresponsibly. The so-called solution works as follows: let us hand over the ownership rights held by this state organisation to another state organisation, which in turn continues to spend the money of the state irresponsibly … We have already tried our hand at simulating quite a number of things. The state-owned firm simulates the behaviour of the profit-maximising firm. Bureaucratic industrial policy, regulating the expansion or contraction of various branches of production, simulates the role of competition. The Price Control Office simulates the market in price determination. The most recent additions to this list are the simulated joint stock companies, the simulated capital market, and the simulated stock exchange. Together, these developments add up to Hungary's Wall Street – all made of plastic! (Kornai 1990a, pp. 71–2).

Now, 'before full privatisation takes place', Lipton and Sachs propose nothing other than another 'pseudo-reform', 'a provisional system of corporate governance that can monitor the management and prevent the managers and workers from squandering the capital income and capital assets of the firms'. If this could be achieved, why would 'full privatisation' still be needed?

The first step offered by Lipton and Sachs is not 'turning back the reel to beginning', because 'inevitably, given a realistic timetable for any privatisation scheme, the initial boards of almost all enterprises will have to be appointed by the government' (Lipton and Sachs 1991, p. 240). What would be the sources of motivation if the managers of state-owned enterprises and the managers of state-owned property boards were appointed by the self-same state? If government-appointed managers of state enterprises could not work, why should the same government-appointed managers of such boards work any better?

Moreover, confronted with so many large state enterprises, Lipton and Sachs' 'full privatisation' becomes a hybrid structure of ownership. They wish the new private owners could be in a strong position to manage their newly acquired assets. However, their new structure of ownership has no choice but to rely heavily on the government (35 per cent of total shares), workers and managers (10 per cent), pension funds (20 per cent), the existing state-owned commercial banks and the insurance sector (10 per cent). The new private owners only have 20 per cent of total shares (1991, pp. 246–7).

PRIVATISATION FOR DEVELOPMENT?

Kornai recommends a group of discriminatory policies for the private and state sectors:

1. *The private sector must be wholly and truly liberated,* [including] freedom to establish a firm; free entry into the production sphere ... Free prices, based on a free contract between the buyer and the seller ... Unrestricted right to rent out privately owned assets ... Unrestricted right to employ people in all cases ... Unrestricted right to accumulate, sell, or buy any article of value ... Unrestricted right to take and bring in domestic and foreign currencies ... Free foreign trade activity, in which the member of the private sector has the unrestricted right to export and import ... Unrestricted right to lend money, with credit terms freely agreed upon between the creditor and the debtor ... Freedom of financial investment in the private ventures of other individuals ... Freedom to sell and buy, at free prices, any privately owned apartment, real estate, or other asset ...
2. *The enforcement of private contracts must be guaranteed by law...*
3. *The absolute security of private property should be emphatically declared...*
4. *The tax system should not constrain private investment...*
5. *Private investment as well as the formation and growth of private capital must be promoted through credit...*
6. *Social respect must be developed toward the private sector.* (1990a, pp. 38–49, italics in original).

In sharp contrast, Kornai also argues:

It is necessary to *restrict* the independence of the state firm ... Most important: the state banking system must strictly control the granting of credit to the state sector ... The wage policies of state firms must not be liberalised ... the state-owned firm's purchases of foreign currency must be restricted by direct administrative means ... The state-owned firm should be independent in those investment decisions that it can finance from its own savings or bank credits, or through funds obtained on the capital market ... The managers of the state-owned firm do not have the right to sell the enterprise. (1990a, pp. 63–7, italics in original).[5]

The reason for such discrimination is obvious. State-owned enterprises are inefficient. The only hope is to develop the private sector. For how long should discrimination against the state sector be implemented? Kornai's answer is 'for the next two decades' (1990a, p. 101). Sachs and Lipton also acknowledge that privatisation 'is likely to take many years' (Sachs and Lipton 1990, p. 101), although they wish to accelerate privatisation as fast as possible.

State-owned enterprises dominate in certain industries. So discrimination lasting for years must affect not only the differential growth rates of the private and state sector, but also the resulting industrial structure. For example, China liberalised private ownership after the early 1980s. Almost ten years later, in 1990, 78 per cent of the total of eight million industrial firms were privately owned. The state only owned 1.3 per cent of all industrial enterprises (SSB 1983, p. 207; 1991, p. 391). Nevertheless, this small number of state-owned enterprises provide basic industrial goods. The non-state sector grew very fast, mainly in the light industries and tertiary industry (see Table 4.2). For example, the top ten state-owned steel makers in 1989 produced 50 per cent of the country's steel (SGDSEMA 1991, p. 10), and 33 state-owned oil and gas fields produced 99.9 per cent of total crude oil and gas in 1990 (SSB 1991, pp. 399–403). Large and medium-size state-owned industrial enterprises accounted for 69 per cent of total industrial profits and taxes. Their 'retained profits' were only 13 per cent of their gross profits and taxes. After deduction of 'retained profits', their financial contribution to the government amounted to 35 per cent of total government revenues (SSB 1991, pp. 209, 401). Just as in advanced economies, large and medium-size enterprises are the backbone of transitional countries. To destroy them would destroy the economy as a whole.

In the face of this simple reality, is it possible to incorporate Kornai's transitional discriminatory policies – promoting the private sector and restricting the state sector – into a development strategy, which favours light and tertiary industries, while undermining the development of basic and heavy industries 'for the next two decades' or even for 'many years'?

SUMMARY

Figure I.1 displays the circular path we have travelled following the logic of privatisation. (1) According to Kornai, the state can never play the role of private owners. This is the reason why all previous reforms and compromised schemes failed. Therefore, (2) state property must be transferred to truly private owners. However, (3) in practice, it is not easy to privatise so many large state-owned enterprises overnight. (4) Since the managers of state-owned enterprises are not told what to do, (5) 'spontaneous privatisation' results. Then we pass through the second stage again: 'spontaneous privatisation' affirms the necessity of not only privatisation, but also the speeding-up of privatisation. (6) In order to speed up privatisation, the proponents of privatisation themselves have to design many impersonalised and even government-appointed agencies. Finally we come back to the original starting point (1): we need privatisation because we cannot

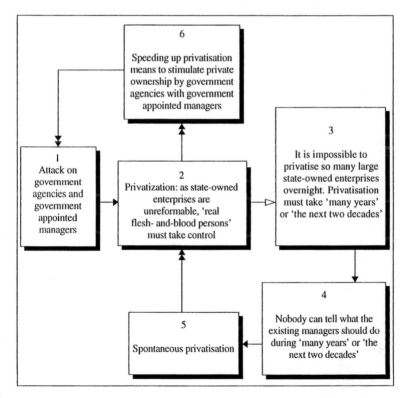

Figure I.1   The circular logic of arguments for privatisation in practice

trust those impersonalised bodies, especially as they are staffed by government-appointed managers.

From this account one can see that the problem of privatisation is practical rather than theoretical. If there is no practicable privatisation scheme for 'real flesh-and-blood persons' to control management in large state-owned enterprises, what is the point of pursuing privatisation?

3 Transcending Private Ownership

Kornai repeatedly emphasises that the main purpose of privatisation is 'to nurture the *incentive force* private ownership provides'. 'Most important, the prime consideration is not legal entitlement to acquire the property but the ability to run it well. In my view, only private property can supply enough incentive to permanently guarantee an effective use of the resources' (1990a, pp. 93 and 91, italics in original). In order to 'run it well':

> It would not be advantageous for that capital to be dispersed among ten thousand different shareholders. In that case the previous, quite impersonal state ownership would be replaced by an equally impersonal private ownership. The desirable thing would be a dominant individual shareholder or small group of shareholders capable of acquiring an appreciable stake in the firm (at least 20 or 30 per cent of the shares) and thus a decisive say in the appointment and supervision of the firm's executives. This aspiration is consistent with the argument already put forward in favour of the need for visible, 'tangible' owners whose private investments (in this case *sizeable* share-holdings) gives them a strong interest in the firm's success. (1990a, p. 91, italics in original)

In short, Kornai's theory of 'turning back the reel to the beginning' consists of three propositions: (1) only private property can supply adequate incentive; (2) therefore, private owners should not only own, but also run, firms; (3) their sizeable share-holding gives private owners a strong interest, and the power, to run firms well. The logic is clear. *Several years have passed. Why is it that Kornai or Sachs, who possess strong motivation and firm belief, have been unable to produce a practicable scheme for privatisation?* The reason is simple. Their idea of privatisation is too far removed from reality. What will be argued below is: (1) nowadays, 'real flesh-and-blood persons' are no longer significant owners of corporations; (2) the owners usually do not actually run firms; (3) private property is not the only resource which can provide incentives for efficient growth of the firm.

PERSONALISATION OR IMPERSONALISATION?

State ownership is the extreme form of property impersonalisation. In contrast, Kornai repeatedly emphasises the 'real flesh-and-blood persons', 'truly private hands', 'natural persons', 'identifiable "flesh and blood" entrepreneurs', and 'identifiable enterprising individuals or groups' (1990a, pp. 85, 70, 57, 50, 75). His privatisation is the opposite extreme: that is, property personalisation. Is it desirable that the transition should personalise nationalised property, thus jumping from one extreme to the other?

Who and Where are the Owners?

Kornai terms impersonalisation 'the germs of socialism' (1990a, p. 76). Table 3.1 shows how seriously 'the germs of socialism' were already present in today's capitalism. Great Britain is the birthplace of capitalism. In the real 'beginning', in the 1920s and 1930s, more than two-thirds of the shares of companies with a stock market quotation were held by individuals. In 1957, individuals held 62 per cent of UK equities. By 1970 their holdings had fallen to 45 per cent (Moyle 1971, pp. 6–7). Currently, less than 20 per cent of total stocks are held by 'real flesh-and-blood persons'. In the USA, institutions hold 46 per cent of the public stock (Wharton 1991, p. 137), about two-thirds of the equity of the 1000 largest US public companies (Lorsch 1991, p. 139).

Table 3.1   Ownership shares of listed companies in the UK, 1987 and 1989 (%)

Type	Share (1987)	Share (1989)
Individuals	18	18
Industrial/commercial companies	5	4
Institutions	67	63
Of which:		
Pension funds	32	–
Insurance companies	25	–
Trusts	10	–
Public sector	3	5
Overseas	5	8
Charities	2	2

Sources: Data for 1987, Schaffer (1990), cited in Blanchard, Dornbusch, Krugman, Layard and Summers (1991), p. 56.
Data for 1989: UBS Phillips and Drew 1990, cited in Pratten (1993), p. 2.

The most important shareholders are institutions. Businesses, especially large firms, no longer belong mainly to 'real flesh-and-blood persons'. For instance, when a corporation goes bankrupt, one cannot simply pursue its main owners among the 'real flesh-and-blood persons' who together hold less than 20 per cent of total shares. Kornai disagrees: 'All things considered, many of institutional investment forms are in the last analysis backed up by an interest by ultimate private owners' (1990a, p. 74). It is clear that he overlooks the dissimilarities between the owners of a firm and the owners of financial products. Even so, his 'ultimate private owners', in the bankrupt example, are not immediately identifiable.

Figure 3.1 presents a history of declining individual ownership. In Japan, from 1949 to 1992, the shares held by individuals declined from 69.1 to 23.85 per cent. Furthermore, the cross-holding in Japan directly

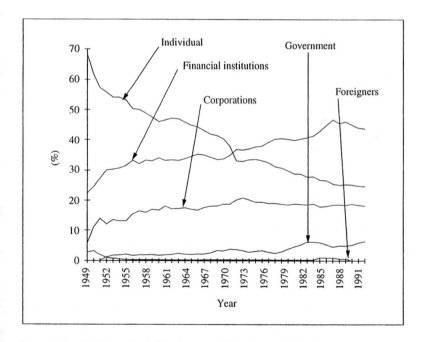

Figure 3.1   Decline of individual ownership in Japan, 1949–92
Sources: Okumura (1993b), p. 326. Data after 1990 from *Weekly Toyokeizai* (1993), p. 81.

questions the very basis of Kornai's 'ultimate private owners'. In Japan, the majority of large companies are members of a small number of industrial groups, the *keiretsu*. 'A *keiretsu* firm usually owns less than two per cent of any other member firm, but it typically has a stake of that size in every firm in the group, so that between 30 and 90 per cent of a firm is owned by other group members' (Drucker 1991, p. 106). These affiliated firms represent about 61 per cent of the market capitalisation of the Tokyo Stock Exchange (Shale 1990, p. 16).[1] Together with the shareholders of financial corporations, on average, Japanese corporations have about 70 per cent of their shares held by other corporations (Aoki 1994, p. 21; Sheard 1994, p. 312). It suggests that the 'ultimate private owners' not only do not control but also actually do not own the firm. For example, as a firm goes bankrupt, with its complex system of cross-holdings, the firm mainly belongs to other firms that mainly belong to other firms. All things considered, it is impossible to deliver the property right of 'other firms' to Kornai's 'ultimate private owners'.

How can Property Rights be Well-Defined?

North and Weingast (1989) have demonstrated the importance of secure property rights for economic development in seventeenth-century England, with its focus on individuals as entrepreneurs who own and operate the firm. This principle underlies the felt need in transitional economies for privatisation. Property rights theory is colourful and insightful in the West. Kornai (1990a) simplifies the rich theory as the theory of well-defined individualised property rights. My question is: if the 'ultimate private owners' are lost in the maze of Japanese cross-holding, why is it necessary to have well-defined individualised property rights for large state-owned enterprises in transitional economies?

Schumpeter views capitalist history as a revolutionary process. In capitalist reality as distinguished from its textbook picture, 'it is not that kind of competition which counts but the competition from the new commodity, the new technology, the new source of supply, the new type of organisation'. He identifies the revolution by the term 'creative destruction' which 'incessantly revolutionises the economic structure *from within*, incessantly destroying the old one, incessantly creating a new one. This process of Creative Destruction is the essential fact about capitalism. It is what capitalism consists in and what every capitalist concern has got to live in' (1950, pp. 84 and 83, italics in original).

As a 'new type of organisation', the joint-stock company represents Schumpeter's 'creative destruction' which 'incessantly revolutionises the economic structure *from within*, incessantly destroying the old one' (the 'personal enterprise'), thus 'incessantly creating a new one' through the separation of ownership and control. The joint-stock company impersonalises individualised property, thereby transgressing the boundary of original private property rights. The impersonalisation has the following aspects.

First, *legal entity*. Assets which belong to real persons do not have the legal rights of real people. When several 'real flesh-and-blood persons' put their property together, establishing a joint-stock company, their property becomes a 'legal person', separate from its owners. In law, the bloodless joint-stock company has equal rights with any real flesh-and-blood person, including its owners. It has full authority to act on its own, regardless of who owned the property originally. By contrast, the real persons lose the right to employ their property. The only thing real persons do is watch, no matter what great ideas they have. This destruction of private property rights brings about 'moral hazard' (Strong and Waterson 1987).

Second, *transferability of ownership*. If 'real flesh-and-blood persons' cannot tolerate watching the bloodless legal person employ their assets, they can simply leave the game; but they cannot withdraw their property. They can only sell their shares: that is, they have to introduce other persons to continue the game. If they cannot find others to take their place, the share prices fall to zero. In other words, they can leave the game by abandoning their property. The 'transferability' of their property is a one-way street, physically irreversible. Once the company is established, the new legal person becomes an indivisible whole. People can never get back their property in its original form. The properties of 'real flesh-and-blood persons' often do not have this kind of transferability. For example, if I borrow US$10 000 from a friend promising to replay US$12 000 later, and then I renege on my promise, my friend lacks property rights to get his money back. The only way for him to quit the game is to sell the receipt signed by me.

Third, *limited liability*. 'Real flesh-and-blood persons' usually have unlimited liability for their debts. For example, I borrow US$10 000 from a friend of mine. If I am insolvent, I cannot just walk away and say: 'I am sorry. There is only ten dollars in my wallet. Please take it and good-bye!' In law, as a 'real flesh-and-blood person', I must be punished for my insolvency, unless I pass away. In the same legal fashion, the joint-stock company with limited liability may only repay its debts insofar as it has assets to do so, as long as the legal bloodless person is willing to die through bankruptcy. These equally legal rights jeopardise the property rights of 'real flesh-and-blood persons'. A great deal of effort is expended in trying to prevent companies cheating 'real flesh-and-blood persons' through bankruptcy.

Fourth, *minority control*. As shares are highly dispersed, the fair principle of 'one share, one vote' results in unfair minority control. In 1945 in the USA, the Temporary National Economic Committee found that as little as 10–20 per cent of the voting power was adequate for 'working control' in large corporations (Gordon 1961, p. 36). A handful of people can seize the decision making rights from the majority of 'real flesh-and-blood persons'.

The joint-stock company has transcended rather than extended the original private property rights. Put another way, the modern history of capitalism is, perhaps, the history of transcending the limits of individualised private property rights. These, in what Goldberg (1980) terms 'relational exchanges',[2] profane the holy 'real flesh-and-blood persons'. They are so blasphemous about private property rights that Marx exclaimed delightedly: 'It is private production without the control of private property ... 'It is the abolition of capital as private property within the framework of capitalist production itself' (1971, pp. 436–8). Schumpeter agrees: 'We should see that gradual socialisation *within the framework of capitalism* is not only possible but even the most obvious thing to expect' (1950, p. 227, italics in original).

Indeed, this destruction of individual property rights transfuses fresh blood into capitalism by bringing many benefits, such as diversifying risk, introducing more capital, enlarging the size (thus yielding economics of scale) and extending the life of enterprises. All these advantages are realised by the distinction between ordinary residual claimants and entrepreneurs.

We lack a clear definition of the concept 'entrepreneur' (Baumol 1968; Soltow 1968; Lewellen 1969). I use the term 'entrepreneur' to refer to the people *who want to operate firms* regardless of whether they are capitalists or managers.[3] In the 'beginning', the concepts 'entrepreneur' and 'residual claimant' are interchangeable. In a 'personal enterprise', an owner-manager single-mindedly operates to maximise profits. If an entrepreneur wants to develop a business, he must have his own new ideas and his own organisational talents to operate a firm with his own capital. His firm often terminates with his death (Chandler 1977, p. 5).

The joint-stock company overcomes the limitations of individualised private property rights by differentiating entrepreneurs from ordinary residual claimants. To entrepreneurs who want to operate a business, the legal entity, transferability of ownership and limited liability can diversify risks, thereby attracting capital and expanding the scale of the firm. To most ordinary investors, especially risk-averse ones, who merely want their capital to grow but do not want to operate a business themselves, the joint-stock company gives them a chance to buy shares. Before the joint-stock company emerged, entrepreneurs could not run a business unless they had sufficient capital to own the firm, while many risk-averse ordinary residual claimants could not make money unless they themselves also ran a firm. The joint-stock company made it no longer necessary for entrepreneurs to be full owners with unlimited liability. They could run the firm as owners, founders, organisers or managers. Meanwhile, ordinary residual claimants no longer needed to operate the firm themselves. They could buy shares, even though they had 'neither the incentive nor ability to assume strategic direction of the companies whose shares they bought' (Lazonick 1991, p. 78).

What is significant to enterprise reform in transitional economies is that the spirit of the joint-stock company is not to strengthen, but to weaken, ownership control over management, *no matter whether it is private or public ownership.* As long as shareholders no longer are entrepreneurs who operate firms themselves, they become monitors or share traders, rather than organisers, operators or managers. When owners become shareholders, the distance between owners and the firm's operation implies a transfer of the operating power from owners to entrepreneurs. The joint-stock company brings forth a division of labour between entrepreneurs who run firms and shareholders who trade shares. As it progresses, both the operation of firms and the trading of shares in the stock market become two different professional careers in separate fields.

Do Owners Run Firms or Trade Shares?

Separation of ownership and control has constituted a classic issue at least since Adam Smith, who worried about the stewardship of the directors of joint-stock companies (1937 [1776], Vol. 2, p. 229).[4] Ever since Berle and Means (1967) observed a managerial revolution in 1932, there have been innumerable theoretical discussions and empirical studies on the separation of ownership and control.[5] For example, Larner (1966) states that, from 1929 to 1963, only about 30 of the 200 largest non-financial corporations in the USA could be classified as truly 'owner-controlled'. Lewellen concludes that 'the era of the owner-manager has passed' (1969, p. 299). None of these arguments affects Kornai's perception. He emphasises: 'most important, the prime consideration is not legal entitlement to acquire the property but the ability to run it well' (1990a, p. 91). How can it be run well? Kornai suggests:

I am fully aware that joint stock companies play a large role in highly developed contemporary capitalist countries, and that there is at most an indirect linkage between the millions of shareholders in corporate business and the control of the corporations. Using Albert *Hirschman's well-known dichotomy*, the small shareholder expresses his disappointment rather by 'exit,' i.e., getting rid of shares that do not appeal to him anymore, than by 'voice,' i.e., directly influencing the management of the firm. (1990a, pp. 75–6, italics in original)

Kornai is not fully aware of the difference between 'voice' and 'exit'. If owners vote with their hands, no matter what they vote for (say, a new manager or a new plan), they are voting on *the matters of the firm*. Their 'voice', no matter whether it is wrong or right, strong or weak, concerns matters internal to the firm. They care about how to improve the firm's performance as owners. Conversely, if owners vote with their feet, the subject on which they are voting has changed. They are no longer voting on matters internal to the firm. *They are voting on their own performance*: that is, whether or not to be the owners of the firm. They are not interested in such questions as who should be the manager, or what strategy the firm should choose. Their concern has become which firm should be the target to invest in.[6] 'What shareholders really own are their shares and not the corporation' (Demsetz 1988, p. 114).[7] For example, Alchian and Demsetz (1972, in Demsetz 1988) find that 'voting and non-voting shares are sold for essentially identical prices, even during some proxy battles' (in Demsetz 1988, pp. 126–7). It indicates that non-voting share holders are simply investors devoid of ownership connotations.

Theoretically ownership control still matters. If large numbers of small, non-voting shareholders are dissatisfied with the size of their dividend, they can easily quit: that is, sell. Selling is usually thought of as a pressure on managers to improve their performance. However, selling shares is not a cost-free transaction. When owners vote with their feet, they have to consider the price at which they can sell. Consequently, whether or not they leave is determined not only by how unhappy they are with the dividend payout, but also by how satisfactory a price they can sell the shares at in the stock market. If share prices fluctuated in direct proportion with the firm's performance, ownership would still matter because their decision to 'exit' would represent a correct valuation of the firm's performance. If it does not, then the story is different.

The development of the stock market makes ownership control further important. In the stock market, *share prices are determined by demand and supply* of stocks. In 1981, Shiller published his famous paper, 'Do stock prices move too much to be justified by subsequent changes in dividends?' Since then, numerous empirical studies have confirmed that stock prices are formed by speculation in fields far beyond a firm's actual performance. All changes can alter the share prices, such as currency exchange rates, interest rates, government monetary and fiscal policies, government intervention on take-over and anti-take-over, changes of government, wars, rumours, political scandals and 'price destabilising speculation' in which traders can themselves create price changes (Hart and Kreps 1986). 'Today's investors attempt to create value by outguessing the market, which is totally unrelated to improving the performance of the companies they own' (Millstein *et al.* 1991, p. 170). Share prices in the stock market become so distant from the firm's actual performance that *The Economist* asserts: 'Prices, after all, reflect not the fundamental values of firms but simply the changing moods and prejudices of investors' (1994a, p. 12).

A perfect market must ensure open and fair trade. A surprising number of laws and regulations greatly restrict shareholders who do anything other than buy and sell tiny holdings (Millstein *et al.* 1991, p. 170). In order to guarantee fair trade, the laws and regulations prevent any one individual from having better access to information than anyone else. Acquiring insider information and insider dealing are strictly prohibited. A range of legislation against monopolies and hostile take-overs legally protects open and fair trade. The more open and fair the trade in the stock market is, *the easier it is for shareholders as traders to trade their shares in the market, and the harder it is for shareholders as owners to monitor the firm.*

A perfect market often encourages subject of the transactions to be as liquid as possible. When shares change hands frequently, so also do the firm's owners. Moreover, portfolio theory tells shareholders to diversify their investments across the securities of many firms. Since shareholders hold the shares of many firms precisely to avoid having their wealth depend too much on any one firm, an individual shareholder generally has no special interest in personally overseeing the detailed activities of any firm (Fama 1980). All these push ownership, no matter whether it is private, public or institutional, away from concern with the firm's operation. Even big institutional shareholders often disperse and 'index' their shares.[8] In the USA, around one-quarter of the shares owned by pension funds are now indexed (*The Economist* 1994a, p. 6). Among the 50 largest US companies, only eight have shareholders who hold 5 per cent or more of the equity. For example, the California Public Employees Retirement System holds equity in 1300 US corporations, plus 300 international ones. Therefore, Lorsch comments that institutional investors neither can nor should function as owners (1991, p. 140).

Summary

First the joint-stock company turns owners into monitors. Then the stock market turns the monitors into share traders. When owners become monitors, they are already outsiders to the firm, but what they vote on with their hands remain inside matters. In the stock market, share traders are interested in the firm's performance only because of share prices. The stock market shifts their monitoring focus from the firm's internal decision-making to share prices, which lies outside the firm. What owners vote for with their feet are no longer inside matters, but share prices in the stock market far removed from the firm's actual performance. The maturation of the stock market makes share trading a professional speculation. A range of legislation, such as the prohibition on acquiring insider information and insider dealing, and the prevention of hostile take-overs, makes the monitoring of a firm's internal operations increasingly difficult, if not impossible. In short, *the nature of separation of ownership and control is a differentiation between the firm's owners and share traders.*

'The most important shareholders today are institutional. And the people running the institutions are salaried employees. Just like company bosses they may have incentives other than to maximise shareholder value' (*The Economist* 1994a, p. 5). The programme of giving shares to managers, and thus buying their loyalty to owners, has clearly symbolised that 'the owners have almost invariably surrendered control' to the managerial regime (Berle and Means 1967, p. 7).[9]

WHAT THE JAPANESE FIRM TELLS US: LESS OWNERSHIP CONTROL, BETTER COMPETITIVENESS?

Japan possesses many characteristics at variance with conventional capitalist economies. After the joint-stock company, the Japanese cross-holding is the second of Schumpeter's instruments of 'creative destruction', essentially eliminating Kornai's 'real flesh-and-blood persons', and thus helping us to think about how to reform state-owned enterprises in transitional economies (Wang and Ji 1988). According to Kornai, 'only private property can supply enough incentive to permanently guarantee an effective use of the resources', and 'the manager is only a paid employee' (1990a, pp. 91 and 67). In Japan, however, not only does individual ownership not rule, but in addition corporate cross-holding relies on a premise of inactivity, leaving management unconstrained (Lichtenberg and Pushner 1992, p. 7).

Blinder complains: 'the Japanese have succeeded by doing everything wrong (according to standard economic theory). That should make economic theorists squirm' (1990, p. 9). Japan became the new leader of industrial advance (Best 1990; Lazonick 1991). On the other hand, Japanese managers enjoy the fullest freedom from ownership control. The contradiction between Kornai's theory of 'turning back the reel to the beginning' and Japanese managerial regimes should make us reflect deeply: is it possible that less ownership control will result in greater competitiveness?

Getting Rid of Ownership Control

As Figure 3.1 showed, Japanese modern business history is one of shrinking individual ownership. Table 3.2 indicates that shares constituted only a small proportion of the sources of corporate finance. In 1971, shares contributed only 7.3 per cent of total corporate capital, while individuals held 37.2 per cent of total shares (Okumura 1993b, p. 326). Therefore individual owners contributed only 2.7 per cent of total corporate capital (7.3 × 37.2). Since the shares held by individuals are usually highly dispersed, the small proportion of individual shares means that 'real flesh-and-blood persons' have no say in Japanese corporations.

Table 3.2   External financial sources of industrial funds in Japan, 1947–81 (annual average, %)

Period	Share	Corporate bonds	Financial institution loans	Government funds	Foreign loans
1947–52	11.5	3.2	71.7	13.6	–
1953–57	16.3	3.6	70.9	9.3	–
1958–62	16.6	3.6	70.1	7.8	1.9
1963–67	8.4	3.6	79.0	8.1	0.8
1968–72	6.5	2.2	82.1	8.0	1.2
1973–77	5.9	4.3	78.5	11.1	–
1978–81	8.3	4.6	73.0	14.2	–

Notes: The 'Government fund' is the sum of the amount supplied by governmental financial institutions and the 'Special Accounts for Financial Purposes'.
Source: Economic Statistics of Japan, cited in Hamada and Horiuchi (1987), Table 8.

Table 3.2 also shows that financial institutions are the main source of finance in Japan. It might be argued that these financial institutions function as monitors. Regarding the question of ownership control, an obvious fact which ought to be taken into account is that financial institutions in Japan have the same ownership structure as non-financial corporations. The difference is that in the financial institutions, the role of the 'real flesh-and-blood persons' is even weaker.

Table 3.3 illustrates the ownership structure of 21 major financial institutions in Japan. In 1991, 92.2 per cent of their total shares were held by financial institutions and other corporations; only 6.2 per cent was individ-

Table 3.3   Ownership structure of the major Japanese financial institutions, 1991 (%)

Banks	Financial institutions	Other corporations	Subtotal	Individual (domestic)
Industrial Bank of Japan	40.1	56.1	96.2	2.2
LTCB of Japan	44.7	51.7	96.4	2.7
Nippon Credit	65.9	30.4	96.3	3.2
Daichi Kangyo	34.7	55.7	90.4	7.5
Hokkaido Takushoku	40.7	46.0	86.7	12.1
Bank of Tokyo	55.7	37.3	93.0	5.7
Sakura	35.9	54.1	90.0	8.2
Mitsubishi	36.2	55.8	92.0	6.7
Fuji	28.8	63.7	92.5	6.0
Sumitomo	28.3	62.4	90.7	6.2
Daiwa	28.4	62.0	90.4	8.0
Sanwa	32.8	58.9	91.7	6.2
Tokai	28.9	61.0	89.9	8.7
Kyowa-Saitama	35.5	54.0	89.5	7.4
Mitsui Trust	23.1	70.0	93.1	5.5
Mitsubishi Trust	22.5	70.4	92.9	4.2
Sumitomo Trust	17.7	74.8	92.5	4.1
Yasuda Trust	26.8	68.9	95.7	3.0
Nippon Trust	31.6	57.6	89.2	10.2
Toyo Trust	33.3	58.1	91.4	7.7
Chuo Trust	29.5	65.7	95.2	3.9
Average	34.3	57.8	92.2	6.2
Average for all listed firms	46.9	25.2	72.1	23.1

Note: 'Financial institutions' include securities companies.
Source: Multiple sources cited in Sheard (1994), Table 3.

ually owned. In other words, cross-holding in financial institutions has the same characteristic as it does in non-financial corporations. The proposition that management rid itself of ownership control through cross-holding is just as relevant to Japanese financial institutions.

Cross-holding is 'stable share-holding'. This colloquial term used in Japanese capital markets indicates that the holder: (1) 'holds the shares as a "friendly" insider sympathetic to incumbent management', (2) 'agrees not to sell the shares to third parties unsympathetic to incumbent management, particularly hostile take-over bidders or bidders trying to accumulate strategic parcels of shares', (3) 'agrees, in the event that disposal of shares is necessary, to consult the firm or at least to give notice of its intention to sell'. 'In economic terms, "stable share-holding" can be interpreted as implicitly contracting away some of the property rights associated with the share-holding, in particular property rights pertaining to the transfer of the shares or the exercise of corporate control' (Sheard 1994, pp. 315–18).

In normal circumstances financial institutions do not exercise explicit control over corporate policy or management selection (Aoki 1990, p. 14; Horiuchi, Packer and Fukuda 1988). The complex share-ownership patterns are not even intended to make managers accountable to shareholders. It forms 'a defensive measure' against ownership control (*The Economist* 1994a, p. 8). Managers in Japan spent US$35 billion annually on entertaining one another. This expenditure was more than they pay out between them in dividends.[10] Such friendly relationships ensure that 'with some 70 per cent of outstanding shares on the Tokyo Stock Exchange in the vaults of friendly business partners, Japanese firms are under little pressure to increase dividends and their management face few fears of being replaced in a sudden stock market coup' (*The Economist* 1991a, p. 54). 'Mutual share-holding may lead to mutual non-intervention. And may lead to interlocking directorships within the group members ... This is a kind of collective defence to maintain the control by management over ownership' (Suzuki 1991, pp. 78–9).

Table 3.4 shows that shareholders only made up 9.4 per cent of total board members (1 + 5). The main reason that people became board members was not because they represented owners, but because they had capability and knowledge in business. No fewer than 77.9 per cent of all board members came from categories 13–19. The bigger the firm, the fewer the shareholders that became board members. When the size of the firm is bigger than 20 billion yen, the percentage of board members of shareholders shrinks to 3.9 per cent (1 + 5), while 85.5 per cent of total board members came from a background of ability and knowledge in business. If we consider the fact that individuals held 46.3 per cent of total

Table 3.4   Reasons for people to become members of the board in 229 Japanese large firms, 1960

Items	*Total*	*Size (total assets in Japanese yen)*			
	(%)	*> 20 billion*	*10–20 billion*	*0.5–10 billion*	*< 0.5 billion*
Total (%)	100.0	100.0	100.0	100.0	100.0
1 major shareholder	5.7	1.6	4.2	8.8	17.4
2 representatives from financial institution	2.3	1.1	2.7	3.1	3.1
3 government representative	0.3	–	1.3	–	–
4 labour representative	0.0	–	–	–	0.4
5 shareholder representative	3.7	2.3	3.3	5.3	5.4
6 buyer representative	1.1	0.2	0.4	1.9	3.1
7 seller representative	0.3	0.4	–	0.4	–
8 representative related to manufacture	0.3	0.1	1.0	–	0.4
9 financial consultant	0.6	0.5	–	0.7	1.3
10 sales consultant	0.2	0.1	0.4	0.1	0.4
11 legal consultant	0.1	–	0.2	0.1	0.4
12 technical consultant	0.4	0.5	0.2	0.6	–
13 knowledge about related causes	37.4	43.5	42.1	30.1	23.1
14 ability in judging business	11.4	12.8	11.9	10.8	6.3
15 ability in leading subordinates	1.4	1.9	0.2	1.7	0.4
16 special knowledge about labour	2.4	2.3	2.1	2.7	2.2
17 special knowledge about techniques	16.0	15.4	17.1	11.8	17.4
18 special knowledge about foreign related aspects	0.8	0.9	0.6	1.0	0.4
19 special knowledge about sales	8.5	8.7	6.3	10.5	9.4
20 no answer	7.1	7.5	5.9	7.3	8.9

Note: '7. seller representative' refers to the seller of materials; '8. representative related to manufacture' refers to people from companies producing components; columns do not necessary add to 100 per cent because of lack of the necessary data.

Soure: Totayo and others assisted by Tokyo Economic Centre, cited in Komiya (1980), p. 264.

shares in 1960 (Okumura 1993b, p. 326), proportionally, there is a 1.8 per cent chance for 'flesh-and-blood persons' to be board members in Japanese large firms in 1960.

By ingeniously exercising property rights as a powerful weapon through the cross-holding process, *Japanese managers hire friendly owners*: that is, their colleagues, thereby *getting rid of not only private ownership control specifically, but also all kinds of ownership control in general.* Gerlach describes this interestingly:

> Unidirectional relationships based on simple flows of equity capital have been replaced by reciprocal relationships based on complex flows of trade in capital, goods, and personnel. The pressures they face from external constituencies come from those over whom they, in turn, have influence. The seemingly crisp categories of principal and agent become fuzzy as the managers of one firm become the owners of another, and in turn are held by managers of that firm. *It is less that management has been separated from control, therefore, than that control has been merged into management.* (1992, p. 238, my emphasis)

Profit Maximisation versus Life-and-Death Struggle

According to Kornai, 'only private property can supply enough incentive to permanently guarantee an effective use of the resources' (1990a, p. 91). In this view, Japanese firms which rid themselves of ownership control must lack 'enough incentive to permanently guarantee an effective use of the resources'. Yet the facts seem otherwise.

In a survey by *Harvard Business Review* of 12 000 world managers in 1991, Nobuyoshi Miki finds: 'It is a common criticism that Japanese companies owe their success to government assistance and the restriction of foreign business in Japan. But *business leaders here think the real source of their success is fierce domestic competition*' (in Kanter 1991, p. 155, my emphasis).

Without domination of ownership by 'real flesh-and-blood persons', can the managers themselves (according to Kornai, they are simply salaried employees) supply sufficient incentive to promote 'fierce domestic competition'?

Managers have their own interests separate from those of the owners, who are residual claimants. There is a series of empirical studies on the differences between owner-controlled and manager-controlled firms in America's largest corporations.[11] I borrow these concepts, and refer to the firm controlled more by 'real flesh-and-blood persons' as the owner-controlled firm, while refering to Japanese firms as manager-controlled firms. In comparing the manager- and owner-controlled firms, there are three interesting hypotheses.

First, it is difficult for the manager-controlled firm being taken over by others. For owners, as long as the dividend increases, they will vote for a merger, whoever will be the new bosses after the merger. For managers, few will keep their jobs after a successful bid. Nothing scares them more than the prospect of being the target of a hostile take-over. The advantage Japanese managers received from eliminating ownership control is the low merger rate. Between 1988 and 1990, the merger rate was 0.3 per cent in Japan, as opposed to 7.8 per cent in the USA (Lichtenberg and Pushner 1992, p. 1). In other words, the possibility of a merger in the USA is 26 times greater than it is in Japan. After the Second World War, there was a famous period, the 'Age of Large-scale Mergers' (Singh 1971). In the UK, nearly 2000 manufacturing companies were quoted on the stock market in the mid-1950s. Of these, nearly 500 disappeared between 1976 and 1982, more than 400 of these through the process of merger. In other words, a quoted manufacturing company had a one-in-five chance of dying through merger over the period. In the mid-1960s, these relatively large firms had a one-in-three chance of dying through merger over a similar period (Hughes and Singh 1983, p. 1). Singh finds that the average merger rate for large firms in the UK among four industries from 1955 to 1960 was 20.5 per cent; from 1967 to 1970 it was 24.2 per cent (1975b, p. 502, Table 2). The Japanese government also tried hard to enlarge firm size through mergers. But 'there are hardly any involuntary take-overs on the stock market' (Singh 1990, p. 175). Among the largest 100 firms, only one in the 1950s, four in the 1960s, and none in the 1970s existed as a result of mergers (Suzuki 1991, p. 94).

Second, the low merger rate should be unfavourable to monopolisation, and should therefore promote competition (Singh 1971, 1975b).

Table 3.5 shows that, reflecting the difficulty of mergers, the proportion of medium and small enterprises in Japan is much higher than that in other

Table 3.5   Industrial enterprises of different sizes in different countries

Size of enterprises (sum of employees)	Proportion of enterprises (%)				
	Japan 1972	USA 1977	Britain 1979	South Korea 1981	India 1976–77
5–32	80.2	56.4	65.2	70.6	51.7
33–74	10.7	20.3	15.7	14.4	35.3
75–188	6.1	12.4	10.8	9.2	7.8
189–242	0.8	3.8	1.4	1.5	0.8
Above 243	2.2	7.1	6.9	4.3	4.4

Source: World Bank (1985), p. 40.

Table 3.6   Degree of economic concentration in different countries (%)

Country	Classification	Degree of concentration
Japan	Total capital of 100 biggest non-financial enterprises	21.4
	Total capital of 100 biggest manufacturing enterprises	33.8
	Sales income of 100 biggest manufacturing enterprises	27.3
USA	Total capital of 100 biggest non-financial enterprises	30.7
	Total capital of 100 biggest manufacturing enterprises	49.0
	Sales income of 100 biggest manufacturing enterprises	41.0
UK	Net output value of 100 biggest manufacturing enterprises	41.0
Germany	Sales income of 100 biggest non-financial enterprises	21.7
	Sales income of 100 biggest manufacturers	45.4

Note: The figures for the USA and the UK are for 1972; Germany for 1973; Japan for 1980.
Source: Senoo Akixu, cited in CESRRI-d (1988), p. 44, Table 1–4.

countries.[12] The domination of small enterprises brings a lower degree of economic concentration in Japan, as Table 3.6 shows.

Third, the low merger rate is accompanied by a high bankruptcy rate. Firms compete against each other to the death. Table 3.7 shows that bankruptcies in Japan are more than twice those in the USA.

In order to estimate the intensity of competition, it is worth emphasising the different implications for a firm of being taken over, and going bankrupt. For example, firm A competes with firm B. When firm A is taken over by firm B, competition between the two is terminated by the merging of the firms. If firm A goes bankrupt, competition is terminated by the death of firm A. There is no deal at all between the two competitors. In the take-over case, firm A could still maintain some competitive potential, since it is alive. In the case of bankruptcy, firm A must desperately compete as it faces death. It can be said that competition ended by take-over is less fierce than competition concluded by bankruptcy.

From the owners' point of view, their firm being taken over by others is a matter of improving the firm's performance and earning more dividends. From the managers' point of view, to be taken over by others is to surrender to their enemies. For their careers as managers, it is a life-and-death struggle: that is, to end or to continue as the bosses. Since there is usually a good chance they will lose their jobs after a take-over, being taken over by others and going bankrupt have the same end-result for managers. In

Table 3.7   Numbers of bankrupt enterprises in Japan and the USA, 1978 and
1979

Industry	1978			1979		
	Japan (1)	USA (2)	(1)/(2) (3)	Japan (4)	USA (5)	(4)/(5) (6)
Total	15 875	6619	2.40	16 030	7564	2.12
Manufacturing	3384	1013	3.34	3095	1165	2.66
Building industry	4771	1204	3.96	4768	1378	3.46
Commercial	5450	3269	1.67	5963	4091	1.46

Note: The numbers for Japan refer to enterprises whose total indebtedness is
above ten million Japanese yen. The numbers for the USA include all bankrupt
enterprises. Therefore, the total bankruptcies in Japan must be even bigger than
this table shows.
Source: Matsumoto Atsuji, cited in CESRRI-d (1988), p. 43, Table 1–3.

order to save their careers, managers must fight until the last minute: that
is, bankruptcy. Competition between two owner-controlled firms can cease
through a comfortable merger. However, competition between two
manager-controlled firms will only end if one of the competitors dies. For
owner-controlled firms, competitions is a process of profit maximisation.
It can be coped with as long as the firm is profitable. For manager-
controlled firms, competition is a life-and-death struggle. They must fight
until the last minute. The bankruptcy numbers in Table 3.7 hints that
this life-and-death struggle may be fiercer than ordinary competition for
profit maximisation.

Fighting Together with Employees

This life-and-death battle forces Japanese managers to build an alliance
with their employees.

   In the life-and-death battle, private owners are potential voters for take-
over. Managers do not have a common interest with these owners.
However, employees often stay in the same firm longer than the shareholders do. To surrender could imperil their job security. This allows managers to build an alliance with their workers. Based on this alliance, in
Japan within the firm, managers form a number of long-term programmes,
in terms of housing, training, lifetime employment and the seniority
system. All these programmes promote the mobilisation of team work,
within which managers can fight with employees until the very end.

Table 3.8   Working days lost through industrial disputes in different countries
(per 1000 employees)

Country	1955–59	1960–64	1965–69	1970–74	1975–80
Japan	254	177	107	151	69
USA	615	301	513	539	389
UK	220	197	175	624	521
France	180	197	163	201	195
Italy	433	932	1204	1404	1434
West Germany	47	23	7	55	41
Sweden	19	6	38	69	222

Source: International Labour Office, cited in Koike (1987), Table 3.

Team work is the most significant innovation of the Japanese firm.
There are numerous studies on this topic. What is interesting for our purposes is that this innovation reinforces the life-and-death struggle.

First, lifetime employment, the seniority system, and non-wage programmes (such as housing, in-firm training and retirement benefits) reduce
labour mobility but introduce a long-term perspective.[13] As workers have a
long-term perspective in the firm, there is a trade-off available between
short-term wage increases and long-term job security and opportunities for
promotion. Hence, as Table 3.8 shows, the level of strikes in Japan is low
and fell over time.[14] Instead, Japanese labour unions and their members
are very interested in having a voice in management (Koike 1987).
Japanese workers often endure hardship in fierce competition and during a
recession (Hashimoto and Raisian 1985; Mincer and Higuchi 1988). For
example, firm A competes with firm B. In normal circumstances, if wages
in firm A fall below a certain standard level, workers will stop work, thus
terminating competition. Manager-controlled firms can reduce the bottom
line as regards wages in the short-term because of a series of long-term
programmes, thus continuing competition a stage further.

Second, the seniority promotion system directly internalises the
manager's career. Table 3.9 shows that 80 per cent of total investigated
public corporations promoted more than 50 per cent of managers from
within the same company. In the larger size group, the first category, this
ratio rises to 89 per cent.

Table 3.10 also demonstrates that the bigger the size, the more managers came from a staff background. As firm size increased to more than
2500 employees, only 2.4 per cent of total managers came from outside.
Externally hired managers are rare. This implies that competition in Japan

Table 3.9   Internalised management in Japanese companies, 1982

Source	Total		Listing size			
			First department		Second department	
	Firms	(%)	Firms	(%)	Firms	(%)
Internal promotion	429	80.0	295	88.9	134	65.7
External hiring	107	20.0	37	11.1	70	34.3
Total	536	100.0	332	100.0	204	100.0

Note: The 'listing size' refers to the firms which issue shares in the stock market. The Japanese stock market is divided into two departments, the first and the second. Firms must register in the second department as they issue shares first. Not until they have reached a certain size can they enter the first department. 'Internal promotion' refers to the firms in which more than half the members of the board are promoted from inside enterprises. 'External hiring' refers to the firms in which more than half the members of board are externally hired.
Source: MITI's Commission of Firm Vitality 1982, cited in CESRRI-d (1988), p. 50, Table 1–6.

Table 3.10   Managers' background in different enterprises by size in Japan

Firm size (person)	Number of firms	Background of managers (%)					
		Founder	Relative of founder	Staff	Other firms	Higher level or government	Other
100–299	89	26.7	34.9	10.5	33.5	19.8	4.7
500–999	40	20.0	20.0	17.5	12.5	27.5	2.5
1000–2499	38	5.3	15.8	34.2	15.8	26.3	2.6
Above 2500	41	4.9	14.6	51.2	2.4	24.4	2.4
Total	208	17.1	24.4	24.4	7.3	23.4	3.4

Source: Ishikauu Akihiro and Inusuka Susumu, cited in CESRRI-d (1988), p. 50.

is a war with no prisoners taken. When a take-over occurred, the careers of managers in the target firm would be killed. They cannot continue to be bosses in the firm which is taken over, and neither can they transfer their managerial careers to other firms. This adds to the difficulty of take-overs, thereby intensifying the already fierce life-and-death struggle.

Different Directions for Competition: Maximising Profit or Maximising Market Share?

From 1976 to 1990, hostile deals, along with leveraged buy-outs and other sales of corporate control, made US shareholders US$750 billion richer (Jensen 1993, p. 837). During the same period, the Japanese government was busy trying to merge firms, and was worried by 'excess competition' (Johnson 1982). Japanese shareholders did not make vast sums of money as the Americans did, while Japanese products greatly increased their share of the world market.

In owner-controlled firms, typically in their old age, the private owners hire managers. Either directly or indirectly, the possibility of take-over provides managers with a competitive threat. If they underperform, owners can sack them.[15] Meanwhile, workers are mobile. They have no long-term expectation from any given firm. The level of wages they can earn is the only reason for them to stay with the firm. Therefore wages are rigid downwards. In owner-controlled firms, both low dividend payout and low wages can put managers in trouble. Their behaviour is constrained by the need to satisfy both owners and workers while competing in the market.

In manager-controlled firms, for example in Japan, cross-holding removes ownership control. Dividend payouts are low and fixed (CESRRI-d 1988). There is no take-over threat. Meanwhile, rigid wages have been made elastic by a series of long-term programmes. There is never the headache of strikes. Managers can wholeheartedly compete in the market, with fewer anxieties at home than those in owner-controlled firms. Managers in manager-controlled firms are far less constrained to do what they want.

What do managers want?[16] Chandler thinks: 'once a managerial hierarchy had been formed and had successfully carried out its function of administrative coronation, the hierarchy itself became a source of permanence, power, and continued growth' (1977, p. 8).[17] As employees, managers and workers alike, 'they may agree to trade wage increases for job security or better opportunities for promotion made possible by the growth of the firm' (Aoki 1987, p. 273).

Table 3.11 bears out Berle and Means' anxiety that 'the corporation has changed the nature of profit-seeking enterprise' (1967, p. 7). Japanese managers see 'share price increase' as the least important target. They have nothing to fear from shareholders. In sharp contrast, American managers think that 'share price increase' is the second most important goal. Best calls Japanese firms 'market-share-dominating corporations' (1990, p. 10). In Table 3.11, there are the four especially sharp differences between the USA and Japan. In terms of 'investment return ratio' and 'share price increase', these are higher in America than in Japan by 1.19

Table 3.11   Corporate objectives in the USA and Japan

Management targets	USA		Japan	
	Comprehensive class	Rank	Comprehensive class	Rank
Return on investment	2.43 (8.1)	1	1.24 (4.1)	2
Share price increase	1.14 (3.8)	2	0.02 (0.1)	9
Market share	0.73 (2.4)	3	1.43 (4.8)	1
Improvement of product portfolio	0.50 (1.7)	4	0.68 (2.3)	5
Rationalisation of production and distribution	0.46 (1.5)	5	0.71 (2.4)	4
Equity ration increase	0.38 (1.3)	6	0.59 (2.0)	6
Ratio of new product	0.21 (0.7)	7	1.06 (3.5)	3
Improvement of company's image	0.05 (0.2)	8	0.20 (0.7)	7
Improvement of working conditions	0.04 (0.1)	9	0.09 (0.3)	8

Note: The columns with parentheses include 291 Japanese companies and 227 US companies ranked factors weighted 10, for first importance, to 1, for least importance.
Sources: Okumuya Akihiyo, cited in CESRRI-d (1988), p. 40, Table 1-1; the columns with parentheses: Economic Planning Agency (1981), cited in Abegglen and Stalk (1985), p. 177.

and 1.12 percentage points respectively. In terms of 'market share' and 'new product ratio', these are higher in Japan than in America by 0.70 and 0.85 percentage points respectively. The former items are linked to the 'residual claimants theory', while the latter are crucial to enterprise expansion.[18] What Japanese managers emphasise is precisely Schumpeterian competition. This is not price competition 'but the competition from the new commodity, the new technology, the new source of supply, the new type of organisation' (Schumpeter 1950, p. 84).

The Lower the Dividend, the Higher the Corporate Accumulation?

The Japanese miracle depends very much on its high rate of investment. Japanese firms acted as if they had 'investment hunger', and often 'over-invested' (Johnson 1982). In the USA, in an empirical study based on 12 year panel data for the *Fortune* 500 largest industrial firms, Monsen, Chiu and Cooley conclude that the 'owner controlled firm provides a much better return on the original investment' (1968, p. 442). In Japan:

> managers were not pressured by stockholders, which meant that they could ignore short-term profitability as a measure of their performance and could concentrate instead on such things as foreign market penetration, quality control, and long-term product development. This became a considerable advantage when Japanese managers began to compete

Table 3.12   Ratio of dividend payout/total profit in different countries, 1963–70 (%)

Industry	Country	1963	1965	1967	1969	1970
Iron and steel	Japan	79.7	98.7	48.4	36.6	43.0
	USA	65.4	45.6	62.9	54.1	88.2
	Germany	95.5	81.5	71.0	52.3	47.5
Machine tools	Japan	43.3	–47.2	24.8	29.6	29.3
	USA	44.0	41.2	47.2	48.6	75.1
Integrated electronic	Japan	89.8	106.1	47.3	37.5	49.6
machines	USA	61.0	57.1	61.2	71.6	67.7
	UK	55.9	43.8	67.7	81.3	55.7
Small sized	Japan	50.7	52.9	25.4	19.7	18.1
electronic machines	USA	47.3	37.8	54.6	44.8	80.9
	UK	–	–	62.8	55.4	57.6
Iron and steel	Japan	79.7	98.7	48.4	36.6	43.0
electronic machines	USA	47.3	37.8	54.6	44.8	80.9
	UK	–	–	62.8	55.4	57.6
Automobiles	Japan	32.6	37.3	25.3	15.2	13.0
	USA	61.2	58.8	75.8	67.6	112.8
	UK	58.6	33.3	–162.2	71.2	215.6
	Germany	74.1	65.9	50.9	47.6	66.5
Synthetic chemicals	Japan	77.1	88.4	51.0	42.3	47.8
	USA	76.9	68.8	70.0	62.8	68.8
	UK	–	–	91.5	62.2	67.7
	Germany	75.7	64.0	85.9	15.8	106.6
Chemical	Japan	40.7	93.5	38.3	30.0	33.1
synthetic fibres	US	44.9	36.4	51.4	25.3	50.9
	UK	64.7	43.0	69.8	63.1	63.5

Source: Takahashi (1983), p. 266, Table 5.

seriously with American firms, since short-term profitability and the payment of dividends were the keys to the availability of capital for American enterprises. (Johnson 1982, p. 204)

Table 3.12 shows that the dividend payout ratio in the USA, the UK, and Germany was usually around 50–60 per cent, compared with 30–40 per cent in Japan. In the remarkable Japanese automobile industry, the dividend payout ratio was especially low. The total dividend payout of all public corporations in Japan was 27.64 per cent in 1989, 30.3 per cent in 1990; this compared with 50 per cent in Germany, 54 per cent in the USA, and 66 per cent in the UK in 1990 (Okumura 1993a, p. 36)

The removal of ownership control means that the unconstrained Japanese managers could ill-treat owners with impunity. Nevertheless, the ill-treatment of owners strengthens the capability of corporate internal accumulation. Not only high rates of individual savings but also *high depreciation rates and corporate savings* drove Japan to achieve the highest investment rate in the world.

As Table 3.13 shows, since the dividend payout could be kept at a low level in Japan, the sum of depreciation and corporate savings could be as

Table 3.13   Structure of Japanese national savings, 1950–60

Year	Total savings	Item (in 100 million Japanese yen)				Ratio of corporate accumulation (%)	
		Depreciation	Corporate savings	Individual savings	Government budget surplus	(3)/(1)	[(2)+(3)] /(1)
	(1)	(2)	(3)	(4)	(5)	(6)	(7)
1957	34 945	10 592	5971	11 891	7590	17.1	47.40
1959	43 712	13 614	6175	14 853	8427	14.13	45.27
1961	76 592	21 659	11 115	23 920	16 971	14.51	42.79
1963	89 947	30 008	10 592	29 591	19 295	11.78	45.14
1965	111 090	41 959	9727	37 591	19 562	8.76	46.53
1967	169 833	58 443	24 139	56 810	28 190	14.21	48.63
1969	253 377	83 893	39 152	77 514	47 313	15.45	48.56
1971	317 483	111 981	46 864	104 160	58 879	14.76	50.03
1972	378 554	143 864	47 731	127 115	68 248	12.61	50.61

Source: Takahashi (1983), p. 267, Table 6.

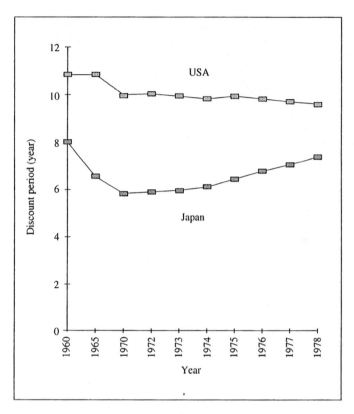

Figure 3.2   Depreciation period of manufacturing industries in Japan and the USA, 1960–78
Source: Japan Development Bank, cited in CESRRI-d (1988), p. 42, Figure 1-1.

high as one-half of total domestic savings. It was even higher than the famous Japanese high rates of individual savings. Figure 3.2 shows that the depreciation ratio in Japan was always much higher than that in the USA. Table 3.14 demonstrates that the highest Japanese investment rates were supported by the highest levels of corporate saving and capital depreciation.

The low dividend payout tends to reduce the incentive for Japanese individuals to buy shares, and tends to increase the incentive for them to

Table 3.14 Composition of savings between Japan and other countries, 1950–60 (%)

Country	Capital depreciation (1)	Individual savings (2)	Net corporate savings (3)	Net government savings (4)	Total domestic savings (5)[a]	Deficit of current account (6)[b]	Total domestic investment (7)
Japan	7.7	10.9	4.9	6.4	29.9	-0.9	29.5
Norway[c]	10.0	10.2	7.2	27.4	2.3	29.6	24.7
Netherlands	9.7	5.8[d]	4.9[d]	6.1	26.8	-1.7	25.8
Finland	5.2	8.3	2.1	10.9	26.7	-0.9	24.0
Germany	9.0	8.7[e]	1.9	6.7	26.0	-2.0	28.6
Australia[f]	6.1	9.7	4.2[g]	6.1[g]	26.0	2.6	24.5
Canada	10.8	5.2	2.7[h]	3.2	22.5	2.6	23.5
New Zealand[i]	6.6	5.7[d]	2.8[d]	5.7	22.2	1.3	21.3
Sweden	..[j]	4.4[j]	12.0[i]	5.1[i]	21.4	-0.1	22.2
Austria[k]	7.2	6.2	1.9	5.8	21.2	1.0	
Italy	9.3	10.7[l]	2.6[m]	20.5	0.4	20.9	
Denmark	6.8	7.5	4.2	18.5	0.3	18.8	
France	9.3	4.3	1.7	3.0	18.4	0.6	18.9
Belgium	9.4	9.4	0.5	-0.7	18.4	-1.3	15.4

Table 3.14 (Continued)

Country	Capital depreciation (1)	Individual savings (2)	Net corporate savings (3)	Net government savings (4)	Total domestic savings (5)[a]	Deficit of current account (6)[b]	Total domestic investment (7)
USA	8.9	5.2	2.1[h]	2.1	18.3	-0.3	18.0
Britain	8.0	1.9	4.6	1.0	15.5	-0.3	15.4
Japan 1955–60	9.2	11.4	5.2	5.7	31.5	-0.2	30.7

Notes: a: (5) equals the sum of (1), (2), (3), (4) theoretically, but it is not always consistent because not all figures in each column are for the same term. (5) plus (6) does not necessary equal (7) because of omissions brought about by statistical errors of savings and investment. b: (6) in the *UN Yearbook of National Accounts Statistics* represents the total net capital input from overseas, which is labelled the overall balance of international payments in *Japanese National Income White Paper*. c: 1951–60. d: 1954–60. e: 1951–60. f: The fiscal year beginning from 1 July. g: State-owned enterprises are included in government. h: Includes the changing evaluation of stockpiled commodities. i: The fiscal year from 1 April. j: Capital depreciation fund includes savings of individuals, corporations and the government. k: not gross domestic produce (GDP) but GNP. l: 1955–60.
Source: UN, cited in Komiya (1980), p. 21.

place their money in banks. This is the reason why Japanese firms rely heavily on bank loans. Without ownership control, internally oriented and immobile managers tend to re-invest profits rather than distribute them (Boltho 1975).

Summary

According to the transaction theory, Williamson summarises:

> three things happen when a transaction is transferred out of the market and is placed under unified ownership: Ownership changes, incentive changes, and governance structures changes. The first – ownership change – occurs by definition. Even if the formal incentive rules (e.g., transfer pricing) are held constant between firm and market, the *effective* incentives changes as a consequence of a change in asset ownership. Accordingly, the formal rules are apt to be adapted. New governance structure will appear in either event to support the integrity of the internal exchange relation. (1985, p. 391, italics in original)

Williamson's 'three things' are useful to our discussion. In the evolution of modern capitalism, the joint-stock company is the first instrument of 'creative destruction' with the ownership changes, incentive changes, and governance structures changes. (1) The legal person with limited liability enabled the joint-stock company to transcend beyond the limitations of individualised private property rights. (2) The incentives change is what distinguishes residual claimants from entrepreneurs. (3) The 'new governance structure' is the separation of ownership and control.

The Japanese cross-holding is the second instrument of 'creative destruction'. (1) Through the 'ownership change' (cross-holdings) it has got rid of ownership control in general.[19] (2) Then the incentive of the firm's development has been changed from profit maximisation to the life-and-death struggle. (3) The 'governance structures change' is the unconstrained managerial autonomy. (See Dore 1987.) The innovations of the Japanese economic miracle are not only state intervention, but also cross-holdings. In short, by using Williamson's 'ownership change', the joint-stock company transcends control of individual ownership, thereby bringing large organisation and professional management into industrial production. The Japanese cross-holding removed all ownership control, thereby bringing unconstrained managerial autonomy, and intensifying competition for market share which is much fiercer than traditional competition for profit maximisation.

THE GOAL OF ENTERPRISE REFORM: PRIVATISATION OR MANAGERIAL AUTONOMY?

In Kornai's eyes, the firm is an abstract and static concept, independently consisting of owners, managers and workers. There is a vertical, endogenous relationship between the three: owners control managers, and managers control workers. This logical relationship implies that only owners themselves really care about their property. As long as owners are not 'real flesh-and-blood persons', the pressure from residual claimants must be weak, and the budget constraint must be awfully soft (Weitzman and Xu 1994).[20] Therefore, both nationalisation in transitional economies and impersonalisation in the West are 'the germs of socialism' (Kornai 1990a, p. 76).

Wood introduce two perspectives from which to observe the firm. 'One is performance-related remuneration of agents. The other is competition among agents' (1991a, p. 20). Indeed, it is not only the vertical line which can characterise the firm, and its internal relationship with owner, manager and worker. For example, when we talk about a firm, factors such as its size, profitability and efficiency are all the result of comparison with other firms. It is not adequate to study only within the area of endogenous 'budget constraints', and to exclude competition exogenous to the firm's organisation and behaviour.

Vertical Budget Constraint versus Horizontal Market Competition

In the early history of industrialisation, international competition occurred between industrialised and pre-industrialised production. A residual claim was a sufficient incentive for capitalists to compete mainly with pre-industrialised production in domestic and colonised economies. After the second industrial revolution, industrial products competed against each other. Mass production professionalized management, thereby bringing about the separation of ownership and control. Today, in the so-called third industrial revolution, competition concentrates more and more on technological innovation, production flexibility, problem-solving at the shop-floor level, collective norms, co-ordination skills and co-operative attitudes. All these are related to team work (Best 1990). Lazonick (1991) calls the three stages, corresponding to the three industrial revolutions, 'proprietary capitalism', 'managerial capitalism' and 'collective capitalism'.

Following Lazonick's three stages of capitalism, we can examine the evolution of the firm in two dimensions. In respect to Kornai's vertical dimension, ownership control becomes progressively weaker. This is especially so for control by 'real flesh-and-blood persons'. In the horizontal dimension, competition outside individual firms becomes progressively fiercer. Which theory of the firm can explain the fact that these two tendencies seem to proceed in different directions? Kornai's theory of 'turning back the reel to the beginning' is an unconvincing attempt to explain this paradox: external competition becomes increasingly fierce, while private ownership, the only source which supplies incentives for firms to compete (Kornai 1990a, p. 91), becomes increasingly impotent.

If Kornai's 'real flesh-and-blood persons' do not provide adequate incentives to intensify competition, what does? In Japan, the answer is clear. Owners, whether individuals or various kinds of institutions, are impotent. The life-and-death struggle is the engine of the extraordinary 'excess competition' which brought about the Japanese miracle.

A firm consists of owners, managers and workers. In principle, all three parties pursue their self-interest through the firm. There is no reason why only owners can be the bosses. For example, *Japanese managers hire owners by cross-holding.*

Who should be the boss depends on who really cares about the firm, or whose interests are closest to what the firm's development needs. Owners, in a former epoch when it was difficult to transfer ownership, had no choice but to be concerned not only with where to invest, but also how they could improve the firm's performance. Compared with workers and managers who could easily quite or be hired and fired, owners typically had to stay in the same firm from beginning to end. At that time, the bosses had to be the owners, because they were the people most interested in the firm's development. With the development of the stock market, owners became share traders. To these share traders, where to invest, and how to improve a firm's performance are separate issues. Today, in the stock market, *ownership is being transferred by computer instantaneously*, matching buyers and sellers. The so-called 'owners' can remain with 'their firms' only through the third party of stock-brokers. They may remain the 'owners' of 'their firms' only for a few minutes.[21] The vast majority of them never see the firms which they 'own'. It is time to investigate 'who may manage the firm in their own interest rather than for that of the owners' (Chandler 1992, p. 489). In contrast to owners, workers, and especially managers, over time tended to work at the same firms for a longer and longer period. Alongside the development of team work, specialisation of labour skills became more widespread, and so firing became more expensive. Indeed, in Japan, life-time employment and many other long-term programmes have made workers' whole lives depend on a given firm.[22] The seniority promotion system internalises the manager's career entirely in a given firm. Managers often act as the representative of the legal entity. This symbolises the fact that, of the three parties, it is the managers' interests rather than that of the owners' which are closest to what the firm needs. Workers' interests come second. As owners typically are interested only in the share price on the stock market, their interests are distant from the firm's development.

Who can fire managers if they underperform? In recent years, there has been increasing criticism of weakly constrained management. In the theory of the firm, who manages the managers (Dalton 1959), who watches the watcher (Millstein *et al.* 1991), and who monitors the monitor (Rowthorn and Chang 1993), are wide, complex and fiercely debated issues that cannot be analysed at length in this work. Aoki notes that, being insulated from take-over, Japanese managers can be monitored by the managers themselves (1987, p. 273). The fact is: it is just *these unconstrained Japanese managers themselves who, having rid of themselves of ownership control, are the locomotive force driving Japan's fierce 'excess competition'.*

Which Reform Path is Shorter and Easier: Privatisation or Managerial Autonomy?

Which way should state-owned enterprises go? There are seemingly two destinations: (1) 'turning back the reel to the beginning', which means going back to primitive capitalism via Kornai's privatisation, in which firms were owned by 'real flesh-and-blood persons'; or (2) 'transcending the logic of private ownership' (Wang 1989), by going for modern impersonalisation, in which firms are owned by impersonalised entities, or (as in Japan) owned by other firms. If outright nationalisation goes 'forward' too far, Kornai's privatisation (that is, personalisation) equally goes 'backward' too far. From this brief analysis of some key features of the firm in modern capitalism, it can be seen that it is possible that the manager-controlled firm is a more effective institution than the owner-controlled firm. The nature of state-owned enterprises is much closer to modern impersonalisation (typically the model of manager-controlled firms through cross-holdings) than to privatisation. Why do we ignore the essential feature of what is right under our eyes, yet try to seek what is far away?

Like the large Japanese firms, large state-owned enterprises in China also provide quasi life-time employment, a quasi seniority-based promotion system, and many quasi long-term benefits, such as housing, in-firm training and retirement pensions (Perkins 1988; Granick 1990). without control by owners, Chinese managers may have a preoccupation with investment, thereby expanding the enterprise. Compared with Japanese firms, there are several similarities which illustrate the possibility that enterprise reform in China can learn much from its Japanese neighbour (Wang and Ji 1988).

The state in China overinterfered in all enterprise activities, including product pricing, input and output distribution, investment, employment, financial arrangement, development plans, and so on. In other words, state-owned enterprises lacked the autonomy necessary to compete with each other. They were state-administered plants or factories, rather than firms or corporations (Nolan 1993, 1994). So the simple answer to reform state enterprises is to give them autonomy, in order to let them compete with each other, irrespective of who owns them.

It is strange that in practice the sequence of privatisation schemes in transitional economies should be the reverse of that in capitalist ones. According to Kornai (1990a), during the transition, apart from restricting the autonomy of state-owned enterprises, there is nothing they can do other than to deliver state property into the hands of 'real flesh-and-blood persons'. In sharp contrast with privatisation in capitalist countries, the ownership reform typically comes at the end of the privatisation process.

The privatisation of the Japanese National Railroad is a typical example. The scheme started in April 1987.[23] The first reform was to establish the Settlement Corporation, a government agent, as the shareholder and the successor to the old Japanese National Railroad. The second reform was to divide the passenger railway division into six companies. A seventh firm handled freight for the entire country. The third reform was to choose managers. The Presidents of the biggest two companies were former high-ranking officials of the Ministry of Transport. The Presidents of the other companies were selected from the management members of the Japanese National Railroad. Other leaders within the old Japanese National Railroad were appointed to influential management posts at the seven new companies. Finally, the fourth reform was that the government planned in April 1992, *five years later*, to sell all the shares of the seven companies within *another four to five years*, when the new companies had met the four exchange requirements of the Tokyo Stock Exchange (Fukui 1992).[24]

The performance of new companies changed dramatically from the outset of the process. In 1985, it was estimated that there were 93 000 redundant workers out of a total of 280 000 employees of the Japanese National Railroad. After corporatisation and division, the number of employees had fallen to 191 000.[25] From 1987 to 1990 the annual increase in passengers and cargo was 5 and 10 per cent respectively. The total annual profit improvement in the seven new companies reached US$21 billion in 1989. Before the reforms, the annual subsidy from the government to the Japanese National Railroad reached US$4.9 billion on average. In 1992, these newly profitable companies paid US$1.2 billion in corporate tax to the government (Fukui 1992). The reforms of corporatisation and division were so successful that the question was raised: 'Would corporatisation alone – without plans to sell shares to private investors – have been sufficient to improve efficiency?' (Fukui 1992, p. 118).

In 1992, three of the six passenger companies met the exchange requirements (Fukui 1992). By October 1993, only one of them had issued shares in the stock market (Tsukada 1994, p. 15). At that time, the only consideration was whether it was profitable for the company to sell the shares. During this reform process, there was no element of ownership reform, in which private owners take over control in order to change the firm's behaviour.

What made the old Japanese National Railroad underperform is not public ownership, but the lack of managerial autonomy. In the case of the National Railroad Public Corporation, for example, managerial autonomy was so highly restricted by legal, bureaucratic and political prescription and interference that Fumio Takagi, president of the corporation from March 1976 to December 1983, complained that his predicament was analogous to that of a swimmer whose arms and legs were tied. Restrictions included (1) legislative control of the rates and fares; (2) political interference in investment programmes; (3) bureaucratic control of personnel policy and pay scales; and (4) sundry other cramping rules, such as refusal to allow the retaining of cash-sales intake for more than a day in station offices (Tsuru 1993, p. 206). The process of privatisation of Japanese railroads shows clearly the continuities in respect to both old public ownership and former managers.[26] It is hard to see how private ownership supplied any incentive. Two measures were decisive: first, breaking up the monopoly, thereby introducing competition, second, releasing government control, thereby giving enterprises managerial autonomy.

The UK had a similar experience. The Thatcher government improved the performance of state-owned enterprises, such as British Steel, the Royal Ordnance factories, the postal service, Telecommunications, Rolls-Royce, British Aerospace, London Transport, HMSO, National Freight Corporation and British Airways, *before* privatisation. A series of 'changes in the internal environment' was carried out before privatisation, which included changes in the organisational structure, objectives, management, labour relations, communication and reporting systems, and the nature and location of the business. Many of these changes were designed primarily to make these firms attractive to potential buyers (Bishop and Kay 1989; Rowthorn 1990; Veljanovski 1992; Parker 1993).[27]

Two further facts are worth keeping in mind: first, having completed privatisation, the government was still the largest single shareholder; second, through this the government kept the strongest voice in these privatised large firms.[28]

Summary

Foreman-Peck and Millward (1994) consider that increasing competition is more important than ownership transfer in generating efficiency gains. Duch (1991) believes that the efficiency of state enterprises depends upon the level of political control. The greater the constraints on financial and management autonomy, the lower the efficiency. If the ideological barriers in transitional economies were not too great, *the logic and the sequence ought to be the same*. The core of reform in large state-owned enterprises ought to be competition and managerial autonomy. If the model of the manager-controlled firms could be made the target, then the reform of state-owned enterprises would be much easier than attempting infeasible privatisation.

4 'Groping for Stones to Cross the River': Enterprise Reform in China

Many East European countries have attempted different types of privatisation schemes. But McDonald finds that privatisation is not sufficient to change the behaviour of state-owned enterprises (1993, p. 49). Privatisation is not the only answer (Vernon-Wortzel and Wortzel 1989). Bruno observes: 'Privatisation can also fail if privatised firms fail to get off the budget hook and continue to keep government credit lines open. In those cases, enterprises will not alter their behavioural norms, despite ownership changes' (1994, p. 3). In contrast, from their careful empirical studies, Pinto, Belka and Krajewski have concluded: 'the state sector is not a write-off, is far from extinct and state-owned enterprise managers are capable of good, market-based performance', even before privatisation (1993, p. 217; also see Pinto 1993). Ferguson suggests 'slow[ing] down the rate at which state enterprises are sold and concentrat[ing] instead on methods of introducing competition and the transfer of market management skills' (1992, p. 503).

A series of empirical studies also reveals the positive reaction of state-owned enterprises in China to enhanced managerial autonomy. This chapter will analyse enterprise reform in China. First, the state sector began to remove itself from downstream industries and concentrate on upstream industries, thus re-drawing the boundary between the state and non-state sectors. Second, there have been four types of enterprise reform in China: the 'contract system', the enterprise group, the joint-venture and the joint-stock company. They all lead to enhanced managerial autonomy rather than privatisation. Third, the 'ownership maze' in China leaves a huge space for the state to intervene. Therefore, reform of the government itself is another core of transition.

RESETTING THE BOUNDARY BETWEEN THE STATE AND NON-STATE SECTORS

Newbery (1991, 1992) advocates redefining the boundary between the public and private sectors in transitional economies.

Growth of the Non-State Sector

Table 4.1   Number of industrial enterprises in China, 1978–93

Ownership	Number of enterprises (10 000)		Increment (10 000)	Growth	Share of the total increment
	1978	*1993*	*1993–78*	*1993/1978*	*(%)*
Total	34.84	991.16	956.32	28.45	100.00
State-owned	8.37	10.47	2.1	0.25	0.22
Urban collective	10.33	17.23	6.9	0.67	0.72
Township and co-operative	16.41	163.13	146.72	8.94	15.34
Private	–	797.12	797.12	–	83.35
Others	–	3.21	3.21	–	0.34

Note: 'Urban collective' means collective-owned enterprises; 'Township and co-operative' refers to township enterprises, village enterprises, joint urban enterprises and joint rural enterprises.
Sources: SSB (1983), p. 207; (1994), p. 373.

Table 4.1 shows that, from 1978 to 1993, the number of industrial firms increased by 26 times. The number of state-owned enterprises increased only slightly, and the non-state sector accounted for 99.73 per cent of the total increased. Today, in 'socialist China', 99 per cent of total industrial enterprises are not owned by the state. Moreover, 80 per cent of the total number of industrial enterprises are, indeed, owned by Kornai's 'real flesh-and-blood persons'.

Figure 4.1 shows that the rapid increase in output in the non-state sector brought about a drastic shrinkage of the share of state industry in total industrial output. In 'capitalist Taiwan' in 1952, public corporations accounted for 56 per cent of total industrial output (Amsden 1979, p. 367). In 'socialist China', by 1992 the state sector's share had fallen to less than 50 per cent industrial output:

> The non-state sector's share in total industrial output has increased from 21 per cent in 1978 to over 48 per cent in 1991. Employment and exports have expanded much faster. Township-village enterprises' share of industrial employment had increased from 22 to 39 per cent in the same period, and their share of exports had grown from 4.8 per cent in 1985 to 24 per cent in 1990. State-owned enterprises that once dom-

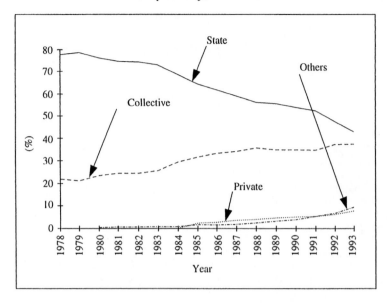

Figure 4.1   Decline of the state sector's share of industrial output value in China, 1978–93

Sources: SSB (1993), p. 414; (1994), p. 375.

inated the commanding weight of the centrally planned economy and accounted for 90 per cent of industrial output in 1966 have been slowly turned into islands in a sea of thriving and dynamic non-state enterprises. (Singh and Jefferson 1993, p. 10)

Division of Labour between the State and Non-State Sectors

What have state-owned enterprises been doing as they 'have been slowly turned into islands'?

As the categories in industrial statistics have altered, it is impossible to examine precisely the structural adjustment in the state sector. If we assume that the state sector dominated most industries in the pre-reform period, Table 4.2 shows a rough pattern in which the state sector withdrew from downstream competitive industries, mainly in the light and processing sectors, where the newly established non-state enterprises were

Table 4.2   Sectoral shares of state-owned and township-village enterprises in China, 1993

Industry	State enterprises	Township-village enterprises
Total	55.65	
Petroleum and natural gas extraction	99.86	0.002
Tobacco processing	97.39	0.33
Logging and transport of timber and bamboo	96.83	10.50
Gas production and supply	94.10	8.84
Petroleum processing and coking products	93.99	6.57
Tape water production and supply	89.19	7.44
Electric power, steam and hot water production and supply	87.27	3.67
Coal mining and processing	78.06	30.04
Smelting and pressing of ferrous metals	77.58	19.46
Non-ferrous metals mining and processing	69.34	36.88
Smelting and pressing of non-ferrous metals	67.99	30.35
Food processing	66.30	35.79
Raw chemical materials and chemical products	62.60	32.83
Medical and pharmaceutical products	61.21	14.21
Transportation equipment manufacturing	60.02	13.72
Beverage manufacturing	59.70	25.25
Special purpose equipment manufacturing	54.68	27.09
Food manufacturing	52.43	69.10
Printing and record pressing	51.53	40.43
Rubber products	51.32	30.22
Ordinary machinery manufacturing	51.11	59.29
Ferrous metals mining and processing	50.13	83.32
Chemical fibres	46.48	19.51
Paper-making and paper products	44.48	55.18
Non-metal minerals mining and processing	43.60	137.22
Non-metal mineral products	43.30	80.21
Instruments, meters, cultural and official machinery	43.04	19.44
Textile industry	42.63	49.48
Electronics and telecommunications	35.35	14.45
Electrical equipment and machinery	34.55	36.97
Timber processing, bamboo, cane, palm fibre and straw products	29.86	81.67
Other minerals mining and processing	22.40	1029.17
Metal products	19.58	83.20
Plastic products	15.87	69.45
Cultural, educational and sports articles	15.62	61.42
Leather, furs, down and related products	14.69	56.43
Other manufacturing	11.97	162.83

Table 4.2   *(Continued)*

Industry	State enterprises	Township-village enterprises
Furniture manufacturing	10.82	96.77
Garments and other fibre products	8.43	69.09

Note: This is the first time the SSB has published the sectoral data of township-village enterprises which has an 'independent account'. There is no reason for the shares of township-village enterprises exceeding 100 per cent of the total output in a sector. And it is also difficult to understand why the sum of the state sector and township-village enterprises exceeds 100 per cent. However, one can still see a general trend of township-village enterprises concentrating on processing industries, although there are obviously some wrong figures.
Source: Calculated from SSB (1994), pp. 374, 378, 395.

booming. Meanwhile, the state sector concentrated on upstream heavy industries that are naturally monopolistic and/or capital intensive.[1] As discussed in Chapter 2, sequential externalities occur where a large upstream plant would induce the entry of downstream firms to make use of new profit opportunities created by the upstream plant but not appropriatable by it. The upstream plant brings greater social benefit, in the form of induced downstream growth, as is reflected in the profit of the non-state sector.

It is not the case that competition from the non-state sector forced the state sector to withdraw from downstream. The World Bank finds that the state actively initiated and carried out a strategic shift: 'Clearly, the central government strategy for mobilising dispersed resources behind a centrally designed program of energy and transport development is part of a solution to pressing problems of shortage. As such, it will play a crucial role in providing the resources for sustained growth now and in future' (1990b, p. 94).

In 1990, state 'budget investment' was only 8.7 per cent of the total national investment, or 13.2 per cent of total investment by state units (SSB 1991, p. 144): 'The decline in the state's direct control over investment decisions let it re-orient its role away from general funding of investment towards priority areas which other Chinese investors would not undertake at the necessary levels, due for example to the project's lumpiness or to the presence of strong positive externalities' (Nolan 1993, p. 89). By the Seventh Five-Year-Plan (1986–90), only 180 prior projects accounted for three-quarters of the central government's spending on 'large-and-medium'

Table 4.3   The state sector's investment in China, 1981–90

Year	Energy (billion RMB) (1)	Transportation, postal and telecommunications (billion RMB) (2)	(1)/state industrial investment (%) (3)	[(1) + (2)]/ total state investment (%) (4)	State investment /total investment (%) (5)	State 'productive' investment/ total 'productive' investment (%) (6)
1981	141.24	65.63	39.34	30.98	69.5	80.93
1982	173.36	88.94	37.78	31.03	68.7	77.35
1983	214.40	114.46	50.78	34.55	66.6	75.42
1984	277.67	156.94	43.26	36.67	64.66	72.39
1985	336.41	226.54	40.10	33.50	66.08	72.82
1986	443.96	257.28	38.28	35.44	65.52	74.85
1987	543.01	282.66	38.59	35.93	63.12	72.71
1988	645.02	317.73	37.36	34.83	61.44	70.52
1989	705.64	271.74	44.19	38.55	61.28	74.40
1990	846.74	348.41	46.78	40.95	65.60	77.55

Sources: (1), (2), (3) and (4) are calculated from SSB (1991), p. 149. (5) and (6) are calculated from SSB (1991), p. 146; (1990), p. 156; (1989), p. 480; (1988), p. 562; (1987), p. 470; (1987b), p. 15.

projects, and of these 91 per cent were in the fields of energy, transportation and raw materials. Energy and transport absorbed close to 50 per cent of total state capital investment (World Bank 1990b, pp. 93–4).

Table 4.3 shows that by 1990 the state sector was still the main resource of 'productive' investment in China.[2] A simple regression analysis reports that state investment had a clear and strong impact on the growth of both light and heavy industry before 1978. By contrast, from 1978 to 1987, state investment had little impact on the growth of light industry, but was still a key determinant of heavy industry (Singh 1992, pp. 48–9). It reflects the industrial restructuring within the state sector.

Restructuring State Enterprises

Alongside industrial restructuring within the state sector, Nolan (1993, 1994) has also drawn attention to a process of restructuring among state-owned enterprises.

Table 4.4 shows that after more than a decade of reform, the growth rate of the state sector as a whole was absolutely lower than that of either of the other sectors or of total industry. Nevertheless, the output of large state enterprises increased significantly, while the government allowed the

Table 4.4   Distribution of industrial output by type of enterprise in China, 1980 and 1992

	1980 (1)	State = 100 (2)	1992 (3)	State = 100 (4)	1992/1980 (5)	Annual growth (6)
Total	100.00		100.00		479.59	13.96
State	75.97	100.0	48.09	100.0	256.62	8.17
Of which:						
Large	31.12	40.97	27.20	56.56	419.13	12.68
Medium	19.84	26.12	15.75	32.74	380.67	11.78
Small	25.01	32.91	5.14	10.70	98.60	–0.12
Collective	23.54	38.04	913.54	20.24		
Individual	0.02		6.76		38 483.35	64.23
Other	0.47		7.11		8 735.98	45.14

Note: (5) = 479.59% × (3)/(1)
Sources: Calculated from SSB (1982), p. 212; (1993), p. 412; (1994), pp. 375–401; (1992b), pp. 34–6; 144–5.

state-owned small enterprises to languish. Consequently, although the non-state small firms very rapidly increased their share of output, the overall share of the small scale sector did not undergo any change whatever, remaining at around half of total industrial output throughout the 1980s. In a sense the non-state sector simply filled the space vacated by the relative shrinkage of state-owned small enterprises. 'The nature of the small scale sector changed hugely, with a great diversity of enterprise sizes and types, doubtless providing large overall efficiency gains, but the role of large and medium sized enterprises did not in any way diminish' (Nolan 1994, p. 9). Columns (2) and (4) in Table 4.4 show that in 1980 small state-owned enterprises account for 33 per cent of total output of the state sector. In 1992, however, large and medium enterprises contributed almost 90 per cent of total output in the state industrial sector. The output of large state-owned enterprises in 1992 was four times that of 1980, with a 12.68 per cent real annual growth rate. If we focus on the growth of the top 500 industrial enterprises, the pace of growth of those state-owned enterprises turns out to be even more significant. From 1988 to 1992, within only four years, the gross sales and total net fixed-assets of the top 500 industrial enterprises had been doubled. Their growth rates were faster than the average of the entire industry as well as that of the fast-growing township-village enterprises (*Management World* 1993, p. 17).

Alongside the growth of large state-owned enterprises, the average scale of large state enterprises also grew. Table 4.5 shows that the average real value

Table 4.5   Average scale of large industrial enterprises in China, 1985–93 (RMB 100 million)

Year	Number	Original value of fixed assets	Gross output value of industry	Average scale	
		(at 1980 price)	*(at 1980 price)*	*Fixed assets*	*Gross output*
1985	2494	2828.30	2327.00	1.1340	0.9330
1988	3178	3610.71	3334.48	1.1362	1.0492
1990	3965	4406.21	4100.82	1.1113	1.0343
1993	4583	6268.35	6890.72	1.3677	1.5035

Sources: Calculated from SSB (1987), p. 325; (1988), p. 312; (1989), pp. 271–3, 320; (1991), pp. 399–401; (1992), pp. 411–13; (1993), pp. 417–19; (1994), pp. 378–9.

of fixed assets in large enterprises in 1993 was 1.2 times that of 1985; the average real value of output in 1993 was 1.6 times that of 1985. The average scale was bigger, and productivity (the ratio of output to assets) was greater.

Summary

In 1993, around 40–50 per cent of joint-ventures in China were reported to be loss-makers (RGCER 1994, p. 23). Perhaps it was the 'attraction' of these losses that caused total contracted foreign investment to rise from US$7.0 billion in 1990 to 111.4 billion in 1993 (SSB 1994a, p. 110). Similarly, over 30 per cent of state enterprises were making losses (SSB 1994a, p. 85). There were several differences between the state sector and joint-venture loss-makers. First, large state-owned enterprises were bearing a very high tax burden. Profit tax and levies might take up 50–75 per cent of an enterprise's net earnings (Gescher 1990). Table 4.6 shows that the tax burden of large state-owned enterprise was more than twice that of foreign investment in 1993. Second, as described in Chapter 2, the state sector supplied underpriced industrial inputs to the economy as a whole throughout the reforms (also see Koo, Li and Peng 1993). Third, state-owned enterprises bore heavy social responsibilities, in terms of pensions, housing and medical care. They even provided free education and employment opportunities for the next generation of workers (Perkins 1988; Minami 1994). In 1991, for example, the expenditure on employment insurance alone in the

Table 4.6　Tax distribution by type of enterprise in China, 1993 (%)

Type of enterprise	Proportion of output	Proportion of tax	Tax/ output	After-tax profit /total profit
Total	100.00	100.00	5.85	40.84
State-owned	55.65	70.54	7.41	33.29
Collective-owned	29.95	20.10	3.93	44.75
Stock ownership	3.68	3.50	5.57	66.92
Foreign investment	4.67	2.86	3.59	66.60
Hong Kong, Macao and Taiwan funded	4.44	1.94	2.55	64.88
Large	37.13	50.60	7.97	40.50
Medium	18.91	20.29	6.27	31.88
Small	43.95	29.12	3.87	46.29

Source: Calculated from SSB (1994), pp. 378–81.

Table 4.7   Loss-makers in the 'Top 500 Industrial Enterprises' in China,
1989–92

Year	Number			RMB10 000		
	Profit makers (1)	Loss makers (2)	(2)/(1) × 100 (3)	Total profits (4)	Total losses (5)	(5)/(4) × 100 (6)
1989	454	46	10.13	7 267 453	408 154	5.62
1990	457*	43	9.41	7 537 268	520 721	6.91
1991	456*	44	9.65	8 713 004	514 123	5.90
1992	457	43	9.41	9 814 697	665 828	6.78

* Includes an enterprise whose profit is zero.
Source: Calculated from *Management World* (1990–93).

state sector reached RMB91.25 billion, which equalled 32.9 per cent of total wages of the state sector, and was twice the size of the total losses of the state industrial sector (SSB 1992, pp. 806, 424).

A large part of the analysis of Chinese industry has argued that the main agent of industrial growth was the small scale non-state sector (usually, erroneously, equated with the private sector). Nevertheless, China's economic progress under reform could hardly have occurred if state industry had served simply as a drag on economic progress (Jefferson and Rawski 1994). Rather, as Nolan observes: 'growth of the large scale, state owned, predominantly heavy industrial sector was at the heart of China's growth in the 1980s' (1994, p. 15). In addition, Table 4.7 shows that loss-makers constituted less than 10 per cent of the top 500 industrial enterprises from 1989 to 1992. This ratio is much lower than that of the *Fortune* 500. In 1992, no fewer than 125 (or 25 per cent) of the *Fortune* 500 suffered from losses (Hadjian and Tritto, cited in Moran and Riesenberger 1994, p. 23).

'MANAGERIAL AUTONOMY' IS THE CORE

Nowhere is this dissonance greater than in China's industrial sector, which has recorded big gains in output, employment, and exports in the absence of privatisation, effective bankruptcy legislation, and other policy innovations widely seen as prerequisites for successful reform (Rawski 1993, p. 1)

A growing awareness that the differences between China's reform and the logic of ownership-based reforms may itself be the cause of favourable outcomes in China leads inexorably to the important question: should the goal of enterprise reform in transitional economies have been ownership reform: that is, privatisation? Oi thinks: 'individuals need not have property rights over enterprise profits for economic growth to occur. Given the large number of formerly socialist systems attempting market reform and economic development, the Chinese model may stand as a less radical but viable alternative to privatisation' (1992, p. 123).

The performance of Chinese large state-owned enterprises challenges Kornai's theory of 'turning back the reel to the beginning'. State enterprises may be reformable. During reform, large state-owned enterprises in China not only developed remarkably, but also were ambitious to become internationally powerful corporations (Nolan 1994).[3] As noted earlier, if one tries to privatise state-owned enterprises, one must confront the impossibility of transferring property rights to Kornai's 'real flesh-and-blood persons'. However, if we turn our focus from ownership to managerial autonomy, there are various practicable measures available, such as the 'contract responsibility system', enterprise group, joint-venture and joint-stock company. During the process of enhancing enterprise autonomy, private ownership is no longer the aim of reforms, but property rights and ownership reform are still powerful weapons enabling state enterprises to escape from government control (that is, state ownership control).

Separation of Ownership and Control

In order to revitalise state enterprises as firms, the Chinese government after 1984 introduced a profit retention scheme, in which enterprises retained a share of the profits to reinvest themselves, and to harness employees' latent, unused, energies. Enterprises were allowed some latitude in procuring inputs, and in producing and selling goods in the market (Granick 1990; Byrd 1991). The immediate reaction of state enterprises, however, disappointed the reformers. They spent as much as possible of their retained profits on bonuses and employee benefits, and little on reinvestment. Nobody took care of state assets (Chen, Wang and Colleagues 1988). The common response to this unexpected phenomena was, as Kornai says: 'public property belongs to all and to none' (1992b, p. 505). Accordingly, the ownership problem was put on to the reform agenda. Innumerable papers and books demonstrated and appealed for well-defined property rights in general, and private property rights in particular (Hsu 1991).

As a step towards well-defined property rights, the establishment of the National Administrative Bureau for State-Owned Property symbolised the victory of the 'ownership' theory. The Bureau was set up in 1988 under the Ministry of Finance. Similar agencies were set up even earlier at provincial and municipal levels. However, it is equivocal whether these bodies should act as holding companies or as legislative/supervisory agencies (Lee and Nellis 1990, p. 9). In order to replace the situation where no one took care of state assets, these bureaux ought to be the representatives of the owner (the state), and thus playing the role of a reliable owner. Following the 'ownership' logic, they ought to have property rights in terms of distributing profits, choosing and promoting managers, hiring and firing workers, pricing products, and making investment decisions. All these necessary ownership functions were already carried out by government agencies at different levels, such as the Bureau of Price Management in the pricing of products, the Department of Finance in the distribution of profits, the State Planning Commission in making investment decisions, the Bureau of Labour in hiring and firing workers, and the Bureau of Personnel in selecting and promoting managers. If the National Administrative Bureau for State-Owned Property should be the owner, all those property rights in hands of different government agencies would have to be transferred to the Bureau. If all those property rights could be in the hands of the newly-established representative of the owner, the Bureau is the existing government, or the existing government with different agencies is the Bureau. What would have changed by the establishment of this new institution? Why should government-appointed officials of the Bureau take care of state assets when officials in different government agencies appointed by the same government do not?

Whether or not people consider it strange or even amusing, China attempted to carry out enterprise reform under the slogan 'separation of ownership and control', in which the government enlarged enterprise's managerial autonomy, in terms of pricing, production-mix, profit distribution, investment and personnel (Wang 1989). Along with welcoming the non-state sector and competition in the market, the state released more and more autonomy to state enterprises. Enlarging enterprise autonomy reinforced competition. This path was opposed to privatisation, in which Kornai and Sachs emphasised the restriction of state-owned enterprises' independence before privatising them. Enlarging enterprise autonomy before privatisation amounts to giving property rights to 'Communist-appointed managers' without ownership control to enforce hard budget constraints.

The Chinese attempted to substitute competition for government control: that is, state ownership control. It is naive to look for ownership control from the National Administrative Bureau for State-Owned Property, but diversifying the ownership structure is a powerful weapon to actualise managerial autonomy. In China property rights play a fundamental role, but in a different way from Kornai's theory which emphasises the need to *to strengthen* ownership control, with its idealistic goal of control by 'real flesh-and-blood persons' over management. Ownership reform in China attempted *to weaken* the control of the sole owner, namely the government. By diversifying the ownership structure, Kornai wanted to make ownership work, while China wanted to make it ineffective.

The 'Contract Responsibility System'

The initial idea of the 'contract responsibility system' was to give management more discretion by specifying the minimum amount of profits that an enterprise was required to remit to the state, and how profits above the minimum were to be shared between the government, the enterprise, and the workers. This was altered in 1986 to bring about further decentralisation. Enterprises were given the right to buy and sell products in excess of planned quotas at market prices. Managers were given increased discretion, and could bargain with the state authorities over profits and taxes to be remitted. By 1988, over 80 per cent of state-owned enterprises had adopted some variant of the system (Yeh 1993, p. 21), and by 1990, 90 per cent (Lee and Nellis 1990, p. 8).[4] In 1994, the government ended the system. All state-owned enterprises have to pay equally the corporate income tax and value-added tax.

As early as the mid-1980s, the 'contract responsibility system' turned enterprises towards profit-seeking (Perkins 1988). This dynamo allowed a widespread release of competitive, entrepreneurial, profit-seeking business activity (Nolan 1991). Sample data reveals a strong correlation between profits, retained earnings and employee bonuses (Jefferson and Rawski 1994). Using panel data from 1984 to 1989 for 80 state-owned enterprises, Jefferson and Rawski (1994) find most new product developments were financed from retained earnings. Workers at unprofitable state enterprises were rarely dismissed (although this began to change in the early 1990s), but they were not immune from financial penalties, which might include low or zero bonuses, leave with partial salary, payment in kind, or removal of free health care (Rawski 1993).

Looking only at the 'contract responsibility system', a superficial view of the Chinese industrial landscape might conclude that nothing had changed in the nature of property rights. However, closer analysis reveals that important changes had occurred within the state sector, leading to large alterations in the nature and exercise of property rights (Nolan 1993, p. 270).

Table 4.8   Losses and subsidies to state-owned enterprises in China, 1986–91
(in billion RMB)

Year	All enterprises			The state industry		
	Loss (1)	Subsidy (2)	(2)/(1) (3)	Loss (4)	Subsidy (5)	(5)/(4) (6)
1986	41.71	32.5	0.78	4.71	3.82	0.81
1987	48.17	37.5	0.78	5.07	3.65	0.72
1988	52.06	44.6	0.86	7.13	5.21	0.73
1989	74.96	59.9	0.80	12.80	9.50	0.74
1990	93.26	57.9	0.62	27.88	11.80	0.42
1991	93.11	50.6	0.54	30.02	14.50	0.48

Note: The figures in brackets are provided by the World Bank.
Sources: Multiple sources cited in Jefferson and Rawski (1994), Table 8.

First, the contract fixed a dividing line of financial responsibility between the state and the enterprise. While increasing enterprise autonomy, the government reduced subsidies to loss-markers. Table 4.8 shows that loss-making state enterprises, formerly eligible for full compensation for losses as part of official administrative routine, faced growing difficulties. Subsidies continued, but the ratio of subsidies to losses dropped from its initial level to below 50 per cent. Workers associated with loss-making enterprises faced a growing probability of sanctions, such as low wage growth, deterioration of bonuses, erosion of health benefits and other perquisites, layoffs, compulsory transfers to ancillary units, and recently, dismissal (Jefferson and Rawski 1994).

Second, the contract fixed a dividing line of investment responsibility between the state and the enterprise. Tables 4.9 and 4.10 show an important change in property rights. After the mid-1980s, over two-fifths of fixed investment undertaken by state enterprises was financed from enterprises' 'self-raised funds', so that a growing share of 'state-owned enterprise' capital stock was its own. Moreover, fixed investment by state-owned units was financed by domestic loans, mainly from banks. It is possible to perceive in embryo similarities with the Japanese system which is cemented by equity holdings with the principal banks (World Bank 1990b, p. 149).

In short, as state enterprises became more and more independent, government subsidies and reinvestment were reduced. In capitalist history, the

Table 4.9   Sources of 'fixed asset investment' in the Chinese state sector, 1985–93 (%)

Year	Total investment	State investment	Domestic loans	Foreign investment	Self-raised funds	Other
1985	100	24.0	23.0	5.3	40.4	7.3
1987	100	20.5	24.6	7.3	47.6	
1989	100	13.4	20.9	10.2	42.8	12.8
1991	100	10.2	28.1	8.3	43.1	10.3
1993	100	6.0	25.4	6.1	48.0	14.5

Sources: Calculated from SSB (1986), p. 468; (1992), p. 150; (1993), p. 146; (1994), p. 140.

Table 4.10   Sources of 'technological reformation investment' in the Chinese state sector, 1985–93

Year	Total investment	State investment	Domestic loans	Foreign investment	Self-raised funds	Other
1985	100	4.4	41.6	1.2	50.3	2.5
1987	100	4.3	40.4	2.3	48.3	4.8
1989	100	1.8	29.6	3.4	55.9	9.4
1991	100	1.7	40.2	3.7	49.7	4.8
1993	100	1.4	36.5	3.9	53.3	4.9

Sources: Calculated from SSB (1986), p. 468; (1992), p. 150; (1993), p. 146; (1994), p. 140.

traditional 'personal enterprise' was replaced by '*de facto* management ownership' (Demsetz 1988, p. 114).[5] In China, from the introduction of the 'contract responsibility system' onwards the state as the sole owner-manager in change of enterprises was being replaced by '*de facto* management ownership'.

Enterprise Group

Building up enterprise groups was another measure through which state enterprises could gain still greater managerial autonomy. In the 1980s there emerged linked plants in related lines of production which began to form company-like groups. Support for the idea of industrial groups became a central plank of government policy for enterprise reform. 'The goal is to form competitive and independently managed industrial giants' (Yao 1992, p. 14). The government identified 55 leading enterprise groups which had been especially successful. They were to be the models for other groups, and were to be targeted for state assistance. The vast bulk of these were in heavy industry (Yao 1992).

One typical example was the Dongfeng Automobile Group, based at the former giant No. 2 Automobile Plant in Hubei Province. By the early 1980s it had 'taken over' around 300 enterprises of different scales. The constituent plants re-oriented production under the guidance of the parent company, which was also the conduit for channelling new technology. They were re-specialised into a variety of processes, such as assembly, special purpose car production and the production of specialised inputs (Yao 1992).

These enterprise groups began to move towards the Japanese *keiretsu* and the South Korean *chaebol* style of organisation (Nolan 1994). Enterprise groups consisted of vast enterprises with different owners, or the same state owner but based in different localities. Enterprise groups diversified the originally unified state ownership. Diversification made enterprise groups more independent than ordinary state-owned enterprises. The 55 leading groups, for example, enjoyed the privilege of being directly responsible to the central government, thus bypassing control from other government agencies. As joint-venture and joint-stock companies developed, most groups formed a variety of mergers through both the old administrative and new commercial measures (Kaye 1992).

The Joint-Venture

The joint-venture, by introducing foreign investors, signalled the start of ownership reform. By 1993 there were 20 055 foreign-invested industrial firms with 2.89 million employees, which produced 9.11 per cent of the total industrial output (SSB 1994, pp. 378 and 98). Many of these foreign-invested firms were joint-ventures with state-owned enterprises. For example, the city of Quanzhou in Fujian Province was famous throughout China for having completely restructured its state sector. All 41 state companies in the city were re-organised in 1992 as a result of a joint-venture between China Strategic Investments, a publicly-listed Hong Kong based company in the Sinar Mas group (which is the third largest conglomerate in Indonesia). In Fuzhou, the capital of Fujian Province, more than half of the total state enterprises were working in joint-ventures by early 1994 (Tracy 1994a, 1994b). By 1993, the biggest 'foreign investor', Hong Kong, which had never employed more than 0.9 million industrial workers before the 1980s, employed 3.65 million in China (Overholt 1993, p. 145).

Tracy surveyed 400 foreign-invested companies in Guangdong and Fujian provinces. He found that between one-third and two-thirds of his sample used expatriate managers to ensure appropriate organisation of production, quality control, and so on (1994a, pp. 12–13).

The Joint-Stock Company Again

As early as 1985, Wood argued for the need to 'rearrange the pattern of state ownership rights. Instead of having particular enterprises belonging to particular ministries or local governments, the ownership of each enterprise would be spread among several different public institutions interested mainly in its profits' (1991b, p. 28; also see World Bank 1985).[6] The joint-stock company, as an instrument of Schumpeter's 'creative destruction', transcended the limits of the traditional private firm: that is, 'an entrepreneur, or owner-manager, who single-mindedly operates the firm to maximise profits' (Fama 1980, p. 288). By the early 1990s in China, the joint-stock company had again become a powerful weapon to transcend the limits of state ownership, enabling the government as the sole owner-manager to operate state-owned enterprises.

The introduction of this form of ownership was welcomed by state-owned firms, 'partly because of the flexibility of the corporate share-holding structure, but more importantly because it gave a separate identity to the secured corporation. The board of directors and shareholders could cushion the enterprise against government intervention, which has always been the biggest problem of state-owned firms' (Hu 1993, p. 11). In July 1984, China's first joint-stock company, the Beijing Tianqiao Department Store Ltd, which consisted of two state-owned department stores and a state-owned wholesale store, was registered in Beijing, and openly issued shares to domestic institutions as well as to individuals. In late 1984, Shanghai, the home of many of the biggest state enterprises, permitted state-owned enterprises to issue stocks to employees or local financial institutions (Singh 1990). By the end of 1991, some 1700 enterprises in Shanghai had issued stocks accounting for more than 30 per cent of the country's total. Institutional investors accounted for more than 70 per cent of the total volume of stock transactions (Wei 1992, p. 16). Shenzhen started issuing shares in 1987. Because of its location near Hong Kong,

Shenzhen attracted a large number of foreigners to set up joint-ventures which were mostly joint-stock companies. This city also tried hard to transform state-owned enterprises into joint-stock ones. By the end of 1991, there were 200 joint-stock companies, 30 of which had been previously state owned. By the end of 1991, corporate equities issued all over the country were estimated at around RMB4.6 billion, involving some 6000 enterprises (Hu 1993, p. 12). In 1993, 2579 industrial joint-stock companies with 1 636 100 employees produced 3.68 per cent of the total industrial output (SSB 1994, pp. 378 and 98). In 1994, the government unveiled a six-point plan to overhaul state-owned enterprises. The scheme aimed to transform them into joint-stock companies with managerial independence from government control (*Transition* 1994, Vol. 5, No. 7, p. 17).

In early 1993, after issuing 'B' shares to overseas investors (Cheng 1992),[7] nine large state-owned companies raised capital by floating shares in Hong Kong. Each of these emerged by taking over other enterprises and/or setting up new ones, gradually taking on the appearance of large multi-plant joint-stock companies. Similar to the privatisation in the West mentioned in Chapter 3, a large proportion of shares was held by government agencies (either local or national), and the remainder were held by a variety of mainly institutional investors.

Summary

From the 'contract responsibility system' to the enterprise group, from the joint-venture to the joint-stock company, one can see progressive ownership reform from what was originally unified state ownership. Under the 'contract responsibility system', the government reduced its subsidies and investment. State-owned enterprises needed to reinvest through 'self-raised funds' and bank loans, thereby transforming the ownership relationship whereby the government was the sole owner-manager. The enterprise group joined enterprises together from different locations with different owners. Many joint-ventures were directly dominated by foreigners. The joint-stock company re-organised state-owned enterprises by the typically capitalist principle of property rights.

Should one understand enterprise reform in China to have been essentially a process of privatisation? Ownership reform in China was subtly different from the logic of privatisation. As ownership reform went deeper and deeper, it was hard to see a path whereby ownership was being changed from public to private. It was also hard to see the newly diversified owners really controlling management. Ownership reform in China was altering the role of the government as the sole owner-manager who operated enterprises. Diversification did not enhance ownership incentives, but rather augmented managerial autonomy. According to Kornai's theory of 'turning back the reel to the beginning', ownership reform in China failed to turn sufficiently far back to reach the 'beginning'. Indeed, diversification of ownership structures in China did not even begin to 'turn back' in the direction of 'real flesh-and-blood persons'. All 'vaguely defined' township-village enterprises, state-owned enterprises and joint-ventures were busy issuing shares into the market. The result was an even more 'vaguely defined', intangible 'ownership maze' (Singh and Jefferson 1993, p. 9). By contrast, from the perspective of managerial autonomy, the picture becomes clearer. As ownership reform went deeper, state-owned enterprises evolved progressively from state-administered plants towards '*de facto* management ownership'. This pattern matches what Wood suggested: the creation of vested interests and rearrangement of public ownership in the joint-stock company in order to transform China's state enterprises into 'independent and efficient economic units' (1991a, p. 1). Hay, Morris, Liu and Yao understand ownership reform in China as follows: 'In practice the main thrust of multiple ownership is not in fact relocation of residual risk, nor even transferability of risk, but a shift in effective decision-taking powers from agencies of the state to managers of enterprises' (1994, p. 432).

If one only examines the degree of ownership privatisation in China, one could conclude that state-owned enterprises were 'virtually unchanged' (Stepanek 1991, p. 453). If one looked at the degree of managerial autonomy, one could not deny the hugely enlarged autonomy in the state sector. By using data from a 1991 survey of over 900 state-owned enterprises and nearly 300 township-village enterprises, Jefferson, Zhao and Lu (1994) construct a composite indicator that combines information along 11 dimensions of management authority. This shows a high degree of decision-making autonomy at enterprise level for less than half of the state-owned enterprises, and nearly two-thirds of the township-village enterprises. They found that *the autonomy of state-owned enterprises was converging towards township-village enterprises.* In the area of the determination of bonus differentials, the managers of state-owned enterprises reported even greater autonomy than township-village enterprises. Using a sample of 200 state-owned and 100 township-village enterprises, Zou concludes that the performance of China's industrial enterprises was 'market-driven rather than ownership-driven' (1992, p. 55). Moreover, Day, Wang and Zou (1991) found a convergence of factor productivity between state-owned and collective (mainly township-village) enterprises.

'OWNERSHIP MAZE' VERSUS 'STATE CORPORATISM'

In China, the introduction of the 'contract responsibility system', enterprise group, joint-venture and joint-stock company did not proceed in a step-by-step logical order. They ran in parallel and interacted with each other. This section attempts to explain the fact that the logic of enterprise reform in China was something other than privatisation, and examines another advantage of the 'ownership maze' which leaves the door open to state intervention.

'Chinese Ownership Maze: Non State, yet not Private' (Singh and Jefferson 1993, p. 9)

The amazing development of the non-state sector in China encouraged support for the 'ownership' theory of reform. However, the so-called 'non-state ownership' cannot be conveniently squeezed into the logic of private ownership.[8] Most of the non-state-owned enterprises, chiefly the famous township-village enterprises, are simply not privately owned (Byrd and Lin 1990; Nee 1992; Oi 1992). 'Altogether, about 12.5 per cent of total industrial output in 1991 was produced by "privately owned" enterprises using this classification, up from five per cent in 1985 ... The rest of China's non-state enterprises are collectively and hence publicly owned and cannot be considered private by normal definitions of ownership' (Singh and Jefferson 1993, p. 9).

The fact that township-village enterprises have grown so fast while not being truly privately owned has caused discomfort. Some have argued, including Kornai, that a 'high proportion of them are clearly private enterprises ... Casual observation shows, however, that the majority of rural collectively owned firms are *de facto* privately owned firms' (Kornai 1992b, p. 442). He gives no evidence as to the proportion of them that were 'clearly private enterprises', and neither does he state the research basis of the 'casual observation' which purports to show that the majority of these firms were '*de facto*' privately owned.

A number of careful field studies give the opposite impression to Kornai's belief. Township-village enterprises were built on the foundation of earlier industrialisation efforts undertaken by local governments (Perkins and Yusuf 1984). Like their predecessors, township-village enterprises of the 1980s and 1990s operated under close supervision from township or village governments which contributed start-up funds, appointed managers and were intimately involved in major strategic decisions (Zweig 1991). A 1990 survey of 285 township-village enterprises found that only 15.8 per cent had the authority to appoint their own leaders. In 60 per cent of cases, the 'supervisory agency' (that is, local government) appointed firm leaders without consultation (Jefferson, Zhao and Lu 1994).[9] Thus from the perspective of property rights, Rawski concludes: 'Local government own and control most collectives. They remain deeply involved in the appointment of managers and in strategic management decisions. Government involvement has increased with the economic importance of collectives, leading some Chinese economists to describe collective industry as the "second state sector"' (1993, p. 1). In fact, township-village enterprises, although different in many respects from state-owned enterprises, are '*public* enterprises' (Jefferson and Rawski 1994, p. 5, italics in original). Based on 222 interviews from 1986 to 1991 in China, Oi labels the local government that co-ordinates economic enterprises in its territory as 'local state corporatism' (1992).[10] Wood defines township-village enterprises as 'rural government-owned enterprises' (1991b, p. 7). Moreover, Walder observes: 'In effect, government property rights over industrial assets are *stronger* in rural jurisdictions because local industrial organisation is simpler, financial incentive clearer, budget constraints more immediate, and the government's capacity to monitor its assets *greater*. Differences in industrial organisation, not in the nature of government property rights, provide the explanation' (1994, p. 2, my emphases). Entrepreneurial performance in the township-village sector has been 'especially remarkable in an environment in which ownership and property rights with respect to industrial assets are not clear and pure private ownership is rare in the smallest concerns' (Byrd 1990, p. 189). Based on 16 years' panel data in more than 400 township-villages, Svejnar finds that the difference between the coefficients of the different ownership dummy variables is statistically insignificant: 'private ownership and community ownership appear to have similar effects on productivity' (1990, p. 253).

What makes township-village enterprises so successful? Walder argues that the main difference between urban and rural public industry is 'not that rural industry is somehow freer from "state" interference, that it is "semi-private" or some kind of hybrid that combines the characteristics of a state firm in a planned economy with a private firm in a market economy'. Township-village enterprises 'compete vigorously in product markets, but they are nonetheless government owned and operated in exactly the same sense as the large state enterprises of the large cities' (1994, pp. 21–2). Singh and Jefferson list six significant differences between state-owned and township-village enterprises: 'better governance, greater autonomy, clear-cut incentives, hard budget constraint, less regulations and social obligations, greater competition' (1993, p. 10). None of these concerns differences in ownership.

Co-Operation of Government and Business

Today competition is already globalised. Economic growth and high employment are widely viewed as the gift of the world market, not of domestic management (Harris 1986). Although Porter (1990) does not like the state directly 'helping' firms, he encourages people to think about international competitiveness *nationally*, because the government can powerfully influence all the determinants of national competitiveness. The consideration of national competitiveness, as opposed to simply making profits, must necessarily be a governmental function, not that of private capitalists:

> The process of accelerated economic growth in the newly industrialis-ing countries appears to be everywhere associated with the expansion of the public sector and the role of the state. It has not been 'free enter-prise' nor multinational capital which has led the process, but the delib-erate and persistent efforts of governments. (Harris 1986, pp. 145, 149)

A succession of careful historical studies of newly industrialising coun-tries has shown that well-directed state action stepping in where the market failed was the main explanation for these countries' success. The relevant issue here is not the necessity of state intervention, but why it is that such states are able to intervene, and why it is that state intervention occurs so frequently in the East, including Japan (Johnson 1982), South Korea (Amsden 1989; Chang 1993), and Taiwan (Wade 1990), all of which are heavily influenced by Confucian orthodoxy, and in which private ownership is, more or less, a 'vaguely defined' maze.

From the perspective of national competitiveness in the world market, Lodge recognises the obsolescence of three Western myths:

> The old idea that firms compete with firms, unencumbered by govern-ment intervention, is shattered by reality ... This fact destroys a second myth, that of the limited state ... That government *is* planning and must do so for better or worse fills some with dread, partly because it threat-ens a third myth, that of property rights. According to the idea of prop-erty rights, corporations are property and the fundamental aim of their managers is to satisfy the property owners, the shareholders. Doing so will be good for the community. Once, when shareholders were a rela-tively small number of easily identifiable persons, the idea made sense. The manager could ask them what they wanted – long-run market share or short-run financial returns – and act accordingly. Today, managers of

the *Fortune* 500 are forced to discern shareholders' desires from the transactions of gifted traders on Wall Street whose objectives are purely financial: a return – and a quick one at that – on what they have invested for their clients, the owners. These traders could scarcely have less interest in the long-run health of the firms their actions sustain or destroy. (1990, p. 6)[11]

Good government relations can be an important competitive advantage (Mahini and Wells 1986). In their consideration of the threat of competition from the East, a substantial amount of evidence suggests a need to restructure government–business relations in order to upgrade the international competitiveness of the UK and the USA (Best 1990; Lodge 1990; Lazonick 1991). There is strong evidence that American managers are thirsty for government support.[12] Compared with Japan, which had 213 government–business councils in 1987,[13] 23 011 lobbyists registered with the secretary of the Senate, 43 for each member of the House and Senate in the same year (as against only 365 in 1961). In 1986, 1300 corporations had Washington offices, compared to only 100 in 1968 (Smith 1988, pp. 29–31). Plainly the characteristics of lobbyists are different from those of Japanese government–business councils. Government–business co-operation is a much broader issue than mere communications (Best 1990, p. 172). For example, the strategy of selective support for certain enterprises is reminiscent of Japan's administrative guidance (Johnson 1982). However, in the USA, Lodge argues: 'If the company's highest priority is short-run shareholder satisfaction, the company's behaviour will almost certainly not be in line with long-run community need as perceived by government' (Lodge 1990, p. 103). In other words, it must be a scandal if the US government offers privileges to a selfish private company, thereby providing income to 'real flesh-and-blood persons'.

How are the Japanese able to do what the Americans cannot? What governments can do is legitimate to the extent that they are in accord with 'public philosophy' (Huntington 1968, p. 27). In Japan, as compared with the USA 'one of the most powerful social supports for private managers' co-operation with the government is that Japanese managers enjoy freedom from being judged exclusively in terms of short-term financial performance' (Johnson 1982, p. 312). Whereas long-term industrial finance in Japan was deeply influenced by the public–private administrative interplay, industrial regulatory policy in the USA presumed the ideal of perfect markets and defined inter-firm co-operation as collusion against the public interest (Best 1990, p. 201).

The complexity of government–business co-operation can be understood fully if cultural differences are taken into account. Lodge distinguishes two ideological paradigms concerning the role of government: '*individualistic*, which stresses the individual over the community, and *communitarian*, in which the reverse is true'. The USA has tended traditionally to be the most individualistic, and Japan the most communitarian. Grounded in communitarian culture, Japan and other Asian countries benefit greatly by acting against the tenets of individualism, simply because their governments and companies practise 'neither free trade nor free enterprise' (1990, pp. 15–16, italics in original). Long-term industrial development in Japan was deeply influenced by the public–private administrative interplay. 'Each case denies the dichotomies of market and plan, private and public, economic and political, that characterise the theories and policies of both the United States and the United Kingdom' (Best 1990, pp. 201–2). In Korea, the mixture goes even further; 'the productive forces in Korea have never been developed according to free market principles' (Amsden 1989, p. 322).

Considering the various national communities, as given in Figure 4.2, Lodge observes four sources of authority for corporate managers: (1) the owners, the shareholders 'who obtain authority via the idea of property rights'; (2) the banks and other debt holders 'that have an interest in safeguarding their loans'; (3) the managed, the corporate membership; (4) the community, as represented by its government. Obviously, American managers would agree that their legitimacy derives from the owners. Debt holders have a secondary position, employees are hired and fired as they

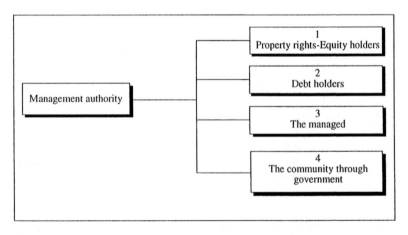

Figure 4.2   Sources of management authority
Source: Lodge (1984), p. 71.

are needed to maximise return to shareholders, and government is an adversary to be kept at arm's length (and avoided entirely if possible). In Germany, however, corporate purpose springs from a well-ordered combination of all four sources, as it does in Japan. For example, an executive of Mitsui, the largest company in the world, describes Mitsui's purpose in the following order of emphasis: '(1) to contribute to Japanese society, to serve the greater glory of Japan; (2) to realise profit for the company so as to promote the welfare and happiness of its employees; and (3) to foster and strengthen the spirit of Mitsui for the future' (Lodge 1990, pp. 40–2).

The words from the Mitsui executive may be hypocritical. One might hear a similar fiction spoken by an American entrepreneur. However, the Japanese public accepts the beautiful words not because of propaganda, but because of the lowest dividend payout in the advanced economies, life-time employment, the seniority system, the housing programmes and the series of social responsibilities shouldered by enterprises. All these, as described in Chapter 3, stem from cross-holding, which ousted the control of 'real flesh-and-blood persons'.[14] In other words, the legitimacy of government intervention, or the legitimacy of businesses receiving government support, depends very much on the enterprise attitudes which are directly or indirectly linked with an 'ownership maze'.

In order to restructure government–business relations, thereby improving public–private co-operation, America needs another example of Schumpeter's 'creative destruction': 'the transition from individualism to communitarianism' (Lodge 1990). Many examples given by Lodge simply demonstrate that 'the old idea that management authority comes from the owners has become un-competitive', while American firms are on their own in competition with both Japanese firms *and* the Japanese government. Lodge calls for reforms in the USA and subtitles his book: '*restructuring business–government relations for world competitiveness*'. It is a tough task. He argues that 'Japan has learned much from the United States since World War II, so theoretically, at least, there is no cultural reason why we cannot learn as much from Japan' (1990, pp. 205 and 203).

What Can We Learn from Lodge?

The success of township-village enterprises relies very much on support from local government in terms of funding, resource allocation, investment and credit, and (in Oi's terms) 'bureaucratic services' which include help in securing licences, certification and prices for products, and tax breaks (Oi 1992, p. 120). At township and village levels, enterprises have closer relations with the community where they are located than do their state-owned counterparts. Lodge's hypothesis about the sources of enterprise authority suggests that the 'ownership maze' may be helpful in the building up of government–business co-operation. It is doubtful whether rapidly privatised township-village enterprises would have left the local authorities with anything like the capacity to raise revenue that occurred under the arrangements which existed in China in the 1980s (Nolan 1993, p. 311).

'Excessive Competition' versus Export

In China, the 'ownership maze' and deep involvement of local governments caused many problems, especially extensive corruption in dealings between enterprises and state officials, and persistent regional protectionism (Huang 1990; Hishida 1991). These problems harmed open and fair competition, although according to Huntington: 'Corruption may be one way of surmounting traditional laws or bureaucratic regulations which hamper economic expansion' (1968, p. 68).

In the same fashion as in Japan, Korea and Taiwan, since the boundary between government and business is insufficiently clear, corruption and under competition are, to a greater or lesser degrees, inescapable. In general, co-operation between government and business must be damaging to competition. Specifically, co-operation between government and enterprise hurts competition *domestically, but not internationally*. Government is an administration located within a fixed boundary. It can only directly affect competition within that boundary. A government may protect its industries domestically, but it cannot directly influence activities in the world market.[15] As competition becomes increasingly globalised, exports become increasingly important, especially for late-comers who need to import technology. In this respect, there is a trade-off. Government–business co-operation hurts competition in the domestic market, but it may strengthen its competitiveness in the world market. Porter comments:

> A country is a desirable global platform in an industry if it provides an environment yielding firms domiciled in that country an advantage in competing globally in that particular industry ... *An essential element of this definition is that it hinges on success outside the country, and not merely country conditions that allow firms to successfully manage domestic competition.* (1986, p. 39, my emphasis)

His important distinction between domestic and international competition suggests that *pursuing perfect competition domestically does not spontaneously bring about international competitiveness.* Government intervention must lead to imperfection in the domestic market, but may promote the country's international competitiveness.

The typical success stories of government–business co-operation are all export oriented economies, including Japan, Korea and Taiwan. For example, many of Taiwan's industries and some of its exports initially would have been unprofitable without state encouragement (Wade 1990, p. 302). Three aspects of policy capacity are relevant to this issue:

> (1) the ability to marshal and direct domestic production factories to take advantage of new commercial opportunities, (2) the ability to organise appraising packages of economic and non-economic incentives to attract desired foreign contributions, and (3) the ability to control, suppress, and avoid domestic and foreign challenges to resource-allocation decisions. In all these respects, the autonomy and strength of the state are critically important.[16]

Chan argues that 'a more pliable work force and more docile business community have enhanced the state's position, and have facilitated its ability to enforce short-term economic sacrifices and to develop long-term industrial plans' (1987, pp. 263–4).

According to Johnson (1982), Japanese government interventions often cause 'overinvestment', and hence 'overproduction' and 'excessive competition'. Porter (1990) also finds that by international standards leading Japanese industries have a relatively large number of competitive producers fighting for a share of the market. If these 'overproducers' can 'overcompete' with each other to export, is there a problem?

Developmental State, Entrepreneurial State, or State Corporatism?

Drawing on these three vaguely defined concepts, the following pages analyse Japan, Korea and Taiwan, as well as China. The later industrialisation comes, the more the government was involved in economic development as a 'developmental state', an 'entrepreneurial state', and in the form of 'state corporatism'.[17] According to Blecher, under a developmental state, 'the role of the state is variously to promote development (through planning, bureaucratic co-ordination, arrangement of finance, procurement of inputs, development of infrastructure, etc.) or to regulate it. But in the entrepreneurial state conceptualisation, bureaux of the state themselves undertake entrepreneurial activity.' In other words, enterprises have greater autonomy under the developmental than the entrepreneurial state (1991, pp. 267–8).

Industrialisation in Britain took over 50 years. As a late-comer, the Japanese government brought public–private co-operation through industrial policies, and was able to compress the process into 25 years. Taiwan and Korea came even later than Japan. Drawing government into deeper involvement in business, they achieved in 15 years what took Japan 25 and Britain over 50 years (Wade 1990, p. 42).

Wade makes the comparison: 'In terms of Chalmers Johnson's model of the developmental state, Taiwan meets the "bureaucratic autonomy" condition but fails to meet the "public–private co-operation" condition' (1990, p. 295). The Japanese developmental state played a 'followship' role, in which the government pilots the market by industrial policies. Government and enterprises are interdependent. Without consensus between government and business, public–private co-operation is a purely scholastic exercise (Best 1990, p. 172). In Taiwan and Korea, the entrepreneurial state played a 'leadership' role. 'Here, leadership is by fiat rather than consensus (which is one way of stating the difference between Taiwan and Japan) ... Until recently the policy network hardly included representatives of private business, and the government retained a striking degree of autonomy in setting the directions and details of policy' (Wade 1990, pp. 226 and 304).[18]

A typical example of government autonomy is the growth of state-owned enterprises which played a small role in Japan. If an agreement could not be reached with businessmen, the government stepped in directly itself. In the early 1970s, at the most difficult time for the overproduction in steel industry, the Korean government bizarrely decided to build the largest steel mill in the world. The World Bank turned down a loan request as it considered the project to be economically infeasible (Amsden 1989, p. 291; Wade 1990, p. 319). Later, the Pohang Iron and Steel Co. Ltd, a state-owned enterprise, became one of the lowest-cost steel-makers in the world.[19]

Taiwan relied even more heavily on public enterprises to make a big push into activities with high entry barriers (Wade 1990). In Japan, as a developmental state, the central bureaucracy directed economic activities and shaped commercial incentives by resorting to those levers available to it in the form of tax treatment, credit provision, currency exchange controls, and the issue of import and export licences. In Amsden's terms, it was an 'interventionist state' (1989, p. 320). Beside being interventionist, the Taiwanese state was further strengthened by its ownership and operation of state-owned enterprises that controlled the allocation of vital factors of production such as raw materials, energy and transportation (Chan 1987, pp. 264–5). Public enterprises concentrated in upstream sectors gave the government an indirect influence over downstream sectors (Wade 1990, p. 179). More importantly, banks were virtually all owned by the government (Wade 1990 p. 162).[20] In terms of Blecher's definition, Taiwan and Korea were more like entrepreneurial states.[21]

China comes even later than Korea and Taiwan. In the last 15 years, with its 1.2 billion population, China's real GNP has grown by an average of almost 9 per cent a year, accompanied by an even more spectacular export growth (Lardy 1992). As a previously command economy, the Chinese government initially was even more deeply involved in business than Taiwan or Korea. Wade has observed that in the West, governments tried to *pick winners*. The governments of Japan, Taiwan and Korea *made winners* (1990, p. 334). Whether or not it is thought to be bizarre or humorous, Chinese local governments today are busy *being winners* themselves, juggling both enterprise reform and decentralisation.[22]

If the ownership of each enterprise could be spread among several different public institutions interested mainly in its profits, as Wood (1991b) suggests, government bureaucrats would have an interest in maximising revenue through helping, and even doing business. In China, under this system, economic bureaucrats and enterprise managers have come to share decision-making powers without clearly defined rules or well-specified divisions of labour (Huang 1990, p. 432). As Oi describes it: 'Local officials have assumed new roles as entrepreneurs, selectively allocating scarce resources to shape patterns of local economic growth ... in the process local governments have taken on many characteristics of a business corporation, with officials acting as the equivalent of a board of directors' (1992, p. 124). Neither concept, 'developmental state' or the 'entrepreneurial state', is adequate to define the web of interests connecting government and business. Oi labels this new institutional development *'local state corporatism'* (Oi 1992, p. 100, italics in original).[23]

Whatever people name it, a 'new institutional development' is there for all to see. Even the success of joint-ventures is reliant on effective cooperation with local officials (Tracy 1994b, pp. 21–2). This is due to the fact that local government capacity to mobilise resources plays an indispensable role in overcoming the obstacle of lack of factor markets. This is essential to a transitional economy. In a command economy with no factor markets, a single centre distributes not only inputs and output, but all factors of production including land, labour and capital. Reform of this system could easily result in a 'neither-plan-nor-market system' (Steinherr 1991, p. 4), in which neither old central planning nor new market mechanisms could work well, simply because developing factor markets is complex and time-consuming. On the one hand, a single centre is capable of distributing factors of production, but unable to follow market signals and competitive principles, because of its central monopolist position. On the other hand, alongside the lack of factor markets, enterprises are not strong enough to re-organise factors of production after the centre gives up its distribution function. This dilemma gives local governments an indispensable role to play in substituting for missing factor markets. Decentralisation empowers localities to allocate resources *following market signals and principles of competition*. Enterprise reform, including the World Bank's suggestion of rearranging ownership structures, powerfully provided local governments with the shareholders' incentive to become more deeply involved in economic development. This is also the pattern at township and village levels. Today, in the state and non-state state sectors, the missing and difficult-to-develop factor markets stimulated all provincial, municipal, township, and village governments to assume the role of the undeniable driving force behind economic growth in general and export growth in particular.

Summary

Based on the 'ownership maze' and vaguely defined property rights, the remarkable growth in China has already lasted for 16 years and seems likely to continue. This growth as a whole, in the state sector, and at township and village levels, has shown that: 'There is, however, no inherent reason why only individuals, as distinct from governments, can be entrepreneurs. Similarly, there is no inherent reason why secure property rights will be an effective incentive only if they are assigned to individuals' (Oi 1992, p. 100). On the contrary, it is the government which is carrying out an intelligent strategy for restructuring state industry, in which the state sector withdraws from downstream areas of competitive light and processing industries, and concentrates on upstream areas of natural monopolised and capital intensive industries. It is the government which is carrying out the restructuring of state-owned enterprises, by allowing small state enterprises to shrink, strengthening large enterprises by intensive investment. Beside enlarging enterprise managerial autonomy, it is also governments at the local level which act as organisers to mobilise resources following market signals in an environment lacking factor markets. Why has China grown so fast when so many conditions thought to be necessary for growth were absent? The reason is because the government is active in the areas where enterprises need help.

Conclusion to Part II: Government Reform is Another Core

Ownership reform in China is going deeper and deeper. However, it is not 'turning back the reel to the beginning' but targeting managerial autonomy. Enlarging managerial autonomy has made the behaviour of state-owned enterprises move towards the relatively efficient behaviour of township-village enterprises. The authority of managerial autonomy in Chinese state-owned enterprises, just as in their township-village counterparts, does not come from private ownership as distinct from the government. The 'owner-ship maze' leaves a huge space for the state to intervene. In the past under the command system, different state agencies, *together* with state-owned enterprises, carried out all economic activities. Nowadays, the newly freed enterprises need government help to overcome the drawback of the deficiencies in factor markets. In this situation it is essential that enterprise reform is combined with the reform of the state itself.

Large problems remain in the state industrial sector in China, such as extensive overmanning and poor work performance, low product quality, continued support for the many loss-making enterprises, and continued evidence of 'investment hunger'. Furthermore, serious problems are raised by 'local state corporatism', especially persistent regional protectionism and extensive corruption in dealing between enterprises and state officials.[1] In 1994, the courts sentenced 20 186 culprits of corruption, including a Vice Minister, 28 bureau directors and 202 branch directors (*Beijing Review*, 27 March–2 April 1995, p. 6). This makes China's future not only economically but also politically so uncertain that one cannot exclude the possibility of the collapse of the Communist regime (Saito 1991).

Amsden finds that economic growth can change the nature of the state:

The Taiwan state, which appeared on its arrival from the Mainland to be an unlikely instrument for the promotion of development, proved to be a most effective one. At the same time, changes in the nature of the state itself appear to have been an important by-product of economic develop-ment. The state, in short, can be said both to have transformed Taiwan's economic structure and to have been transformed by it. (1985, p. 101)

After 16 years of reforms and miraculous growth, the Chinese government has not only transformed the economic structure, but has itself also 'been transformed by it'. Many different government agents, used to being components of the command system, have been reformed into a new mixed system. Some of them have been downgraded: for example, in 1994, the State Bureau of Price Management and the Ministry of Materials, extremely important agents of the planning regime, were incorporated separately into the State Planning Commission and the Ministry of Domestic Trade. Some of them have been commercialised as companies: for example, the former material and commerce distribution systems and most former industrial ministries have become companies. Some of them have been changed into professional social organisations: for example, the Ministry of Electronic Industry has given up all administrative control of enterprises and become an industrial association. Some of them have been combined with others: for example, with 'quota purchases' dramatically reduced, the Ministry of Grain, the Ministry of Trade and the General Commune of Supply and Sales have been merged into the new Ministry of Domestic Trade. Some new agents have been established: for example, the Commission for Security Supervision with authority over the newly established stock and future markets. There is a mushrooming of, in White's terms, 'quasi-state institutions' which are 'most often in the form of companies or corporations, designed to act as an intermediary between enterprises and state agencies proper ... They inhabit a new hybrid institutional world which is *neither fully state nor enterprise but a fusion of both*' (1991, p. 12, my emphases). Prominent examples are many labour service companies attached to local labour bureaux, six newly established investment companies attached to the Planning Commission, and many industrial trade companies established under the Ministry of Foreign Economic Co-operation and Trade. Meanwhile, there is a huge change in local governments and a large increase in the competence of Chinese officials at all levels of government. In short, the most noticeable fact is that China's outstanding growth in the last decade relied not only on enterprise reform but also reform of the government itself.

Both transition and growth in China are continuing. During this dynamic process, it is difficult to conclude which government agency ought to be closed, and which ought to be strengthened. It is a progressive process corresponding to the progressive process of enterprise reform. Typically the function of many 'quasi-state institutions' cannot be defined precisely or copied from a textbook. The combination of enterprise reform and government reform also is a process of 'groping for stones to cross the river'.

Since 'turning back the reel to the beginning' is not an option, China must explore a new way to survive. In other words, China should seek a new theoretical interpretation transcending conventional theory, in order to understand both the relatively successful past and the uncertain future.

Conclusion: Development Orientation versus Transitional Innovation

Why did China choose its own way to carry out the transition? What is the logical future of the Chinese 'gradual approach'?

DEVELOPMENT ORIENTATION

'Returning to Europe', as Sachs and Lipton have repeatedly stressed, is the clear slogan that guides reforms in many the East European countries (Sachs 1992a, p. 20; see also Sachs 1991, Sachs and Lipton, 1990, p. 46). Even the former Soviet Union had the same goal in mind (Soros 1990). Although the real economic systems in Western Europe are most unlike the simplified picture presented by Sachs and Kornai, that is the direction in which they intend to move.

Unfortunately, there is no 'Europe' for China to return to. Even though China has been heavily influenced by the West since 1978, there is no finite end for China's transition. 'Groping for stones to cross the river' becomes a symbol of ambiguity, because there is no clear conception about where the opposite bank is. Without a clear guideline, transition in China has been heavily led by a purely pragmatist philosophy: 'It does not matter whether the cat is black or white, as long as it can catch rats.' Deng Xiaoping's funny adage was the real guideline of policy-making. The well-known ideological debate in 1978 concluded that practical effects are the sole criterion of the truth.

Over the three decades before 1979, the Chinese people had been fanatically enthused by many idealist 'truths' and paid extraordinarily high prices for these fabulous ideas. In particular the ten-year 'Cultural Revolution' destroyed any belief in a Utopian goal. The ordinary Chinese people had already suffered greatly. With their painful experiences, the 'truth' for them was simply to be able continuously to improve their standards of living, including not only economic but also cultural and political aspects. They were tired of paying for the pursuit of something beautiful but painful. *It would also have been unfair to make them pay again.* It was worth trying to find a way which could avoid Sachs' 'valley of tears' which necessarily accompanies the big bang (Sachs 1991, 1992a, 1992b).

Both pragmatist philosophy and the desire of ordinary people meant that the transition in China followed the path of improving people's living standards step by step. Transition in China was started by the poorest peasants at the lowest grass-roots level. In the remote countryside, reform was their only way out of starvation. In this it differed from transition in the former Soviet Union where a great politician introduced the 'New Thinking' in the parliamentary building in the capital city. This important difference resulted in transition in China being a practical development issue rather than a form of political or ideological struggle.

The big-bang and privatisation protagonists, chiefly Sachs and Kornai, forcefully introduced their political outlook and ideological beliefs into the policy-making debates of economic system transition (Kornai 1990a; Lipton and Sachs 1990; Sachs and Lipton 1990). Kornai declared openly: 'In fact, I could call it may prejudice, since my opinion is clearly based on a value judgement' (1992a, p. 5). By contrast, in China, time and again, many policy-making debates were first conducted on the basis of initial experimentation, the practical consequences of which were then examined carefully. This method was the consequence of the absence of a clear political and ideological destination: 'Theory had nought to do with choice; the driving force was the replication of experience' (Murrell 1992, p. 90). This made the transition in China short-sighted. From a long-term view, China's reform is definitely at the 'halfway' stage. There is still a long way to go though the final destination is unclear. Some questions are, nevertheless, still crucial: Where is the end? What is a sufficient transition? What are the criteria for judging which direction, how far, when and how China should go? The theories of big bang and 'turning back the reel to the beginning' are poor guides. Those theories, especially the ones found in Kornai's book, *The Road to a Free Economy*, have difficulty in explaining why Japan (for example, Johnson 1982), South Korea (for example, Amsden 1989; Chang 1993), and Taiwan (for example, Wade 1990) are not still toddling in their 'halfway' stage to a free economy, or why they too do not need drastic 'surgery' in the form of the big-bang programme and privatisation by 'turning back the reel to the beginning'.

From a definitional point of view, like a multicoloured cat, Chinese reform is neither socialist nor capitalist, nor even the real 'third way' Market Socialism.[1] Perhaps China is 'groping for stones' to find its own way, which not only mixes the three in a muddle but also has been richly coloured by the progress of the newly industrialising countries of East Asia (Perkins 1986, 1991b; Nolan 1993). This muddle makes academic research a complex task. There is a long way to go before China reaches the end of its transition.

The question of how to improve living standards from poverty to affluence is more comprehensible than the question of how to transform the economy from heterodox planning to a textbook free market, perfectly-competitive economy. Perkins has characterised the essence of transition in China, as being so simple that many economists have overlooked it:

> Between 1984 and 1988 the Chinese labour force grew by 61.4 million people. Of that huge number, 48 million (78 per cent) were employed outside of agriculture. In 1989 and 1990 the labour force increased by 24.1 million and 18.5 million (77 per cent) had to be absorbed by agriculture. One uses the word absorbed rather than employed because one hundred million or more members of the agricultural labour force were already in some sense superfluous. By the year 2000 the Chinese labour force will increase by another 150 million people and China cannot afford politically to add three quarters of these to the surplus labour pool in the countryside. *To avoid this, China's GNP must grow at a rate that is at least six to eight per cent year.* But a high rate growth in an unreformed economy could re-trigger inflation followed by a renewed round of credit rationing. To avoid this kind of stop and go growth, China needs a market oriented financial system as well as a marketised industry. (1992, p. 26, my emphasis)

This is the reason why China could not stop the transition, no matter who won the political game. This is also the reason why China could not adopt the big bang and privatisation by 'turning back the reel to the beginning', which would be spectacular, but practically infeasible.

TRANSITIONAL INNOVATION

Development is a dynamic and time-consuming process. The transition unfolded in China as a 'gradual approach', which is also both a dynamic and time-consuming process. China has simply combined the gradual development process with the 'gradual approach' of transition. Introducing development issues into the transition is the key to understanding China's miraculous growth in the past and the failures elsewhere of the big-bang programme and privatisation by 'turning back the reel to the beginning'.

Two further points are worth emphasising. First, the word 'gradual' should not be understood as *slow*. For example, rural reform in China as early as the end of the 1970s was a really big bang. The 'household production responsibility system' cut all the farm land into tiny pieces and transferred them to individual peasant families. It went further than most East European countries and Russia have gone today in their rural reforms. The nature of the Chinese 'gradual approach' is not to carry out the transition slowly, but rather to carry out the transition carefully to *meet the needs of development*. For example, as discussed in Chapter 2, China did not implement price liberalisation but first adjusted the industrial structure, thus releasing the 'golden period of reform'. Once the existing excessively 'heavy' industry had shifted its production capability from heavy to light industries, previously scarce consumer goods became over-supplied. At that point, China decontrolled prices one by one from the situation of a buyer's market, thus causing the price of these goods to fall.

Second, the Chinese 'gradual approach' should not be understood as a 'slow approach', simply because *it does not have the same direction* as the big-bang programme and privatisation by 'turning back the reel to the beginning'. In Eastern Europe, transition means transforming a command economy to a market economy. *In China, transition means moving from being poor to becoming richer*. In Eastern Europe, Steinherr asserts: '*A market economy without private ownership is a body without a brain*, a beautiful and static Florentine David instead of the creativity of the Michelangelos one would like to see born' (1991, p. 4, italics in original). In China, Deng Xiaoping asserts: 'It does not matter whether the cat is black or white, as long as it can catch rats.' 'Groping for stones to cross the river', in order to meet the needs of development, is the real nature of the Chinese 'gradual approach' which takes no direction at all, but aims for growth of GNP. In contrast to Kornai, who states many times what he firmly believes in, the Chinese do not have a belief in mind except development. Therefore, China did not concern itself with what it *should* do, but rather with what it *could* do; it tried whatever measures would propel economic growth. For example, as discussed in Chapter 4, the Chinese government does not concern itself with whether local governments or enterprises themselves *should do* business. It is concerned only with what local governments and enterprises *are capable of doing*. Consequently, local authorities are deeply involved in business, playing the role of entrepreneurs.

The fact of progressing with no clear guideline gave the Chinese government the chance to make a lot of mistakes, *but also the opportunity to innovate*. In China, people concerned with policy-making considered and discussed all of Sachs' and Kornai's suggestions, including the big-bang programme and privatisation by 'turning back the reel to the beginning'. China did not adopt these radical measures, simply because they could not increase GNP. Under pressure to increase GNP, China created the notorious dual-track price system. The gamble was that, as was discussed in Chapter 2, growth itself could transform a command economy into a market one.

Fortunately, modern capitalist history also gradually evolved through Schumpeter's 'creative destruction' which essentially destroyed the old systems. In the process of capitalist evolution, the joint-stock company arising in the UK destroyed the traditional 'personal enterprise', thereby making large scale production possible. Then the Japanese got rid of ownership control through managers cross-holding shares in each other's firms, thereby enabling manager-controlled firms to put into practice the famous team work to intensify fierce 'excessive competition'. What the British in the nineteenth century and the Japanese in the twentieth century did was not implement the so-called 'second best', but to *beat* the previously existing 'best'. Many people now realise that feasible schemes of transition cannot be directly copied from textbooks. This means that the existing 'best' cannot be put into practice in the transition. What can one expect from the transition? In Poland, the minimum involvement of foreign investors and the low level of involvement of domestic private capital led to 'the domination of employee ownership in the pattern of companies created by way of the liquidation procedure' (Olko-Bajienska, Pankow and Ruszkowski 1992, p. 40). The Hungarian privatisation programme also encouraged employee share ownership (Bonin 1992, p. 721). Privatisation in Russia means that more than 70 per cent of large industrial enterprises with over 2000 employees appeared to be involved in 'management or employee buy-out' (Buck, Filatotchev and Wright 1993, p. 13). The consequences encouraged Hankiss to predict the logical outcome of privatisation in East Europe:

> when a state enterprise is transformed into a joint-stock company, shares are bought by other companies and banks. At the same time, the company in question buys share in these companies and banks. By this 'cross-ownership' an almost uncontrolled power is acquired by the managerial class, cross-owning and cross-protecting itself. (Quoted from Cui 1991, p. 9)

Considering what is happening in China's joint-stock companies where institutional share-holders dominate, ought we to imagine a future for transition in China in which it beats the existing 'best' by a new form of 'creative destruction'?

With the centre restructuring the state sector, grounded in the 'ownership maze' and 'local state corporatism', China with its 1.2 billion population has become the second largest country in terms of foreign capital inflow and the eleventh largest exporting country. The total trade of China, Hong Kong (which will be reunified with China in 1997) and Taiwan together exceeds Japans and accounts for 10 per cent of total world trade. If China, the centre and birthplace of Confucianism, survives successfully, then the experience of 'groping for stones to cross the river' may come to be seen as the latest example of 'creative destruction', which destroyed not only the old command system but also the theories of the big bang and 'turning back the reel to the beginning'.

Notes

Introduction: The Inconsistencies of the Big Bang

1. In 1989, the compensation received by employees from their employers was 65 per cent of total personal income in the USA (Ehrenberg and Smith 1991, p. 1) whereas, in Chinese cities, the same measurement was 98 per cent in 1982 (Li, Yang and He 1985, p. 18), because few people had personal incomes from private property in a socialist economy.

1 Why did China avoid the Big Bang?

1. Obviously profitability is determined by a variety of factors far beyond price distortions. My oversimplified assumption is simply for the sake of logical argument here.
2. Since the discussion here is about price liberalisation in general, the effects of substitution and different elasticity have been ignored.
3. Kornai also writes:

   In the case of a soft budget constraint the income effect does not materialise. If the firm has a demand for any input which is in shortage, it will buy that input in spite of the higher price. Where the increased costs cannot be covered within the limits of its budget constraint, it will sooner or later charge them to the buyer or the state. (1980, pp. 325–6, italics in original)

4. Erhardt's reform in 1948 in West Germany is always the example cited by proponents of big bang (Kornai 1990b, p. 90).
5. Kornai points out: '*the majority of our propositions concerned with responsiveness to price will be given as a function of the degree of hardness of the budget constraint*' (1980, p. 323, italics in original).
6. Compared with the former USSR, in 1980, 68 per cent of all hiring was done directly by enterprises or other units. In Russia in 1978, 16 per cent of all industrial manual workers left their jobs. This figure is close to that from American data for all full-time employees in manufacturing (Granick 1987, pp. 100–10).
7. According to the command economic system, statistics in China distinguish between 'productive' and 'non-productive' investment. 'Productive' investment does not include investment in education, medicine, social facilities, housing and tertiary industry, such as real estate, hotels or shopping malls.
8. From personal experiences when I worked for the Chinese Economic System Reform Research Institute (CESRRI) under the State Council's Committee for Restructuring Economic Systems, during 1985–9.
9. The two figures appeared in SSB (1988, 1989, 1990), but are different in SSB (1991): see Table 1.2.

10. 'RMB' is the name of the Chinese currency, 'Ren Min Bi'. All comparisons appearing thus, unless stated otherwise, are calculated at the exchange rate of eight RMB per US dollar.
11. Calculated from *Financial Times* [Chinese], 6 October 1991.
12. The Office of 'Eliminating Triangular-Debt' under the State Council declared that one unit of additional working fund injected could cancel 3.28 units of triangular debt from 15 August to 31 October 1991 (*Liberation Daily* [Chinese], 11 November 1991).
13. Similar price structures could also be found in other transitional economies (Blanchard, Dornbusch, Krugman, Layard and Summers 1991, pp. 14–17; Frydman and Wellisz 1991, p. 145; Kenen 1991, p. 251).
14. According to Lipton and Sachs, in Poland's big bang:

> Energy prices, which had fallen sharply in real terms over the course of 1989, shot up, with regulated coal and electricity prices rising between 300 and 600 per cent and gasoline and other petroleum prices freed from price controls. Apparently the energy price increases were swiftly passed through to final goods prices of industrial goods, distribution charges, and retail prices. (1990, p. 114)

15. For example, Poland's steel industry used 4.3 times as much energy as the world average (OECD, cited in Amsden 1992, p. 13).
16. Bleaney (1992) criticises the validity of the Lipton–Sachs model in theory and practice; see also Alexeev (1991).

2 'Groping for Stones to Cross the River': Price Reform in China

1. Many factors are responsible for the fall in output during transition. First, as discussed earlier, stabilisation reduced output rather than suppressed prices. Second, Sachs advocates that the fall in output in Eastern Europe is largely attributed to the collapse of the trade with the former Soviet Union (Sachs 1991, p. 28; Berry and Sachs 1992, pp. 153–5). My focus here is *only* on the industry which 'is vastly overgrown, as a result of the forty years of the Stalinist development model. It is therefore in need of substantial reduction in scale as well as restructuring and modernisation' (Sachs 1991, p. 28).
2. I am grateful to Nolan for suggesting this point here.
3. I am grateful to Nolan for suggesting the name which symbolises precisely this phase of price reform in China.
4. In China, all that Lipton and Sachs predicted has already occurred before their 'coming decade'. Beside a shift of production from heavy to light industry, services and housing construction also boomed before price liberalisation was completed (SSB 1991, p. 269).
5. Sachs asserts: 'The proper long-term solutions to the industrial sector problems are clear. The enterprises should be privatised, and then restructured under private control' (1991, p. 29).
6. The 'staff of the ministries' in the former Soviet Union numbered around 1.6 million in 1986 (Aslund 1991, p. 27).
7. Gomulka reckoned in 1989 that a shock programme in Poland would 'bring supply and demand into balance, and therefore reduce shortages. However,

they will be reduced not by any substantial increase in supplies but by demands falling to the levels of available supplies' (1989, p. 5).

8. This section is concerned with, but does not include, the issue of the interaction between the two markets, the planned and the parallel free market. There are theoretically three possibilities: first, according to the textbook, prices are determined by the marginal unit of demand and supply. Raising planned prices or releasing planned price control should not change the parallel market prices. Second, under the dual-track price system, market prices mainly met the demand of the non-state sector which was relatively small in the mid-1980s. Therefore, releasing planned price control could result in a significant price increase. Third, since demand for materials in the state sector was exaggerated by low planned prices, releasing planned price control ought to reduce this demand, thereby reducing market prices as well. There were few sophisticated analyses of this issue in China at that time. Parallel markets is an issue worthy of further study. I am grateful to Thoburn for recommending to me the papers written by Roemer (1986) and Azam and Besley (1989). Their papers, especially Roemer's, are helpful in understanding the dynamic of China's dual-track price system.

9. If we look back at Figure 2.2, the function of the new entrants with respect to the gradual dynamics of price liberalisation was genuinely constructive. The right end was the most profitable industry. As the new entrants crowded into the industries from right to left one by one, price liberalisation advanced.

10. Lardy argues correctly that the trade ratio is not an appropriate measure of the degree of openness of the Chinese economy, because of the changes in the official exchange rate. A comparison of growth rates of trade and GNP can reflect the openness more precisely (1992, pp. 150–5).

11. Calculated from SSB (1991), pp. 40, 230, at 1950 prices.

12. The highest growth rate of productivity in the USA was 2.25 per cent annually from 1959 to 1968, and in Japan it was 2.59 per cent from 1964 to 1973 (Okimoto and Saxonhouse 1987, p. 386).

13. See also the final section of Chapter 4.

14. It looks like a similar dual-track system in Korea. 'The argument that relative prices in Korea were distorted but in the right direction (that is, toward exports) is therefore itself distorted. Price were distorted in all directions in Korea – both for import substitutes and for exports – and often for one and the same product in the two categories' (Amsden 1989, p. 155).

15. Coal and crude oil accounted for 6.5 per cent of total exports in 1990 (SSB 1991, pp. 624, 616).

16. I am grateful to Adrian Wood and Dwight Perkins for giving me a view of both sides of this issue.

Introduction: The Self-Contradictory Privatisation

1. See Nolan (1993, ch. 6) for 'the impossibility of rapid privatisation and the possibility of improving state enterprises performance'. See Chang and Singh (1993, Section 6) for the practical problems of privatisation in general and in developing countries.

2. See Kornai (1990a), pp. 96–100 and 72; (1992b), pp. 461–511; Sachs and Lipton (1990), p. 47; Lipton and Sachs (1991), pp. 237–8.
3. These figures relate to aggregate values of all 'independent accounting' industrial enterprises, excluding those industrial enterprises which are sub-ordinates of non-industrial enterprises.
4. From experiences of privatisation in East Europe, Portes observes:

> The role and prospects of state-owned enterprises were under-estimated ... There was no coherent policy toward them, except to privatise as rapidly as possible or to make them fold by cutting off finance, so little thought went into trying consciously to modify their behaviour before privatisation. This trap was 'state desertion,' sometimes going so far as to involve explicit tax and other discrimination against state-owned enterprises *vis-à-vis* private firms ... Recent research suggests that many of the state-owned enterprises can in fact adapt, at least enough to warrant reconsidering policies that explicitly seek to starve them quickly. The key is to stop open-ended subsidies and to create incentives with the prospect of ultimate privatisation that will not necessarily involve sacking all managers. But in many countries comprehensive privatisation of state-owned enterprises is still not a prospect, and the examples of rapid privatisation in Czechoslovakia and Russia are at best problematic. (1994, p. 14)

> Pinto, Belka and Krajewski find: 'The focus in Poland has always been on rapid privatisation of manufacturing; restructuring state-owned enterprises and clarifying managerial accountability and rewards has received little attention' (1993, p. 4).

5. Pinto, Belka and Krajewski (1993) find that in Poland many felt that the only goal of the government in the transition was to destroy state-owned enterprises.

3 Transcending Private Ownership

1. Though there is no German equivalent of the Japanese *Keiretsu*, companies own over 40 per cent of German equities (*The Economist* 1994a, p. 8). The country's three major banks have long controlled around 60 per cent of the share capital of the larger companies (Drucker 1991, p. 107).
2. The theory of property rights treats the firm as long-term, complex and multiparty contractual (or contract-like) relationships. See, for example, Goldberg (1976, 1977); Williamson (1975, 1985), Wachter and Williamson (1978); Klein, Crawford and Alchian (1978); Alchian and Demsetz (1972, in Demsetz 1988); Cheung (1983); Jensen and Meckling (1976); Hart and Moore (1990); and Moore (1992).
3. The concept of 'entrepreneur' used here blurs the distinction between the concepts of 'ownership' and 'management'. In most literature about the principal–agency problem, and the issue of separation of ownership and control, the 'management' is opposed to the 'principal'. In this conceptualisation, managers are unlikely to be entrepreneurs. Manne defines disciplining management as an 'entrepreneurial job' (1965). Who, why, and how, should be the 'principal' has been heavily clouded by the existence of the dispersed,

changeable and non-voting shareholders. However, the concepts of 'property rights', 'residual claimant' and 'ownership' are still exclusively opposed to the concept of 'management'.

In fact, entrepreneurs stand out from ordinary money-makers, or 'residual claimants'. According to Schumpeter, most new firms 'are founded with an idea and for a definite purpose' (1939, p. 94). Hence, Penrose uses the term 'entrepreneur' in a functional sense to refer to:

Individuals or groups within the firm providing entrepreneurial services, whatever their position or occupational classification may be. Entrepreneurial services are those contributions to the operations of a firm which relate to the introduction and acceptance on behalf of the firm of new ideas, particularly with respect to products, location, significant changes in technology, to the acquisition of new managerial personnel, to fundamental changes in the administrative organisation of the firm, to the raising of capital, and to the making of plans for expansion, including the choice of method of expansion. Entrepreneurial services are contrasted with managerial services, which relate to the execution of entrepreneurial ideas and proposals and to the supervision of existing operations. The same individuals may, and more often than not probably do, provide both types of service to the firm. (1959, pp. 31–2, footnote 1)

Based on this definition, Best elaborates: 'The entrepreneur is an organiser, carrier, and/or implementer of new ideas ... The entrepreneur is not driven to maximise profits by substituting amongst homogeneous factors of production for a given product, but to revolutionise existing product designs, production processes, and organisational forms.' He terms the Japanese firm (the typical manager-controlled firm) the 'entrepreneurial firm' (Best 1990, p. 120 and ch. 5).

4. Smith warns:

The directors of such companies, however, being the managers rather of other people's money than of their own, it cannot well be expected that they should watch over it with the same anxious vigilance with which the partners in a private copartnery frequently watch over their own. Like the stewards of a rich man, they are apt to consider attention to small matters as not for their master's honour, and very easily give themselves a dispensation from having it. Negligence and profusion, therefore, must always prevail, more or less, in the management of the affairs of such a company. It is upon this account that joint stock companies for foreign trade have seldom been able to maintain the competition against private adventurers. (1937 [1776], Vol. 2, p. 229)

5. Berle and Means comment:

In examining the break up of the old concept that was property and the old unity that was private enterprise, it is therefore evident that we are dealing not only with distinct but often with opposing groups, ownership on the one side, control on the other – a control which tends to move further and further away from ownership and ultimately to lie in the hands of the management itself, a management capable of perpetuating its own position. (1967, p. 116)

6. Having analysed the difference between shareholders and bondholders, Alchian and Demsetz (1972, in Demsetz 1988) find:

> If we treat bondholders, preferred and convertible preferred stockholders, and common stockholders and warrant holders as simply different classes of investors – differing not only in their risk averseness but in their beliefs about the probability distribution of the firm's future earnings, why should stockholders be regarded as 'owners' in any sense distinct from the other financial investors? The entrepreneur-organiser, who let us assume is the chief operating officer and sole repository of control of the corporation, does not find his authority residing in common stockholders (except in the case of a take over).

They emphasise: 'Non-voting share holders were simply investors devoid of ownership connotations' (in Demsetz 1988, pp. 126–7 and footnote 14).

7. Fama understood this from a different direction: 'However, ownership of capital should not be confused with ownership of the firm ... Unless the bonds are risk free, the risk bearing function is in part borne by the bondholders, and ownership of capital is shared by bondholders and stockholders' (1980, p. 291). Risk bearing, nevertheless, cannot explain who owns Japanese cross-holding firms, and neither can it explain whether stockholders will bear the risks of changes of stock prices or changes of enterprise performances, as the two are highly disconnected. In Japan, dividend payout is often fixed. So Abegglen and Stalk ask: *'Does the shareholder own the Japanese company?'* (1985, p. 183, italics in original). If we are talking about the function, not the name, of ownership, as long as shareholders are not entrepreneurs who actually operate the firm, they are share traders. They trade their shares rather than own the firm.

8. According to the 'efficient market theory', because share prices reflect all available information, there is no point in investors trying to 'beat the market' by searching for firms whose shares will outperform others in future. Instead, an investor should reduce firm-specific risk by diversifying across a wide range of shares. See Schall (1972); Mossin (1973); Fama (1970, 1976); and Jensen (1978). For criticisms, see Grossman and Stiglitz (1976), Stiglitz (1981).

9. For example, in the ten largest firms in the *Fortune* 500 in 1975, the average share of stock owned by managers over ten years was only slightly over 2 per cent. But an average of 20 firms (ten in the middle and ten at the bottom of the 500 list) reveals that corporate managers owned about 20 per cent of outstanding shares (Demsetz 1988, p. 199). Also Lewellen (1969) calculates managers' remuneration for the 55 largest US manufacturing firms from 1940 to 1963. He finds that stock-based compensation for the top executives exceeded their after-tax wages four times, and for the top five executives it was almost five times as large as their wages.

10.　According to the 1981 Survey of Corporations by the National Tax Agency, the total expense accounts of all corporations come to US$3.1 trillion in 1980, equal to 13.3 per cent of total profits and exceeding the total dividends payout which amounted only to 9.8 per cent of total profits (Aoki 1987, p. 622).

11.　For example, Larner (1966); Kamerschen (1968); Monsen, Chiu and Cooley (1968); Lewellen (1969); Demsetz and Lehn (1985, in Demsetz 1988).

12.　Small and medium-sized enterprises in Japanese manufacturing are defined as having less than 300 employees and less than 100 million yen in capital. Small enterprises in manufacturing are those with 20 or less employees and 10 million yen or less in capital (Small and Medium Enterprise Agency 1986, cited in Best 1990, p. 240, footnote 1).

13.　The duration of employment tends to be relatively long for Japanese workers. See Hashimoto and Raisian (1985); Mincer and Higuchi (1988).

14.　Enterprise-based Japanese unions are commonly viewed as weak, with a negligible or even negative effect on wages (Kalleberg and Lincoln 1988; Freeman and Rebick 1989), and as co-operative with management (Koike 1987). Muramatsu (1983) finds that Japanese unions do indeed increase productivity. Nevertheless, by using data on 979 union and non-union Japanese manufacturers, Brunello (1992) finds unions reduced both productivity and profitability, although they also reduced regular wages.

15.　Many have criticised hostile take-overs:

> Even if it were true that individual firms (and their shareholders) benefited from a hostile take-over, the threat of one could push managers in all firms to sacrifice long-term performance to boost their short-run share price – a common complaint in America and Britain. Prices, after all, reflect not the fundamental values of firms but simply the changing moods and prejudices of investors. So firms could be taken over, and bosses fired, not because they are doing badly but because the market mis-prices the firms' shares. Bosses who fear that they will not be judged on merit therefore try to keep their share price high rather than to maximise long-term shareholder value. (*The Economist* 1994a, p. 12)

16.　What managers want remains a topic beyond pure economics analysis but worth exploring further, because it links directly with the firm's growth. In the USA, Monsen and Downs (1965) suggest that the self-interest of managers in managerial-oriented firms lies in maximising the managers' life-time income. The concept of 'life-time income' is a long-term expectation linked with the firm's growth. Clarke (1987) finds that managers tend to go for growth maximisation simply for 'risk-reducing reasons'. Further more, from a series of empirical studies on take-over, Singh (1971, 1975b) finds that the motivation of power is very important. Managers are pursuing power, so they expand firms more and more. Drucker finds: 'In Europe and Japan, stock ownership is a means to non-financial ends ... The *keiretsu's* first concern is power – power in the market, power over suppliers and subcontractors, power and influence with ministries and civil servants' (1991, p. 107).

17. Chandler also concludes:

> In making administrative decisions, career managers preferred policies that favoured the long-term stability and growth of their enterprises to those that maximised current profits. For salaried managers the continuing existence of their enterprises was essential to their lifetime careers. Their primary goal was to assure continuing use of and therefore continuing flow of material to their facilities. They were far more willing than were the owners (the stockholders) to reduce or even forego current dividends in order to maintain the long-term viability of their organisations. They sought to protect their sources of supplies and their outlets. They took on new products and services in order to make more complete use of existing facilities and personnel. Such expansion, in turn, led to the addition of still more workers and equipment. If profits were high, they preferred to reinvest them in the enterprise rather than pay them out in dividends. In this way the desire of the managers to keep the organisation fully employed became a continuing force for its further growth. (1977, p. 10)

18. Penrose identifies various endogenous pressures for growth of the firm. She further distinguishes the conceptual difference between 'economies of size' and 'economies of expansion'. The latter, including, for example, new products, is identical with Schumpeter's innovation.

> The great prestige of the large firm rests on its ability to explore, to experiment, and to innovate; it is this ability, together with the market position (carefully cultivated by advertising) that its reputation, and the reputation of its products, can command, which give rise to many of its economies of expansion. (1959, p. 262)

> Standing within the same line, Best (1990) terms the Japanese firm the 'entrepreneurial firm'. Takahashi (1983) terms the Japanese firm the 'expansively entrepreneurial firm'.

19. Before the Second World War, Japanese ownership structure was similar to the American one (Johnson 1982; Takahashi 1983; CESRRI-d 1988).

20. For criticisms of this misleading concept of 'soft budget constraint', see Chang (1994); Chang and Singh (1993).

21. Pratten estimates that the equivalent of 30 per cent of total share volume was traded in 1989 in the UK (1993, p. 2). This implies that the average owner's association with one firm is little more than three years. In China, the owner's association with a firm is even shorter. In 1990, 85 043 340 shares of five public companies were traded in the Shenzhen stock market. The five companies issued a total of 80 656 450 shares. This indicates that every owner has changed 1.06 times within one year. In other words, the average period that a owner stays at each firm is 11 months (calculated from Jin, Xiao and Xu 1991, pp. 20–60, 105).

22. In Japanese team work, 'employees are network-specific assets'. 'Corporate decisions would have an impact on workers' short-term and long-term positions in the rank hierarchies that define their life-time earnings' (Aoki 1990, p. 19).

23. Tsuru states a different schedule: 'The actual move for privatisation began, as stated earlier, in the spring of 1981 and took four (for the Nikon Telephone and Telegraph Company) to six (for the Nikon National Railroad) years for consummation' (1993, p. 207).

24. The Exchange requirements are:

   (1) Net assets must be twice as large as paid-in-capital; (2) Both current and pre-tax profits in the financial period immediately before listing must be more than 40 per cent of paid-in-capital and more than 30 per cent of paid-in-capital in the two preceding periods; (3) A dividend must have been paid in the immediately receding period; (4) The company must have been in business continuously for at least five years. (Fukui 1992, p. 14)

25. A total of only 1 050 employees, 11.7 per cent of the total redundant workers, were ultimately dismissed because they refused to move to newly allotted placements offered by both the public and private sector (Fukui 1992).

26. Privatisations in the UK also 'have kept public sector management teams intact' (Filatotchev, Buck and Wright 1992, p. 508). See also Veljanovski (1992).

27. For other similar examples in developing countries, see Chang and Singh (1993); Bienen and Waterbury (1989); Vernon-Wortzel and Wortzel (1989).

28. In Taiwan, privatisation was first proposed in the mid-1980s. Up to 1992, in all privatised state enterprises, the government was still the largest single shareholder (Baum 1992).

4 'Groping for Stones to Cross the River': Enterprise Reform in China

1. It is interesting to compare this with Taiwan.

   By the early 1980s, the share of the public sector in manufacturing production had fallen to less than 20 per cent. Nevertheless, the government remains dominant in such fields as heavy machinery, steel, aluminium, shipbuilding, petroleum, synthetics, fertilisers, engineering, and, recently, semiconductors. Almost every bank in Taiwan is also wholly or partially owned by the state (foreign banks were not allowed to establish operations until 1969). The lending activities of all financial institutions have been under strict state supervision. (Amsden 1985, pp. 91–2; see also Wade 1990, pp. 159–82)

2. There was a similar story in Taiwan too:

   Although the state's share of gross domestic investment has fallen from a high of 62 per cent in 1958, it still amounted in 1980 to as much as 50 per cent. State spending has gone largely to finance ten major development projects in infrastructure, integrated steel, shipbuilding, and petrochemicals, which contributes to the fact that manufacturing in Taiwan has progressed in breadth (the percentage of manufacturing in GDP) and in depth (the percentage of 'sophisticated' products and processes in total manufacturing output). (Amsden 1985, p. 93)

   In the period 1975–8, Taiwan government investment stood at about 30 per cent of GNP (Wade 1990, p. 173).

3. This section draws heavily on Nolan's work (1993, 1994).
4. By October 1988, 93 per cent of large and medium size enterprises and 83 per cent of enterprise under government budget had adopted the contract responsibility system (*People's Daily* [Chinese], 2 November 1988). See Lee (1990) for an analysis on a variety of this system in detail, Koo, Li and Peng (1993) for an evolutionary process, and Byrd (1992) for a case study.
5. Demsetz comments:

   De facto management ownership and limited liability combine to minimise the overall cost of operating large enterprises. Shareholders are essentially lenders of equity capital and not owners, although they do participate in such infrequent decisions as those involving mergers. What shareholders really own are their shares and not the corporation. Ownership in the sense of control again becomes a largely individual affair. The shareholders own their shares, and the president of the corporation and possibly a few other top executives control the corporation. (1988, p. 114)

6. See Singh (1990) for a similar suggestion. In 1985 Ji and I doubted the logic of ownership in general, and suggested there was something to learn from the extraordinary ownership structure of Japanese firms, in which (no matter whether they are public or private) ownership is impotent (Wang and Ji 1988). Technically, in 1985, state enterprises had no autonomy in product pricing. One could not expect too much from any kind of ownership change. Now I agree with Wood that ownership reform is a necessary weapon to change the sole owner-manager situation, thus yielding managerial autonomy.
7. By 1992, foreigners and overseas Chinese had already set aside US$2 billion for Chinese stocks (Kaye and Cheng 1992, p. 48).
8. Weitzman and Xu (1994) term township-village enterprises 'vaguely defined co-operatives'. Murrell and Wang use the term 'private ownership' in the sense of absence of ownership and control by the state (1993, p. 1).
9. An earlier survey shows that more than 80 per cent of managers of township-village enterprises were appointed by local governments (Song 1990, p. 399).
10. Also see Oi (1988, 1989) in detail. Others have drawn similar analyses from local government and business entities. See Wong (1987, 1992); articles in Byrd and Lin (1990); Walder (1992, 1994).
11. The analyses of this section draw heavily on the work of Lodge (1990) and Best (1990).
12. A survey carried out by the *Harvard Business Review* of 11 678 managers in 25 countries asks whether there should be free trade between nations, along with minimal protection for domestic firms. In reply, 78 per cent of American managers agreed that there should, as did 95 per cent of German, 86 per cent of Japanese, and 83 per cent of British managers. In America especially, however, that free-trade facade swiftly cracks. Of American managers, 60 per cent believed their government should 'give preference to' domestic firms when deciding what to buy; 74 per cent reckoned the government should 'actively help' those firms to succeed internationally; and 38 per cent wanted limits on foreign ownership of corporate assets. 'What of Japan? On paper, it looks to be the country most committed to free trade – only nine per cent of Japanese managers, for instance, believed

that their government should prefer to buy from Japanese companies' (Kanter 1991).

13. MITI sponsored 20, the Ministry of Finance 14, other ministries the rest (Lodge 1990, p. 50).

14. Blinder says: 'Japanese businesses seek profits, to be sure, but not for their stockholders. They want them, instead, as the wellspring of growth, which they see as an integral part of nation-building' (1990, p. 9).

15. Of course, international competition is always disturbed by government activities. That is a different issue from what we are discussing.

16. For related discussions, see Amsden (1985); Wade (1990); Duvall and Freeman (1981, 1983); Evans, Rueschemeyer and Skocpol (1988); Krasner (1978); and Skocpol (1979).

17. I use these terms here only analytically. For the different definitions of the concepts, see Johnson (1982); Duvall and Freeman (1983); White and Wade (1985); Wade (1990); White (1988); Blecher (1991); and Oi (1988, 1989 and 1992).

18. In Taiwan, the legacies of Japanese colonialism, the Chinese civil war, the Kuomingtang's autocratic rule, and US support to foster a strong anti-Communist regime all contributed to the formation and persistence of an autonomous and powerful state (Amsden 1979, 1985; Hamilton 1983; Gold 1986). See Chang (1994) for the Korean 'hard state'.

19. See Amsden (1989, ch. 12) for details.

20. See Amsden (1989) and Chang (1993, 1994) for a similar banking system in Korea.

21. Wade also calls the Taiwanese government 'state corporatism' (1990, pp. 294–5).

22. Decentralisation is another highly debated issue even before Chinese reform has been processed. See Schurmann (1968); Meisner and Blecher (1982); White (1983); Solinger (1984); and Ness and Raichur (1983).

23. The original dedication of corporatism, for example, Schmitter defines as:

> A system of interest representation in which the constituent units are organised into a limited number of singular, compulsory, non-competitive, hierarchically ordered and functionally differentiated categories, recognised or licensed (if not created) by the state and granted a deliberate representational monopoly within their respective categories in exchange for observing certain controls on their selections of leaders and articulation of demands and supports. (1974, pp. 93–4)

Fewsmith uses a version of Schmitter's understanding of corporatism to describe China during the Republican period (1985). Oi uses the concept of 'corporatism' differently from its use in previous studies. 'By local state corporatism I refer to the workings of a *local* government that co-ordinates economic enterprises in its territory as if it were a diversified business corporation' (1992, p. 100, italics in original; also see Oi 1988, 1989). It is worth mentioning that for the same emphasis on state activism, Harris identifies the 'state-organised economy' of Britain in the 1930s and 1940s as corporatism, in which the state re-organised the domestic economy by means of tight import controls to protect a domestic monopoly of the market, and exchange controls to force British finance into investment in Britain (1986, pp. 155–6). Wade prefers to call the European form 'social corporatism', in order 'to distinguish it from Taiwan's "state corporatism", the principal criterion being the balance of power between the state and interest groups'. According to his interpretation: 'The "state corporatist" power structure has facilitated the government's efforts to pursue a "leadership" role in important industries, rather than simply a "followship" role' (1990, p. 295).

Conclusion to Part II: Government Reform is Another Core

1. Co-operation of government and business in Japan, Korea and Taiwan also contained corruption: see Johnson (1982); Amsden (1989); Wade (1990); Chang (1993).

Conclusion: Development Orientation versus Transitional Innovation

1. Singh points out interestingly: 'In contrast with the Mao era, the main focus of the post-Mao Chinese leadership is clearly not socialism as such but the development of the "forces of production", or more specifically the "four modernisations" adumbrated by Deng Xiaoping a decade ago' (1990, p. 175).

Bibliography

English Works Cited

Abegglen, James C. and George Stalk, Jr (1985) *Kaisha: The Japanese Corporation* (New York: Basic Books).

Abramovitz, Moses (1989) *Thinking about Growth and Other Essays on Economic Growth and Welfare* (Cambridge: Cambridge University Press).

Albouy, Yves (1991) 'Coal pricing in China: Issues and reform strategy', *World Bank Discussion Papers*, No. 138.

Alexeev, Michael (1991) 'If market clearing prices are so good then why doesn't (almost) anybody want them?', *Journal of Comparative Economics*, Vol. 15, pp. 380–90.

Amsden, Alice A. (1979) 'Taiwan's economic history: A case of Etatisme and a challenge to dependency theory', *Modern China*, Vol. 5, No. 3, pp. 341–79.

Amsden, Alice A. (1985). 'The state and Taiwan's economic development', in Peter B. Evans, Dietrich Rueschemeyer and Theda Skocpol (eds), *Bringing the State Back In* (Cambridge: Cambridge University Press), pp. 78–106.

Amsden, Alice A. (1989) *Asia's Next Giant: South Korea and Late Industrialisation* (New York and Oxford: Oxford University Press).

Amsden, Alice A. (1992) 'Can Eastern Europe compete by "getting the prices right?"' *Working Papers Series*, No. 37, The Graduate Faculty of Political Economy, New School for Social Research.

Amsden, Alice A., Jacek Kochanowicz and Lance Taylor (1994) *The Market Meets its Match: Re-industrialising Eastern Europe* (Cambridge, Mass.: Harvard University Press).

Aoki, Masahiko (1987) 'The Japanese firm in transition', in Kozo Yamamura and Yasukichi Yasuba (eds), *The Political Economy of Japan*, Vol. 1 (Stanford: Stanford University Press), pp. 263–88.

Aoki, Masahiko (1990) 'Toward an economic model of the Japanese firm', *Journal of Economic Literature*, No. 28, pp. 1–27.

Aoki, Masahiko (1994) 'The Japanese firm as a system of attributes: A survey and research agenda', in Masahiko Aoki and Ronald Dore (eds), *The Japanese Firm: The Sources of Competitive Strength* (Oxford: Oxford University Press), pp. 11–40.

Aslund, Anders (1991) 'Gorbachev, Perestroyka, and economic crisis', *Problems of Communism*, January–April, pp. 18–41.

Azam, Jean-Paul and Timothy Besley (1989) 'General equilibrium with parallel markets for goods and foreign exchanges: Theory and application to Ghana', *World Development*, Vol. 17, No. 12, pp. 1921–30.

Balassa, Bela (1985) *Change and Challenge in the World Economy* (London: Macmillan).

Balassa, Bela (1987) 'China's economic reforms in a comparative perspective', in Bruce L. Reynolds (ed.), *Chinese Economic Reform: How Far, How Fast?* (Boston, Mass.: Academic Press), pp. 120–36.

Baum, Julian (1992) 'On the block: Taiwan's sell-off of state assets gathers momentum', *Far Eastern Economic Review*, 23 January, p. 55.

Baumol, J. William (1968) 'Entrepreneurship in economic theory', *American Economic Review*, Vol. 58, No. 2, pp. 64–71.

BBC Monitoring (1992–3) *Summary of World Broadcasts* (London: British Broadcasting Corporation).

Berle, Adolf A. and Gardiner C. Means (1967) [1932] *The Modern Corporation and Private Property*, rev. edn (New York: Harcourt, Brace & World).

Berry, Andrew and Jeffrey Sachs (1992) 'Structural adjustment and international trade in Eastern Europe: The case of Poland', *Economic Policy*, Issue 14, pp. 117–74.

Best, Michael H. (1990) *The New Competition: Institutions of Industrial Restructuring* (Cambridge: Polity Press).

Bienen, Henry and John Waterbury (1989) 'The political economy of privatisation in developing countries', *World Development*, Vol. 17, No. 5, pp. 617–32.

Bishop, Matthew R. and John A. Kay (1989) 'Privatisation in the United Kingdom: Lessons from experience', *World Development*, Vol. 17, No. 5, pp. 643–57.

Blanchard, Olivier, Rudiger Dornbusch, Paul Krugman, Richard Layard and Lawrence Summers (1991) *Reform in Eastern Europe* (London: MIT Press)

Bleaney, Michael (1992) 'Why is there a tendency to excess demand in consumer goods markets in planned economies?', *Economics of Planning*, No. 25, pp. 237–46.

Blecher, Marc (1991) 'Developmental state, entrepreneurial state: The political economy of socialist reform in Xinju Municipality and Guanghan County', in Gordon White (ed.), *The Chinese State in the Era of Economic Reform: The Road to a Crisis* (London: Macmillan Press), pp. 265–91.

Blinder, Alan (1990) 'There are capitalists, then there are the Japanese', *Business Week*, 8 October, p. 9.

Boltho, Andrea (1975) *Japan: An Economic Survey, 1953–73* (Oxford: Oxford University Press).

Bonin, John P. (1992) 'Privatisation and efficient contracts: The workers' stake in the transition', *Journal of Comparative Economics*, Vol. 16, pp. 716–32.

Brechling, F.P.R. and R.G. Lipsey (1963) 'Trade credit and monetary policy', *Economic Journal*, Vol. 73, No. 4, pp. 619–41.

Brunello, Giorgio (1992) 'The effect of unions on firm performance in Japanese manufacturing', *Industrial and Labour Relations Review*, Vol. 45, No. 3, pp. 471–87.

Bruno, Michael (1994) 'Our assistance includes ideas as well as money', *Transition*, Vol. 5, No. 1, pp. 1–4.

Bruno, Michael and Jeffrey Sachs (1985) *Economics of World-Wide Stagflation* (Oxford: Basil Blackwell)

Buck, Trevor, Igor Filatotchev and Mike Wright (1993) 'Buy-outs and the transformation of Russian industry', *Discussion Papers*, School of Management and Finance, University of Nottingham.

Byrd, William (1987) 'The role and impact of markets', in Gene Tidrick and Chen Jiyuan (eds), *China's Industrial Reforms* (Oxford: Oxford University Press), pp. 237–75.

Byrd, William (1988) 'The impact of the two-tier plan/market system in Chinese industry', in Bruce L. Reynolds (ed.), *Chinese Economic Reform: How Far, How Fast?* (Boston, Mass.: Academic Press) pp. 5–18.

Byrd, William A. (1990) 'Entrepreneurship, capital and ownership', in William A. Byrd and Lin Qingsong (eds), *China's Rural Industry: Structure, Development, and Reform* (Oxford and New York: Oxford University Press), pp. 189–218.

Byrd, William A. (1991) *The Market Mechanism and Economic Reforms in China* (Armonk, NY and London: M.E. Sharpe).

Byrd, William A. (ed.) (1992) *Chinese Industrial Firms under Reform* (Oxford: Oxford University Press).

Byrd, William A. and Lin Qingsong (eds) (1990) *China's Rural Industry: Structure, Development, and Reform* (Oxford and New York: Oxford University Press).

Byrd, William and Gene Tidrick (1984) 'Adjustment and reform in the Chongqing Clock and Watch Company', *World Bank Staff Working Paper*, No. 652.

Byrd, William and Gene Tidrick (1987) 'Factor allocation and enterprise incentives', in Gene Tidrick and Chen Jiyuan (eds), *China's Industrial Reforms* (Oxford: Oxford University Press), pp. 60–120.

Byrd, William and N. Zhu (1990) 'Market interactions and industrial structure', in William A. Byrd and Lin Qingsong (eds), *China's Rural Industry: Structure, Development and Reform* (New York and Oxford: Oxford University Press), pp. 85–111.

Calvo, Guillermo A. and Fabrizio Coricelli (1992) 'Stagflationary effects of stabilisation programs in reforming Socialist countries: Enterprise-side and household-side factors', *World Bank Economic Review*, Vol. 6, No. 1, pp. 71–90.

Chan, Steve (1987) 'The mouse that roared: Taiwan's management of trade relations with the United States', *Comparative Political Studies*, Vol. 20, No. 3, pp. 251–92.

Chandler, Alfred D. Jr (1977) *The Visible Hand: The Managerial Revolution in American Business* (Cambridge, Mass.: Harvard University Press).

Chandler, Alfred D., Jr (1992) 'What is a firm? A historical perspective', *European Economic Review*, Vol. 36, pp. 483–92.

Chang, Ha-joon (1993) 'The political economy of industrial policy in Korea', *Cambridge Journal of Economics*, Vol. 17, No. 2, pp. 131–57.

Chang, Ha-joon (1994) *The Political Economy of Industrial Policy* (London: Macmillan).

Chang, Ha-joon and Ajit Singh (1993) 'Public enterprises in developing countries and economic efficiency – A critical examination of analytical, empirical, and policy issues', *UNCTAD Review 1993*, No. 4 (Geneva: United Nations Conference on Trade and Development).

Chen, K., Gary H. Jefferson, Thomas G. Rawski, Wang Hongchang and Zheng Yuxin (1988) 'New estimates of fixed investment and capital stock for Chinese state industry', *China Quarterly*, No. 114, pp. 243–66.

Chen, K., Gary H. Jefferson and Inderjit Singh (1992) 'Lessons from China's economic reform', *Journal of Comparative Economics*, No. 16, pp. 210–25.

Chen Yizi, Wang Xiao-qian and Colleagues (1988) 'Reform: Results and lessons from the 1985 CESRRI survey', in Bruce L. Reynolds (ed.), *Chinese Economic Reform: How Far, How Fast?* (Boston, Mass.: Academic Press), pp. 172–88.

Chenery, Hollis, Sherman Robinson and Moshe Syrquin (1988) *Industrialisation and Growth: A Comparative Study* (Oxford: Oxford University Press).

Cheng, Elizabeth (1992) 'Welcome back: Foreign institutions snap up China's B shares', *Far Eastern Economic Review*, January, p. 39.

Cheung, Steven N.S. (1983) 'The contractual nature of the firm', *Journal of Law and Economics*, Vol. 26, pp. 1–21.

Clarke, Roger (1987) 'Conglomerate firms', in Roger Clarke and Tony McGuinness (eds), *The Economics of the Firm* (Oxford: Basil Blackwell), pp. 107–32.

Crawford, Paul (1992) 'A survey of the trade credit literature', *Discussion Paper*, No. 92/324, Department of Economics, University of Bristol.

Cui Zhiyuan (1991) 'Reflections on Eastern European Transformation: Compared with China', *China Report*, Vol. 2.

Dalton, Melville (1959) *Men who Manage: Fusion of Feeling and Theory in Administration* (New York, London and Sydney: John Wiley & Sons).

Day, H. Richard, Wang Zhigang and Zou Gang (1991) 'A dynamic analysis of Chinese enterprise behaviour under alternative reform', mimeograph.

Demsetz, Harold (1988) *Ownership, Control, and the Firm: The Organisation of Economic Activity*, Vol. 1 (Oxford: Basil Blackwell).

Dore, Ronald (1987) *Taking Japan Seriously: A Confucian Perspective on Leading Economic Issues* (Stanford: Stanford University Press).

Dornbusch, Rudiger and Stanley Fischer (1991) *Macroeconomics*, 4th edn (New York: McGraw-Hill).

Drucker, Peter F. (1991) 'Reckoning with the pension fund revolution', *Harvard Business Review*, Vol. 69, No. 2, pp. 106–14.

Duch, M. Raymond (1991) *Privatising the Economy: Telecommunications policy in Comparative Perspective* (Ann Arbor: University of Michigan Press).

Duvall, Raymond D. and John R. Freeman (1981) 'The state and dependent capitalism', *International Studies Quarterly*, Vol. 25, No. 1, pp. 99–118.

Duvall, Raymond D. and John R. Freeman (1983) 'The techno-bureaucratic elite and the entrepreneurial state in dependent industrialisation', *American Political Science Review*, Vol. 77, pp. 569–87.

The Economist (1991a) 'Japan's industrial structure: Inside the charmed circle', 5 January, p. 54.

The Economist (1991b) 'Eastern Germany's energy industry enters a new era', 23 February, p. 62.

The Economist (1991c) 'Soviety economic reforms: Plenty of shock, no therapy', 27 April, p. 71.

The Economist (1992) 'China: The titan stirs', 28 November, pp. 3–22.

The Economist (1994a) 'Corporate governance', 29 January, pp. 3–18.

The Economist (1994b) 'Picking losers in Japan', 26 February, p. 91.

Ehrenberg, Ronald G. and Robert S. Smith (1991) *Modern Labour Economics: Theory and Public Policy* (New York: HarperCollins).

Evans, Peter B., Dietrich Rueschemeyer and Theda Skocpol (eds) (1988) *Bringing the State Back In* (Cambridge: Cambridge University Press).

Fama, Eugene F. (1970) 'Efficient capital markets: A review of theory and empirical work', *Journal of Finance*, Vol. 25, No. 2, pp. 383–417.

Fama, Eugene F. (1976) *Foundation of Finance: Portfolio Decisions and Securities Prices* (Oxford: Basic Books).

Fama, Eugene (1980) 'Agency problems and the theory of the firm', *Journal of Political Economy*, Vol. 88, pp. 288–307.

Fama, Eugene F. and Merton H. Miller (1972) *The Theory of Finance* (Hinsdale, Ill.: Dryden Press).

Ferguson, R. Paul (1992) 'Privatisation options for Eastern Europe: The irrelevance of Western experience', *World Economy*, Vol. 5, No. 4, pp. 487–504.

Fewsmith, Joseph (1985) *Party, State and Local Elite in Republican China: Merchant Organisations and Politics in Shanghai, 1890–1930* (Honolulu: University of Hawaii Press).

Filatotchev, Igor, Trevor Buck and Mike Wright (1992) 'Privatisation and entrepreneurship in the break-up of the USSR', *World Economy*, Vol. 15, No. 4, pp. 505–24.

Foreman-Peck, James and Robert Millward (1994) *Public and Private Ownership of British Industry, 1820–1990* (Oxford: Clarendon Press).

Freeman, Richard B. and Marcus E. Rebick (1989) 'Crumbling pillar? Declining union density in Japan', *Journal of the Japanese and International Economies*, Vol. 3, No. 4, pp. 578–605.

Frydman, Roman and Stanislaw Wellisz (1991) 'The ownership-control structure and the behaviour of Polish enterprises during the 1990 reforms: Macroeconomic measurers and microeconomic responses', in Vittorio Corbo, Fabrizio Coricelli and Jan Bossak (eds), *Reforming Central and Eastern European Economies: Initial Results and Challenges* (Washington, DC: World Bank), pp. 141–56.

Fukui, Koichiro (1992) 'Japanese National Railways privatisation study: The experience of Japan and lessons for developing countries', *World Bank Discussion Paper*, No. 172.

Gao Shangquan, Chen Yizi and Wang Xiao-qiang (1988) 'Investigation of reforms in Hungary and Yugoslavia', *Chinese Economic Studies*, Vol. 22, No. 3, pp. 80–8.

Gerlach, Michael L. (1992) *Alliance Capitalism: The Social Organisation of Japanese Business* (Berkeley, Los Angeles and Oxford: University of California Press).

Gescher, Jeanne-Marie C. (1990) 'A legal opinion', *China Trade Report*, Vol. 28, pp. 6–7.

Gold, Thomas B. (1986) *State and Society in the Taiwan Miracle* (Armonk, NY: M.E. Sharpe).

Goldberg, Victor P. (1976) 'Relation and administered contracts', *Bell Journal of Economics*, Vol. 7, No. 2, pp. 426–8.

Goldberg, Victor P. (1977) 'Competitive bidding and production of pre-contract information', *Bell Journal of Economics*, Vol. 8, No. 1, pp. 250–61.

Goldberg, Victor P. (1980) 'Relational exchange: Economics and complex contracts', *American Behavioural Scientist*, Vol. 23, No. 3, pp. 337–52.

Gomulka, Stanislae (1989) 'Shock needed for Polish economy', *The Guardian*, 15 August, p. 5.

Gordon, Robert A. (1961) *Business Leadership in the Large Corporation* (Washington, DC: Brookings Institution)

Granick, David (1987) 'The industrial environment in China and the CMEA countries', in Gene Tidrick and Chen Jiyuan (eds), *China's Industrial Reforms* (Oxford: Oxford University Press), pp. 103–31.

Granick, David (1990) *Chinese State Enterprises: A Regional Property Rights Analysis* (Chicago: University of Chicago Press).

Grossman, Sanford L. and Joseph Stiglitz E. (1976) 'Information and competitive price systems', *American Economic Review*, Vol. 66, No. 2, pp. 246–53.

Guo Jiann-jong (1992) *Price Reform in China, 1979–86* (London: Macmillan).

Hamada, Koichi and Akiyoshi Horiuchi (1987) 'The political economy of the financial market', in Kozo Yamamura and Yasukuchi Yasuba (eds), *The Political Economy of Japan*, Vol. 1 (Stanford: Stanford University Press), pp. 223–60.

Hamilton, Clive (1983) 'Capitalist industrialisation in East Asia's four little tigers', *Journal of Contemporary Asia*, Vol. 13, No. 1, pp. 35–73.

Hare, Paul G. (1990) 'From central planning to market economy: Some microeconomic issues', *Economic Journal*, Vol. 100, No. 401, pp. 581–95.

Hare, Paul and Tamas Revesz (1992) 'Hungary's transition to the market: the case against a 'big bang', *Economic Policy*, Issue 14, pp. 227–65.

Harris, Nigel (1986) *The End of the Third World: Newly Industrialising Countries and the Decline of an Ideology* (London: I.B. Tauris).

Hart, Oliver D. and David M. Kreps (1986) 'Price destabilising speculation', *Journal of Political Economy*, Vol. 94, No. 4, pp. 927–52.

Hart, Oliver D. and John Moore (1990) 'Property rights and the nature of the firm', *Journal of Political Economy*, Vol. 98, No. 4, pp. 1119–58.

Hashimoto, Masanori and John Raisian (1985) 'Employment tenure and earnings profiles in Japan and the United States', *American Economic Review*, Vol. 75, No. 4, pp. 721–35.

Hay, Donald, Derek Morris, Guy Liu and Shujie Yao (1994) *Economic Reform and State-Owned Enterprises in China, 1979–1987* (Oxford: Clarendon Press).

Hishida, Masaharu (1991) 'The phenomenon of corruption in China', *Journal of International Economic Studies*, No. 5, pp. 21–9.

Horiuchi, Akiyoshi, Frank Packer and Shin'ichi Fukuda (1988) 'What role has the "main bank" played in Japan?', *Journal of the Japanese and International Economies*, Vol. 2, No. 2, pp. 159–80.

Hsu, Robert C. (1991) *Economics Theories in China, 1979–1988* (Cambridge: Cambridge University Press).

Hu Yebi (1993) *China's Capital Market* (Hong Kong: Chinese University of Hong Kong).

Huang Yasheng (1990) 'Web of interests and patterns of behaviour of Chinese local economic bureaucracies and enterprises during reforms', *China Quarterly*, No. 123, pp. 431–58.

Hughes, Alan and Ajit Singh (1983) *Mergers, Concentration, and Competition in Advanced Capitalist Economies: An International Perspective* (Cambridge: Department of Applied Economics, Cambridge University).

Huntington, Samuel P. (1968) *Political Order in Changing Societies* (New Haven, Conn.: Yale University Press).

Hutton, Will (1992) 'Selling the capitalist miracle', *The Guardian*, 2 March.

IMF, World Bank, OECD and EBRD (1990) *The Economy of the USSR – Summary and Recommendations* (Washington, DC: World Bank).

Jefferson, Gary H. and Thomas G. Rawski (1994) 'A model of endogenous innovation, competition and property rights reform in Chinese industry', *Working Paper*, No. 289, Department of Economics, University of Pittsburgh.

Jefferson, Gary H., Thomas Rawski, and Zheng Yuxin (1991) 'Growth, efficiency, and convergence in China's state and collective industry', *Economic Development and Cultural Change*, Vol. 40, No. 1, pp. 239–66.

Jefferson, Gary H., Zhao John Zhiqiang and Lu Mai (1994) 'Reforming property rights in Chinese industry', mimeograph, Harvard Institute of International Development.

Jensen, Michael C. (1978) 'Some anomalous evidence regarding market efficiency', *Journal of Financial Economics*, Vol. 6, No. 1, pp. 95–101.

Jensen, Michael C. (1993) 'The modern industrial revolution, exit, and failure of internal control systems', *Journal of Finance*, Vol. 48, No. 3, pp. 831–80.

Jensen, Michael C. and William H. Meckling (1976) 'Theory of the firm: Managerial behaviour, agency costs, and ownership structure', *Journal of Financial Economics*, Vol. 3, No. 1, pp. 305–60.

Johnson, Chalmers A. (1982) *MITI and the Japanese Miracle* (Stanford: Stanford University Press).

Kalleberg, Arne L. and James R. Lincoln (1988) 'The structure of earnings inequality in the United States and Japan', *American Journal of Sociology*, Vol. 94, supplement, pp. S121–53.

Kamerschen, David R. (1968) 'The influence of ownership and control on profit rates', *American Economic Review*, Vol. 58, No. 3, pp. 432–47.

Kanter, Rosabeth Moss (1991) 'Transcending business boundaries: 12 000 world managers view change', *Harvard Business Review*, Vol. 69, No. 3, pp. 151–64.

Kaye, Lincoln (1992) 'Chinese merger shows weakness of government policy: Corporate hybrid', *Far Eastern Economic Review*, 13 February, pp. 48–9.

Kaye, Lincoln and Cheng Elizabeth (1992) 'Babes in the bourse: China embarks on its most daring economic experiment. Will socialism survive?', *Far Eastern Economic Review*, 16 July, pp. 48–50.

Kenen, Peter (1991) 'Transitional arrangements for trade and payments among the CMEA countries', *IMF Staff Papers*, Vol. 38, No. 2, pp. 235–67.

Kester, W. Carl (1991) *Japanese Take-Overs: The Global Contest for Corporate Control* (Boston, Mass.: Harvard Business School Press).

Klein, Benjamin, Robert G. Crawford and Armen Alchian (1978) 'Vertical integration, appreciable rents and the competitive contracting process', *Journal of Law and Economics*, Vol. 21, pp. 297–326.

Koike, Kazuo (1987) 'Human resource development and labour–management relations', in Kozo Yamamura and Yasukuchi Yasuba (eds), *The Political Economy of Japan*, Vol. 1 (Stanford: Stanford University Press), pp. 289–330.

Komiya, Ryutaro (1987) 'Japanese firms, Chinese firms: Problems for economic reform in China, Part II', *Journal of the Japanese and International Economies*, Vol. 1, No. 2, pp. 229–47.

Koo, Anthony Y.C., Elizabeth Hon-Ming Li and Zhaoping Peng (1993) 'State-owned enterprise in transition', in Walter Galenson (ed.), *China's Economic Reform* (San Francisco: 1990 Institute).

Kornai, Janos (1980) *Economics of Shortage* (Amsterdam, New York and Oxford: North-Holland).

Kornai, Janos (1990a) *The Road to a Free Economy* (New York: W.W. Norton).

Kornai, Janos (1990b) *Vision and Reality, Market and State – Contradictions and Dilemmas Revisited* (Budapest: Corvina Books).

Kornai, Janos (1992a) 'The post-socialist transition and the state: Reflection in the light of Hungarian fiscal problems', *The American Economic Review*, Vol. 82, No. 2, pp. 1–21.

Kornai, Janos (1992b) *The Socialist System: The Political Economy of Communism* (Oxford: Clarendon Press).

Kornai, Janos (1993) 'Anti-depression cure for ailing post-communist economies', *Transition*, Vol. 4, No. 1, pp. 1–4.

Kornai, Janos (1994) 'Painful trade-offs in post-socialism', *Transition*, Vol. 5, No. 5, p. 5.

Krasner, Stephen D. (1978) *Defending the National Interest: Raw Materials Investments and US Foreign Policy* (Princeton, NJ: Princeton University Press).

Lardy, Nicholas R. (1992) *Foreign Trade and Economic Reform in China, 1978–1990* (Cambridge: Cambridge University Press).

Larner, Robert J. (1966) 'Ownership and control in the 200 largest non-financial corporations, 1929 and 1963', *American Economic Review*, Vol. 56, No. 4, pp. 777–87.

Lazonick, William (1991) *Business Organisation and the Myth of the Market Economy* (Cambridge: Cambridge University Press).

Lee, Barbara and John Nellis (1990) 'Enterprise reform and privatisation in Socialist economies', *World Bank Discussion Papers*, No. 104.

Lee, Keun (1990) 'The Chinese model of the socialist enterprise: An assessment of its organisation and performance', *Journal of Comparative Economics*, Vol. 14, No. 3, pp. 384–400.

Leibenstein, Harvey (1968) 'Entrepreneurship and development', *American Economic Review*, Vol. 58, No. 2, pp. 72–83.

Lewellen, Wilbur G. (1969) 'Management and ownership in the large firms', *Journal of Finance*, Vol. 24, No. 2, pp. 299–322.

Li Ping (1992) 'Price reform: The progressive way', *Beijing Review*, Vol. 35, No. 18, pp. 4–10.

Li Xueseng, Yang Shengming and He Juhuang (1985) 'The structure of China's domestic consumption: Analyses and preliminary forecasts', *World Bank Staff Working Paper*, No. 390.

Lichtenberg, Frank R. and George M. Pushner (1992) 'Ownership structure and corporate performance in Japan', *NBER Working Papers Series*, No. 4092, National Bureau of Economic Research.

Lipton, David and Jeffrey Sachs (1990) 'Creating a market economy in Eastern Europe: The case of Poland', *Brookings Papers on Economic Activity*, No. 1, pp. 75–147.

Lipton, David and Jeffrey Sachs (1991) 'Privatisation in Eastern Europe: The case of Poland', in Vittorio Corbo, Fabrizio Coricelli and Jan Bossak (eds), *Reforming Central and Eastern European Economies: Initial Results and Challenges* (Washington, DC: World Bank), pp. 231–51.

Lodge, George C. (1984) *The American Disease* (New York: Alfred A. Knopf).

Lodge, George C. (1990) *Perestroika for America: Restructuring US Business-Government Relations for Competitiveness in the World Economy* (Boston, Mass.: Harvard Business School Press).

Lorsch, Jay W. (1991) 'Real ownership is impossible', *Harvard Business Review*, Vol. 69, No. 6, pp. 139–41.

Mahini, Amir and Louis T. Wells, Jr (1986) 'Government relations in the global firm', in Michael E. Porter (ed.), *Competition in Global Industries* (Boston, Mass.: Harvard Business School Press), pp. 291–312.

Management World Editorial Dept (1991–93) *Listing of China's Largest Enterprises* (Beijing: Management World).

Manne, Henry C. (1965) 'Mergers and the market for corporate control', *Journal of Political Economy*, Vol. 73, No. 2, pp. 110–20.

Marx, Karl (1971) [1894] *Capital: A Critique of Political Economy*, Vol. 3 (Moscow: Progress).

McDonald, Kevin R. (1993) 'Why privatisation is not enough', *Harvard Business Review*, Vol. 71, No. 3, pp. 49–59.

Mcmillan, John and Barry Naughton (1991) 'How to reform a planned economy: Lesson from China', mimeograph, School of International Relations and Pacific Studies, University of California.

Meisner, Mitch and Marc Blecher (1982) 'Administrative level and agrarian structure, 1975–1980: The county was focal point in Chinese rural development policy', in Jack Gray and Gordon White (eds), *China's New Development Strategy* (London: Academic Press), pp. 55–84.

Millstein, Ira M., Sarah A.B. Teslik, Michael T. Jacobs, John Pound, Dale M. Hanson, Jonathan P. Charkham, Martin Lipton and Steven A. Rosenblum, Howard D. Sherman, Elizabeth Holtzman and Elmer W. Johnson (1991) Debate on 'Can pension funds lead the ownership revolution?' in *Harvard Business Review*, Vol. 69, No. 3, pp. 166–83.

Minami, Ryoshin (1994) *The Economic Development of China: A Comparison with the Japanese Experience*, translated by Wenran Jiang and Tanya Jiang with assistance from David Merriman (London: Macmillan).

Mincer, Jacob and Yoshio Higuchi (1988) 'Wage structures and labour turnover in the United States and Japan', *Journal of the Japanese and International Economies*, Vol. 2, No. 2, pp. 97–133.

Monsen, Joseph R. and Anthony Downs (1965) 'A theory of large managerial firms', *Journal of Political Economy*, Vol. 7, No. 3, pp. 221–36.

Monsen, Joseph R., John S. Chiu and David E. Cooley (1968) 'The effect of separation of ownership and control on the performance of the large firm', *Quarterly Journal of Economics*, Vol. 82, No. 3, pp. 435–51.

Moore, John (1992) 'The firm as a collection of assets', *European Economic Review*, Vol. 36, Nos 2/3, pp. 493–507.

Mossin, Jan (1973) *Theory of Financial Markets* (Englewood Cliffs, NJ: Prentice-Hall).

Moyle, John (1971) 'The pattern of ordinary share ownership 1957–1970', *Occasional Papers*, No. 31, University of Cambridge, Department of Applied Economics.

Muramatsu, Kuramitsu (1983) 'The effect of trade unions on productivity in Japanese manufacturing industries', in Masahiko Aoki (ed.), *The Economic Analysis of the Japanese Firm* (Amsterdam: North Holland).

Murrell, Peter (1992) 'Evolutionary and radical approaches to economic reform', *Economics of Planning*, No. 25, pp. 79–95.

Murrell, Peter and Wang Yijiang (1993) 'When privatisation should be delayed: The effect of Communist legacies on organisational and institutional reforms', *Working Paper Series*, No. 93-1, Department of Economics, University of Maryland.

Naughton, Barry (1991) 'Inflation in China: Patterns, causes and cures', in Joint Economic Committee at US Congress (ed.), *China's Economic Dilemmas in the 1990s: The Problems of Reforms, Modernisation, and Interdependence*, Vol. 1, pp. 135–59.

Naughton, Barry (1992) 'Implications of the state monopoly over industry and its relaxation', *Modern China*, January pp. 42–71.

Nee, Victor (1992) 'Organisational dynamics of market transition: Hybrid forms, property rights, and mixed economy in China', *Administrative Science Quarterly*, No. 37, pp. 1–27.

Nellis, John (1991) 'Improving the performance of Soviet Enterprises', *World Bank Discussion Papers*, No. 118.

Ness, Peter Van and Satish Raichur (1983) 'Dilemmas of socialist development: An analysis of strategic lines in China, 1949–1981', in The Bulletin of Concerned Asian Scholars (eds), *China from Mao to Deng: The Politics and Economics of Socialist Development* (Armonk, NY: M.E. Sharpe).

Newbery, David M. (1991) 'Sequencing the transition', *CEPR Discussion Paper*, No. 575.

Newbery, David M. (1992) 'The role of public enterprises in the national economy', *Asian Development Review*, Vol. 10, No. 2, pp. 1–34.

Nolan, Peter (1991) 'Prospects for the Chinese economy', *Cambridge Journal of Economics*, No. 15, pp. 113–24.

Nolan, Peter (1992a) 'The peculiarities of China's post-Mao political economy', mimeograph, Faculty of Economics and Politics, University of Cambridge.

Nolan, Peter (1992b) 'Reforming the Stalinist system: Chinese experience', mimeograph, Faculty of Politics and Economics, University of Cambridge.

Nolan, Peter (1993) *State and Market in the Chinese Economy – Essays on Controversial Issues* (London: Macmillan Academic and Professional Press).

Nolan, Peter (1994) 'Large firms and industrial reform in former planned economies: The case of China', *Cambridge Journal of Economics*.

North, Douglass C. and Barry R. Weingast (1989) 'Constitutions and commitment: The evolution of institutions governing public choice in 17th century England', *Journal of Economic History*, Vol. XLIX, No. 4, pp. 803–32.

Oi, Jean C. (1988) 'The Chinese Village, Inc.', in Bruce L. Reynolds (ed.), *Chinese Economic Policy: Economic Reform at Midstream* (New York: Paragon House Press), pp. 67–87.

Oi, Jean C. (1989) *State and Peasant in Contemporary China: The Political Economy of Village Government* (Berkeley: University of California Press).

Oi, Jean C. (1992) 'Fiscal reform and the economic foundations of local state corporatism in China', *World Politics*, Vol. 45, No. 1, pp. 99–126.

Okimoto, Daniel I. and Gary R. Saxonhouse (1987) 'Technology and the future of the economy', in Kozo Yamamura and Yasukuchi Yasuba (eds), *The Political Economy of Japan*, Vol. 1 (Stanford: Stanford University Press), pp. 385–419.

Olko-Bajienska, Teresa, Julian Pankow and Pawel Ruszkowski (1992) *Privatisation of State Enterprises 1990–91: Results of Empirical Studies* (Warsaw: Zmiany Ltd, Research and Consulting Institute).

Overholt, William H. (1993) *China: The Next Economic Superpower* (London: Weidenfeld & Nicolson).

Parker, David (1993) 'Ownership, organisational changes and performance', in Thomas Clarke and Christos Pitelis (eds), *The Political Economy of Privatisation* (London: Routledge), pp. 31–53.

Penrose, Edith (1959) *The Theory of the Growth of the Firm* (Armonk, NY: M.E. Sharpe).

Perkins, Dwight H. (1986) *China: Asia's Next Economic Giant?* (Seattle and London: University of Washington Press).

Perkins, Dwight H. (1988) 'Reforming China's economic system', *Journal of Economic Literature*, Vol. 26, pp. 601–45.

Perkins, Dwight H. (1991a) 'Price reform vs. enterprise autonomy: Which should have priority?' in Joint Economic Committee at US Congress (ed.), *China's*

Economic Dilemmas in the 1990s: The Problems of Reforms, Modernisation, and Interdependence, Vol. 1, pp. 160–7.

Perkins, Dwight H. (1991b) 'The transition from central planning: East Asia's experience', paper presented at the 21st Anniversary Symposium, Korea Development Institute, Seoul, Korea.

Perkins, Dwight H. (1992) 'China's "gradual" approach to market reforms', paper presented at the conference 'Comparative Experiences of Economic Reform and Post-Socialist Transformation', El Escorial, Spain.

Perkins, Dwight H. and Shahid Yusuf (1984) *Rural Development in China* (Baltimore and London: Johns Hopkins University Press).

Pinto, Brian (1993) 'Brian Pinto explains why Polish state firms are restructuring', *Transition*, Vol. 4, No. 7, pp. 4–5.

Pinto, Brian, Marek Belka and Stefan Krajewski (1993) 'Transforming state enterprises in Poland: Evidence on adjustment by manufacturing firms', *Brookings Papers on Economic Activity*, No. 1, pp. 213–70.

Porter, Michael E. (1986) *The Competitive Advantage of Nations* (London: Macmillan Press).

Portes, Richard (1992) 'Structural reform in Central and Eastern Europe', *European Economic Review*, Vol. 36, pp. 661–9.

Portes, Richard (1994) 'Now that the transformation traps have been recognised, there should be less likelihood of getting caught', *Transition*, Vol. 5, No. 8, pp. 13–14.

Pratten, Cliff (1993) *The Stock Market* (Cambridge: Cambridge University Press).

Prybyla, Jan S. (1991) 'The road from socialism: Why, where, what, and how', *Problem of Communism*, January–April, pp. 1–17.

Rawski, Thomas G. (1993) 'Chinese industrial reform: Accomplishments, prospects, and implications', *Working Paper* No. 287, Department of Economics, University of Pittsburgh.

Reynolds, Bruce L. (ed.), prepared by the staff of the Chinese Economic System Reform Research Institute (CESRRI-a) (1987) *Reform in China: Challenges and Choices* (Armonk, NY and London: M.E. Sharpe).

Roemer Michael (1986) 'Simple analytics of segmented markets: What case for liberalisation?', *World Development*, Vol. 14, No. 3, pp. 429–39.

Rowthorn, Bob (1990) 'Privatisation in UK', mimeograph, Faculty of Economics and Politics, University of Cambridge.

Rowthorn, Bob and Ha-joon Chang (1993) 'Public ownership and the theory of the state', in Thomas Clarke and Christos Pitelis (eds), *The Political Economy of Privatisation* (London and New York: Routledge), pp. 54–69.

Sachs, Jeffrey (1987) 'Trade and exchange rate policies in growth-oriented adjustment programs', in Vittorio Corbo, Morris Goldstein and Mohsin Khan (eds), *Growth-Oriented Adjustment Programs* (Washington, DC: IMF and World Bank), pp. 291–325.

Sachs, Jeffrey (1991) 'Crossing the valley of tears in East European reform', *Challenge*, September–October, pp. 26–32.

Sachs, Jeffrey (1992a) 'Building a market economy in Poland', *Scientific American*, March, pp. 20–6.

Sachs, Jeffrey (1992b) 'The economic transition of Eastern Europe: The case of Poland', *Economics of Planning*, No. 25, pp. 5–19.

Sachs, Jeffrey (1992c) 'Privatisation in Russia: Some lessons from Eastern Europe', *American Economic Review*, Vol. 82, No. 2, pp. 43–8.

Sachs, Jeffrey (1994) 'Russia's struggle with stabilisation', *Transition*, Vol. 5, No. 5, pp. 7–9.

Sachs, Jeffrey and David Lipton (1990) 'Poland's economic reform', *Foreign Affairs*, Vol. 69, No. 3, pp. 47–66.

Sachs, Jeffrey and Wing Thye-Woo (1994) 'Structural factors in the economic reforms of China, Eastern Europe, and the former Soviet Union', *Economic Policy*, Vol. 18, pp. 102–45.

Saito, Minoru (1991) 'The collapse of Soviet-type Socialism in Europe and the lessons for China', *Journal of International Economic Studies*, No. 5, pp. 1–19.

Samonis, Valdas (1991) 'From plan to market in Eastern Europe: Poland's big bang', mimeograph, University of Toronto.

Schall, Lawrence D. (1972) 'Asset valuation, firm investment, and firm diversification', *Journal of Business*, Vol. 45, No. 1, pp. 11–28.

Schmitter, Phillippe C. (1974) 'Still the century of corporatism?', in Fredrick B. Pike and Thomas Stritch (eds), *The New Corporatism: Social-Political Structures in the Iberian World* (Notre Dame: University of Notre Dame Press), pp. 85–131.

Schonfelder, Bruno (1990) 'Reflections on inflationary dynamics in Yugoslavia', *Comparative Economic Studies*, Vol. 32, No. 4, pp. 85–106.

Schumpeter, Joseph (1939) *Business Cycles: A Theoretical, Historical, and Statistical Analysis of the Capitalist Process* (New York and London: McGraw-Hill).

Schumpeter, Joseph (1950) [1942] *Capitalism, Socialism and Democracy*, 3rd edn (New York: Harper).

Schurmann, Franz (1968) *Ideology and Organisation in Communist China*, 2nd edn (Berkeley and Los Angeles: University of California Press).

Shale, Tony (1990) 'Reawakening the sleeping giant', *Euromoney*, November, pp. 14–23.

Sheard, Paul (1994) 'Interlocking share-holdings and corporate governance', in Masahiko Aoki and Ronald Dore (eds), *The Japanese Firm: The Sources of Competitive Strength* (Oxford: Oxford University Press), pp. 310–49.

Shiller, Robert J. (1981) 'Do stock prices move too much to be justified by subsequent changes in dividends?', *American Economic Review*, Vol. 71, No. 3, pp. 421–36.

Simoneti, Marko (1993) 'A comparative review of privatisation strategies in four former socialist countries', *Europe-Asia Studies*, Vol. 45, No. 1, pp. 79–102.

Singh, Ajit (1971) *Take-Overs: Their Relevance to the Stock Market and the Theory of the Firm* (Cambridge: Cambridge University Press).

Singh, Ajit (1975a) 'An essay on the political economy of Chinese development', *Thames Papers in Political Economy*, School of Social Sciences of Thames Polytechnic.

Singh, Ajit (1975b) 'Take-overs, economic natural selection and the theory of the firm: Evidence from the post-war United Kingdom experience', *Economic Journal*, Vol. 85, pp. 497–515.

Singh, Ajit (1990) 'The stock-market in a socialist economy', in Peter Nolan and Tung Fujeng (eds), *The Chinese Economy and its Future: Achievements and Problems of Post-Mao Reform* (Cambridge: Polity Press), pp. 161–78.

Singh, Inderjit (1992) 'China: Industrial policies for an economy in transition', *World Bank Discussion Papers*, No. 143.

Singh, Inderjit J. and Gary H. Jefferson (1993) 'State enterprises in China: Down to earth from commanding heights', *Transition*, Vol. 4, No. 8, pp. 8–10.

Skocpol, Theda (1979) *State and Social Revolutions: A Comparative Analysis of France, Russia, and China* (New York and Cambridge: Cambridge University Press).

Smith, Adam (1937) [1776] *The Wealth of Nations*, Cannan edn (New York: Modern Library).

Smith, Hedrick (1988) *The Power Game: How Washington Works* (New York: Random House).

Solinger, Dorothy (ed.) (1984) *Three Visions of Chinese Socialism* (Boulder, Col.: Westview Press.

Soltow, H. James (1968) 'The entrepreneur in economic history', *American Economic Review*, Vol. 58, No. 2, pp. 84–98.

Song, Guoqing and Zhang Weiying (1990) 'Theoretical questions concerning macroeconomic balance and macroeconomic control', *Chinese Economic Studies*, Vol. 23, No. 3, pp. 23–45.

Song, Lina (1990) 'Governance: A comparison of township firms and local state enterprises', in William A. Byrd and Lin Qingsong (eds), *China's Rural Industry: Structure, Development, and Reform* (Oxford and New York: Oxford University Press), pp. 392–412.

Soros, George (1990) *Opening the Soviet System* (London: Weidenfeld & Nicolson).

State Statistical Bureau (SSB) (1981–) *Statistical Yearbook of China* (Hong Kong: Economic Information Agency).

Steinherr, Alfred (1991) 'Essential ingredients for reforms in Eastern Europe', *Moct-Most*, No. 3, pp. 3–28.

Stepanek, James B. (1991) 'China's enduring state factories. Why ten years of reform have left China's big state factories unchanged', in Joint Economic Committee at US Congress (ed.), *China's Economic Dilemmas in the 1990s: The Problems of Reforms, Modernisation, and Interdependence*, Vol. 2, pp. 440–54.

Stiglitz, Joseph E. (1981) 'The allocation role of the stock market: Pareto-optimality and competition', *Journal of Finance*, Vol. 36, No. 2, pp. 235–51.

Strong, Norman and Michael Waterson (1987) 'Principles, agents and information', in Roger Clarke and Tony McGuinness (eds), *The Economics of the Firm* (Oxford: Basil Blackwell), pp. 18–41.

Suzuki, Yoshitaka (1991) *Japanese Management Structures 1920–80* (London: Macmillan).

Svejnar, Jan (1990) 'Productive efficiency and employment', in William A. Byrd and Lin Qingsong (eds), *China's Rural Industry: Structure, Development, and Reform* (Oxford and New York: Oxford University Press), pp. 243–54.

Tracy, Noel (1994a) 'The overseas Chinese and China: The critical linkage', mimeograph, School of Social Sciences, Flinders University of South Australia.

Tracy, Noel (1994b) 'The Southeast: The cutting edge of China's economic reform', mimeograph, School of Social Sciences, Flinders University of South Australia.

Tsuru, Shigeto (1993) *Japan's Capitalism: Creative Defeat and Beyond* (Cambridge: Cambridge University Press).

Veljanovski, Cento (ed.) (1992) *Privatisation and Competition: A Market Prospectus* (London: Institute of Economic Affairs).

Vernon-Wortzel, Heidi and Lawrence H. Wortzel (1989) 'Privatisation: Not the only answer', *World Development*, Vol. 17, No. 5, pp. 633–41.

Wachter, Michael L. and Oliver E. Williamson (1978) 'Obligational market and the mechanics of inflation', *Bell Journal of Economics*, Vol. 9, No. 2, pp. 549–71.

Wade, Robert (1990) *Governing the market: Economic Theory and the Role of Government in East Asian Industrialisation* (Princeton, NJ: Princeton University Press).

Walder, Andrew G. (1992) 'Local bargaining relationships and urban industrial finance', in Kenneth G. Lieberthal and David M. Lampton (eds), *Bureaucracy, Politics, and Decision Making in Post-Mao China* (Berkeley: University of California Press), pp. 308–33.

Walder, Andrew G. (1994) 'The industrial organisation of Zouping County: Agency and ownership in local public enterprise', mimeograph, Department of Sociology, Harvard University.

Wang Xiao-qiang (1989) 'Transcending the logic of private ownership', *Chinese Economic Studies*, Vol. 23, No. 1, pp. 43–56. Original Chinese version: *Economic Development and Reform*, No. 4 (1988), pp. 27–48.

Wang Xiao-qiang and Ji Xiaoming (1988) 'Thoughts on the model of non-stock enterprise', *Chinese Economic Studies*, Vol. 22, No. 2, pp. 38–46. Original Chinese version: *Economic Development and Reform*, No. 1 (1985), pp. 13–26.

Wei Wenyuan (1992) 'Steady development of Shanghai stock exchange', *Beijing Review*, 24 February–1 April, pp. 16–18.

Weitzman, Martin L. and Xu Chenggang (1994) 'Chinese township-village enterprises as vaguely defined co-operatives', *Journal of Comparative Economics*, No. 18, pp. 1–25.

Wharton, Clifton R. (1991) 'Just vote no', *Harvard Business Review*, Vol. 69, No. 6, pp. 137–9.

White, Gordon (1983) 'Chinese development strategy after Mao', in Gordon White, Robin Murray and Christine White (eds), *Revolutionary Socialist Development in the Third World* (Brighton: Wheatsheaf Books), pp. 155–92.

White, Gordon (ed.) (1988) *Developmental States in East Asia* (London: Macmillan).

White, Gordon (1989) 'Restructuring the working class: Labour reform in Post-Mao China', in A. Dirlik and M. Meisner (eds), *Marxism and the Chinese Experience* (Armonk, NY, and London: M.E. Sharpe), pp. 153–68.

White, Gordon (1991) 'The road to crisis: The Chinese state in the era of economic reform', in Gordon White (ed.), *The Chinese State in the Era of Economic Reform: The Road to a Crisis* (London Macmillan), pp. 1–20.

White, Gordon and Robert Wade (eds) (1985) *Developmental States in East Asia: A Research Report to the Gatsby Charitable Foundation* (Brighton: Institute of Development Studies).

Williamson, Oliver E. (1975) *Market and Hierarchies: Analysis and Antitrust Implications* (New York and London: Free Press).

Williamson, Oliver E. (1985) *The Economic Institutions of Capitalism: Firms, Markets, Relational Contracting* (New York and London: Free Press).

Wong, Christine P.W. (1987) 'Between plan and market: The role of the local sector in Post-Mao China', *Journal of Comparative Economics*, Vol. 11, pp. 385–98.

Wong, Christine P.W. (1992) 'Fiscal reform and local industrialisation: The problematic sequencing of reform in Post-Mao China', *Modern China*, Vol. 18, No. 2, pp. 197–227.

Wood, Adrian (1991a) 'Joint stock companies with rearranged public ownership: invigoration of China's state enterprises further considered', mimeograph, Programme of Research into the Reform of Pricing and Market Structure in China, London School of Economics, CP No. 11.

Wood, Adrian (1991b) 'China's economic system: A brief description, with some suggestions for further reform', mimeograph, Programme of Research into the Reform of Pricing and Market Structure in China, London School of Economics, CP No. 12.

World Bank (1985) *China: Long-Term Development Issues and Options* (Baltimore and London: Johns Hopkins University Press).

World Bank (1988a) *China: External Trade and Capital* (Washington, DC: World Bank).

World Bank (1988b) *China: Finance and Investment* (Washington, DC: World Bank).

World Bank (1990a) *China: Between Plan and Market* (Washington, DC: World Bank).

World Bank (1990b) *China: Macroeconomic Stability and Industrial Growth under Decentralised Socialism* (Washington, DC: World Bank).

World Bank (1991) *World Development Report* (New York and Oxford: Oxford University Press).

Wu Jinlian and Zhao Renwei (1988) 'The dual pricing system in China's industry', in Bruce L. Reynolds (ed.), *Chinese Economic Reform: How Far, How Fast?* (Boston, Mass.: Academic Press), pp. 19–28.

Yao Jianguo (1992) 'Experimenting with enterprise groups', *Beijing Review*, Vol. 35, No. 19, pp. 14–19.

Yeh, Kung-Chia (1993) 'Economic reform: An overview', in Walter Galenson (ed.), *China's Economic Reform* (San Francisco: 1990 Institute).

Yeasts, Alexander J. (1991) 'China's foreign trade and comparative advantage: Prospects, problems, and policy implications', *World Bank Discussion Papers*, No. 141.

Zinser, Lee (1991) 'The performance of China's economy', in Joint Economic Committee at US Congress (ed.), *China's Economic Dilemmas in the 1990s: The Problems of Reforms, Modernisation, and Interdependence*, Vol. 1, pp. 103–18.

Zou Gang (1992) 'Enterprise behaviour under the two-tier plan/market system', mimeograph, School of Business Administration, University of Southern California.

Zweig, David (1991) 'Internationalising China's countryside: The political economy of exports from rural industry', *China Quarterly*, No. 128, pp. 716–41.

Chinese Works Cited

Anshan Steel Company (1991) 'Report outline for the State Council', mimeograph, 5 June.

Deng Yintao and Luo Xiaopeng (1987) 'The limitation of cross quantity analyses and policies in China's economic theory and practice', *Economic Study*, No. 6.

Development Research Office of Chinese Economic System Reform Research Institute (CESRRI-b) (1988) *The Structural Problem in Industrial Growth* (Chengdu: Sichuan People Press).

Headquarters of Urban Social and Economic Survey, State Statistical Bureau (SSB) (1988c–91c) *Statistical Yearbook of China's Prices* (Beijing: China's Statistical Press).

Industrial and Transportation Department, State Statistical Bureau (SSB) (1985b–90b) *Statistical Yearbook of China's Industrial Economy* (Beijing: China's Statistical Press).

Jin Jiandong, Xiao Zhuoji and Xu Shunxin (eds) (1991) *China's Security Market (1991)* (Beijing: China Finance Press).

Microeconomics Research Office of Chinese Economic System Reform Research Institute (CESRRI-c) (1988) *The Market Structure and Enterprise System in Reform* (Chengdu: Sichuan People Press).

Moran, Robert T. and John R. Riesenberger (1994) *The Global Challenge – Building the New World-Wide Enterprise* (London: McGraw-Hill International). Translated by Hong Ruilin (1996) (Taipei: McGraw-Hill).

Office of Investment, State Statistical Bureau (SSB) (1987d) *China's Fixed Asset Investment 1950–1985* 1950–1985 (Beijing: China's Statistical Press).

Qu Bipong (1992) 'Where is the outlet of electronic fan production', *China's Machinery and Electronic*, 29 January, p. 3.

Research Group of the Centre of Economic Research, Planning Commission (RGCER) (1994) 'Research report about foreign direct investment in China', mimeograph.

Special Group for 2000 Development Strategy and Economic Management of Angang (SGDSEMA) (1991) 'General outline of 1991–2000 development strategy of Angang – 1991–2000', *Management of Angang*, supplementary issue, pp. 3–19.

State Statistical Bureau (SSB) (1981–94) *Statistical Yearbook of China* (Beijing: China's Statistical Press).

State Statistical Bureau (SSB) (1994a) *Summary of Statistical Yearbook of China* (Beijing: China's Statistical Press).

Study Group to Japan, Chinese Economic System Reform Research Institute (CESRRI-d) (1988) *The Enlightenment of the Japanese Model: The Firms, Government, and Middle Organisations* (Chengdu: Sichuan People Press).

Japanese Works Cited

Komiya, Ryutaro (1980) *Study on Modern Japanese Economy* (Tokyo: Tokyo University Press).

Okumura, Hiroshi (1993a) *Is Corporate Departmentalism Collapsing?* (Tokyo: Yan Bo Press).

Okumura, Hiroshi (1993b) *The Structure of Corporate Capitalism* (Tokyo: Social Thinking Press).

Takahashi, Kamekichi (1983) *The Basic Reasons for the Japanese Economy Leaping Forward after the Second World War* (Tokyo: Japan Economic News Press).

Tsukada, Kishi (1994) '"Budget-first-ism" destroys the market: NTT, JR-East Japan, JT issue shares as "people speculation"', *Weekly Toyokeizai*, 17 September, pp. 14–17.

Weekly Toyokeizai, supplement/Data Bank (1993) 'Comprehensive review of all enterprises 1994 – 94'.

Index